The Structure of Written Communication

Studies in Reciprocity
between Writers and Readers

The Structure of Written Communication

Studies in Reciprocity between Writers and Readers

Martin Nystrand

The University of Wisconsin
Madison, Wisconsin

With Contributions by

Margaret Himley
Anne Doyle

1986

ACADEMIC PRESS, INC.

Harcourt Brace Jovanovich, Publishers
Orlando   San Diego   New York   Austin
Boston   London   Sydney   Tokyo   Toronto

ACADEMIC PRESS, INC.
Orlando, Florida 32887

United Kingdom Edition published by
ACADEMIC PRESS INC. (LONDON) LTD.
24–28 Oval Road, London NW1 7DX

Library of Congress Cataloging in Publication Data

Nystrand, Martin.
    The structure of written communication.

    Bibliography: p.
    Includes index.
    1. Written communication.   I. Himley, Margaret.
II. Title.
P211.N97   1986   001.54'3   86-13979
ISBN 0—12—523482—1 (alk. paper)

PRINTED IN THE UNITED STATES OF AMERICA

86 87 88 89   9 8 7 6 5 4 3 2 1

Contents

3. What Writers Do   59

4. A Critical Examination of the Doctrine of Autonomous Texts   81
MARTIN NYSTRAND, ANNE DOYLE, and MARGARET HIMLEY

5. Necessary Text Elaborations   109

Part II
LEARNING TO WRITE

6. Genre as Generative: One Perspective on One Child's Early Writing Growth   137
MARGARET HIMLEY

Preface

In the last decade, writing and reading researchers have increasingly drawn closer together in their common emphasis on the cognitive character of writing and reading. Researchers see both writing and reading as constructive, interpretive activities in which both writer and reader test hypotheses about possible meanings in terms of elements of text. Writers are said to represent and evaluate their intentions continuously in the conventions of written text, and readers are said to confirm and/or alter expectations and interpretations which they bring to the text. What is not always recognized, however, is that writers and readers interact not only with the text but also with each other by way of the text. Writers gauge their intentions in terms of the expectations of their readers, and readers measure their understanding in terms of the writer's intentions. Communication between writers and readers requires that the text they share configure and mediate these respective interests and expectations. This requirement means that the skilled writer's choices and options at any point in the composing process are determined not just by what the writer wants to say but also by what the text has to do and, in turn, by what the reader may reasonably expect the text to do. Both writer and reader make sense, as recent research clearly affirms—the one *in* print (or text), the other *of* print (or text). More fundamentally, each presupposes—indeed counts on—the sense-making capabilities of the other. There is a condition of reciprocity between conversants that undergirds and continuously regulates discourse at every turn.

This book presents a series of inquiries exploring the implications of this principle for writing and reading, and especially how the character of discourse is shaped by the premise of reciprocity between writer and reader. In particular, this volume examines the implications of the reciprocity principle for writers. Part I, including Chapters 1–5, examines the writing process. Part II, including Chapters 6–8, examines the process of learning to write. The reader should not expect to find the sequential development of a single argument here; this is not that sort of book. This set of explorations—some theoretical in character, others empirical—reads more like spokes on a conceptual hub than episodes in a thematic narrative.

Part I. Chapter 1 reviews recent research on the composing process and examines reader expectations as an essential factor in the writer's task. We see that accounting for the interaction of writer and reader is essential for understanding the relationship between the writing process and the written text. Chapters 2 and 3 formally examine reciprocity as a principle of discourse. Chapter 3 presents a reciprocity-based grammar of written text, introducing the concepts of genre, topic, and commentary, and in addition examines the writer's task in terms of this grammar. Chapter 4 examines the doctrine of autonomous texts and shows the important role context plays in the explicitness of any text. Chapter 5 presents two studies on the role of text elaborations and distinguishes between topic-level elaborations and commentary-level elaborations, particularly as these elaborations relate to the needs of knowledgeable and unknowledgeable readers.

Part II. Chapter 6, by Margaret Himley, is a case study of a first grader learning to write. In this chapter Himley examines the process of socialization which learning to write represents. Chapter 7 carefully examines the development of orthography in one preschooler's writing and shows the important role the discourse community plays even in the problem of spacing text. Chapter 8 presents research showing the effectiveness of peer group work in college expository writing classes and examines how many students learn to write by talking with their readers about what they have written. We understand the importance of readers in the process of learning to write here as we examine the substantial role that group discussion plays in shaping the writers' premises about composing and also the revisions which authors subsequently make in light of the discussions. All three chapters in Part II examine the social foundations of text functionality. (For a more detailed outline of volume contents, the reader is referred to pp. 15–18 of the Introduction.)

This book is written for researchers, graduate students, and the many educators concerned with writing and reading and especially their relationship. It will be useful in courses in educational psychology, applied linguistics, semiotics and the philosophy of language, discourse analysis, rhetoric, and the linguistics of literacy.

Acknowledgments

I am indebted to far more people than I can acknowledge adequately. Much of the present discussion benefited from discussions with Robert Gundlach of Northwestern University, Richard Buchanan, and Martin Steinmann, Jr., at the University of Illinois–Chicago, and Deborah Brandt and Nick Doane at the University of Wisconsin–Madison. I could not have undertaken the research presented in Chapter 4 without the essential collaboration of Anne Doyle and Margaret Himley. Glenda Bissex and her son Paul generously provided the texts analyzed in Chapter 7. Beth Black, Ellen Berry, Barbara Glatt, and Carolyn Perez provided important research assistance; special thanks go to Jean Walia. I appreciate the comments and suggestions of Anne Doyle of the University of Illinois–Chicago, Lester Faigley of the University of Texas at Austin, Margaret Himley of Syracuse University, Maya Hickmann of the Max Planck Institute for Psycholinguistics, Rosalind Horowitz of the University of Texas at San Antonio, Dale Liebert and John Kean of the University of Wisconsin–Madison, Sheldon Rosenberg of the University of Illinois–Chicago, and Michael Stubbs of the University of London Institute of Education. I thank my editor at Academic Press for his support. Students from both the University of Illinois–Chicago and the University of Wisconsin–Madison—too many to name—have made innumerable contributions; I especially thank the graduate students whose class comments often helped me with my own learning and the scores of undergraduates who served as subjects in the studies reported here. I am indebted to Anne Doyle and Carl Stach, who carefully edited the entire volume.

The graduate schools of both the University of Illinois–Chicago and the University of Wisconsin–Madison provided key grants supporting research presented in Chapters 5 and 7. Chapter 8 is the final report of "Increasing Student Awareness of Their Composing Processes," research funded by the Wisconsin Center for Education Research (W.C.E.R.), 1025 W. Johnson Street, Madison, Wisconsin 53706. From 1980 to 1985, W.C.E.R. was supported in part by grant no. NIE-G-84-0008 from the National Institute of Education; the opinions expressed in Chapter 8 do not necessarily reflect the position, policy, or endorsement of the National Institute of Education.

Most of all, I am indebted to the support of my wife, Nancy. This book is dedicated to Stephen Nystrand, who, more than most, has recently taught me important insights about the development of discourse. To all our friends and family who supported this work in too many ways to count (and which they ultimately discovered was a saga, not a "set of inquiries"), I say thank you.

The Structure of Written Communication

Studies in Reciprocity between Writers and Readers

Introduction

From 1975 to 1977, I was project director of the Eastern Ontario Language Arts Assessment Project, and though the studies in this volume have little to do with assessment and testing, most of the ideas presented here about writing nonetheless originated and developed out of my work on problems related to language arts assessment in Ontario. In this introduction I review this work and say something about how, after more than a decade of subsequent research and reflection, rather narrowly conceived issues of educational testing gave way to insights concerning written communication and semiotics.

In 1975 the Ontario Ministry of Education funded a criterion-referenced language arts assessment project at the Trent Valley Centre of the Ontario Institute for Studies in Education. The original context and impetus for the project were largely social and political, the most important factor being a general conviction that the language skills of the region's youth had declined in recent years, as well as a special confidence in possibilities for remedying the situation through more systematic management of more objectives and more testing. Much like their American neighbors, Canadians in the mid-1970s sensed a decline in the quality and efficacy of their schools, a sentiment clearly articulated in an influential 1975 *Newsweek* article titled "Why Johnny Can't Write," which stated that "the U.S. educational system is spawning a generation of semiliterates [December 8, 1975, p. 58]." In the Ontario project, the back-to-basics movement expressed itself in three central questions: Why can't Johnny write? Why can't Johnny read? Why isn't Johnny doing as well on tests as he used to?

The proposal for the Ontario project was a result as well of several years' involvement by the Trent Valley Centre in other assessment projects, following a 4-year criterion-referenced mathematics project reported by Leithwood et al. in *The Peterborough Project* (1976). In 1972, the Trent Valley Centre had undertaken the development of comprehensive criterion-referenced tests for basic computational skills, resulting in 600 behavioral objectives (specific target behaviors in addition, subtraction, multiplication,

1

division, fractions, decimals, integers, and exponents), as well as a pool of 10 test items per objective. These tests purportedly allowed schools to determine proportions of students mastering given objectives in a given class, school, or system.

It was within this context, then, that the Ontario Ministry of Education funded the Trent Valley Centre's 2-year criterion-referenced assessment project in 1975. The objectives of the project were (a) an array of behavioral objectives (or target behaviors) that would adequately define the basic skills of written language, (b) a pool of 5–10 equivalent test items to measure performance on each objective, and (c) a battery of criterion-referenced tests incorporating these items. In the fall of 1975, six boards of education throughout the region officially joined the Centre for the start of the project. Eventually 5 other counties joined; in all there were 11.

Just which aspects of reading, writing, speaking, and listening were selected for test development was determined by the expressed preferences of the individual school board representatives. One school district, for example, chose to work on objectives and test items for *sentence-level skills*, another chose *reference materials*, another chose *explicit and implicit comprehension*, another chose *sound–symbol relationships*, another chose *the paragraph and prose*, and one school district chose *listening and speaking*.

This process of identifying objectives and writing test items involved several assumptions about language and testing, some explicit and other inherent:

1. Objectives were judged for their adequacy with respect to specificity and consensus among the curriculum specialists writing objectives and test items.
2. Test results were to allow for instructional "diagnosis," "treatment," and "prescription" so that teachers and schools might identify weak performances on "critical" objectives. In this respect, language arts instruction was seen as a medical problem of sorts.
3. Procedures for testing mastery were considered universally applicable to all curriculum areas, and in this respect language was no different from mathematics. Only 2 years were allocated to the language project, compared to 4 years for math, on the grounds that the latter project involved "substantial problems" whose "solution" (i.e., the experience of the Centre) abbreviated the need for fundamental inquiry into language.
4. Writing objectives and test items were considered neutral with respect to curriculum and instruction. Test items were thought not to affect what was taught; rather, they only reported what was learned.

Education was viewed largely as a management problem requiring effective reporting of individual performances on well-catalogued, cross-referenced objectives. Learning was defined not psychologically but rather pedagogically as "the mastery of objectives." Hence, what was learned was essentially "what was taught." As one investigator commented, "We're not interested in their 'learning to write'; we're interested in their mastery of our objectives."

5. At the same time that these procedures were intended to be neutral with respect to curriculum and instruction, the design requirements of the tests inevitably compartmentalized, fragmented, and sequenced the character of writing and reading in very particular ways. Writing and reading were divided conceptually as well as geographically throughout the region.

Of particular significance in the project's brief history were links established in the spring of 1976 with the Bureau of School and Cultural Research of the New York State Department of Education in Albany. Robert P. O'Reilly, then bureau chief, had for several years with his associates also been involved in major evaluation and assessment projects. Like the Trent Valley Centre, the New York group had completed a comprehensive criterion-referenced mathematics project, Comprehensive Achievement Monitoring (CAM), and chose as follow-up to apply its evaluation skills to language arts. The results were nearly 5000 behavioral objectives with five test items each.

In preparing criterion-referenced tests for language arts—indeed after having written several thousand behavioral objectives—the New York group experienced difficulty in articulating satisfactory objectives for reading comprehension. As O'Reilly explained, "The basic problem [was] not with the desirability of having objectives but with their limitations. Objectives neither sufficiently define the measurement situation; nor do they contribute much to clarifying what is being measured.... Any set of reading objectives results in an arbitrary definition of reading that has been heavily influenced by existing reading tests and texts. The question is, Which of the objectives represented in a reading test actually test reading comprehension?... The problem of defining the behavioral components of comprehension will not be solved by listing, sorting, and organizing objectives.... [O'Reilly, personal communication, 1976]."

Philosophically, criterion-referenced measurement is a revival of logical positivism. Positivists, Sir Karl Popper notes, "wish to admit, as scientific or legitimate, only those statements which are reducible to elementary (or 'atomic') statements of experience.... [1959, p. 35]." The ontological status of individual objectives is as unproblematic for the criterion referencer as is that of "observable particulars of experience" (i.e., facts) for the logical positivist: Objectives and facts respectively are "mere neutral particulars" subject to and necessary for generalization.

Yet objectives and facts—no matter how apparently specific—are always generalizations. Popper explains: "The statement, 'Here is a glass of water' cannot be verified by any observational experience. The reason is that the *universals* which appear in it cannot be correlated with any specific sense-experience.... By the word 'glass', for example, we denote physical bodies which exhibit a certain *law-like behaviour*, and the same holds for the word 'water'. Universals cannot be reduced to classes of experience; they cannot be 'constituted' [1959, p. 95]." On this same score, criterion-referenced measurement fares no better. Mastery of objectives ("Here is a fluent consonant blend reader"; "Here is a regular capitalizer") cannot be verified by direct, immediately given observation, such as consistent response to test items. Like the protocol statements of logical positivism, all objectives—no matter how specific—are formulations purporting certain regular properties which are never immediately given by or directly verifiable in behavior. Objectives *are* generalizations, each naming a *class* of behavior. Hence, even though statements such as "Student will read consonant blends fluently" or "Student will capitalize proper nouns regularly" may be treated by test makers as single objectives, the possibility of writing many test items to measure the achievement of each clearly shows the intent of the test maker to assess a *generic class of behaviors*. The logic of criterion-referenced measurement, then, is not that of inferring universals from particulars. Rather the logic of criterion-referenced measurement is that of inferring generalizations from other generalizations—in short, infinite regress.

The reliability problems of criterion-referenced measurement are due precisely to this inductive logic. How many consonant blends must be read fluently, for example, before the reader is judged a fluent reader of consonant blends? How many proper nouns must be capitalized? All? Some? An "adequate sample"? Currently available criterion-referenced tests assess performance on many objectives at one administration. These tests rely on only three or four items to assess mastery of each objective. Yet the power of the tests cannot be increased by using more test items. The point is simply this: Consistent performance on a few test items tagged to particular objectives no more justifies inferences regarding target behaviors than does observation of a few white swans, to cite Popper's example, warrant the conclusion that all swans are white.

The same inductive logic leads to validity problems. An arbitrary set of objectives simply does not constitute an adequate account of any given phenomenon. There is no end of things that can be counted in language, and the extent to which they relate to the phenomenon in question is hardly assured by "adequate specificity" (avoiding a few "vague" verbs such as *understand, know, learn, develop*), along with consensus as to their importance among test users. There are as many criterion-referenced tests of reading and writing ability as there are combinations of objectives and test items. Which of these many tests actually measures reading and writing ability? Is everything worth counting? How should we assess the objectives themselves? Can we assume that all banks of objectives and test items are equal and that all will foster literacy equally well? Can we even know the answers to these questions if the tests measure only mastery of unexamined and arbitrarily assembled sets of objectives? A major hazard of criterion-referenced measurement is the appeal of one particular assumption: That specification, cataloging, and mastery of objectives will result in authentic achievement that can be measured by tests tied to the objectives. This modus operandi cannot even tell what's worth counting in the first place.

Mastery of an arbitrary set of reading and writing objectives simply does not add up to reading with comprehension and writing effectively. Hence, we do not know whether mastery of a particular set of reading–writing objectives is anything more than performance on a test. Clear questions about the focus of assessment—about *what* is measured—go unanswered and typically are not even asked (Messick, 1975). This logic here is humpty dumpty ex cathedra: Reading–writing ability is whatever the school says it is, and the proof is evidence showing the school does what it says!

Given these problems, difficulties in interpreting criterion-referenced test scores are hardly surprising. As long as measures are derived not from principled accounts of writing and reading but merely from what schools say they want to accomplish—that is, as long as *what is learned* remains merely *what is taught*—mastery levels and passing scores can only be arbitrary, and the data they yield will necessarily be ambiguous. Given their atheoretical, arbitrary character, the resulting test scores lack empirical content, meaning that their results bear on little other than themselves. Results from such tests will reveal many things Johnny and Mary can and cannot do but fail to account for these behaviors *vis-à-vis* the phenomena in question, reading and writing.

Any concerted effort to assess learning must certainly involve the test makers in fundamental questions regarding the nature of skill acquisition and assessment. Questions which need consideration *before* test development include the following:

1. What is important and why?
2. What is the nature or character of the phenomenon in question?
3. What is acceptable evidence regarding presence, absence, status, and extent of the phenomenon?

For example:

1. What is the character of writing?
2. What constitutes reading?
3. What is evidence of learning to read or write?

Such questions are logically asked prior to meaningful data collection. Construct validity is fundamental. Construct validity is to educational measurement what theory is to scientific inquiry. And for good reason: Educational measurement is a form of empirical inquiry, specifically one concerning the interpretation of educational phenomena. Popper writes that "the logical analysis of scientific knowledge ... is concerned not with *questions of fact* (Kant's *quid facti?*), but only with questions of *justification or validity* (Kant's *quid juris?*) [1959, p. 31]." *Mutatis mutandis*, the critical evaluation of student learning is concerned not with questions of protocol, observational statements, or objectives, but only with questions of justification or validity, i.e., lucid interpretations of data arising from specified procedures. As Cronbach notes, "One validates, not a test, but *an interpretation of data arising from a specified procedure* [1971, p. 447: Emphasis in original]."

As a science, educational measurement aims to attribute meaning and significance to data about learning. As Shotter (1971) notes about empirical inquiry generally, this task "does not lie in just discovering new facts, but in discovering an orderly arrangement for many, many facts, one which depicts the nature of all their interconnections. . . . A 'fact' only has significance if an individual possesses a way of interpreting it; otherwise it is literally nonsense. A 'scientific fact' is not, as Cassirer (1944) says, 'given in any haphazard observation or in mere accumulation of sense data. The facts of science always imply a theoretical, which means symbolic, element [p. 232]." It follows, then, that the task of educational measurement and evaluation is analogous: To generate, test, and implement applications of relevant theories and constructs so as to bring student responses within the scope of such theories, specifically for the purpose of understanding the educational significance of the responses.

In the Ontario project, we therefore soon found that experience at writing test items for mathematics did not after all represent adequate preparation for evaluating reading or writing. Before creating useful assessment procedures, test makers must grapple with fundamental questions about the nature of what they are examining, in our case writing and reading. Just what makes someone able to write and read? Why do some texts work better than others? What is essential to learning to write and read?

As part of the formulation of the College Entrance Examination Board Test of Writing Ability, Paul Diederich (Diederich, French, and Carlton, 1961) conducted an investigation of issues concerning the nature of good writing. Working from the premise that the key variables in good writing lie in the text (Faigley et al., 1985), he made multiple copies of student writing samples and then distributed each paper to a number of readers, not all of whom were teachers, for reading, marking, and marginal annotations. Readers varied enormously in their judgments, and virtually every paper received every possible mark, from Superior to Failing. A factor analysis of comments written on the papers revealed five major clusters among the judgments: ideas, mechanics, organization, style, and spelling. When panels of readers treated each of these factors equally—ideas no more important than organization or anything else, style no more important than spelling or anything else, and so on—highly reliable readings of papers giving a normal distribution were obtained.

It is not surprising that these assessment procedures, which force readers to treat each factor equally and consistently, improved the reliability of College Board assessments. But why did readers differ so much in their original estimates? Did many readers simply misread or misjudge? Does such variation necessarily indicate a fundamental inconsistency among readers? Or is such variation perhaps rather predictable when readers, who, with normally varied and varying expectations, encounter a text not really written for them and about which they know nothing?

Diederich's original finding that readers vacillate highly in their judgments of texts no doubt relates more closely to the nature of reading and written communication than the consistent results of the College Board's trained panel. The meaning and import of any text will normally vary from reader to reader—and even from reading to reading for the same reader—depending on the purposes, expectations, and understandings that the readers bring to the text. In short, the meaning and import of a text depends not just on what the writer says, nor on some categorical set of text features. Rather, the text uniquely configures writer and reader interests. From the time a child learns to form letters of the alphabet—indeed from the time a child becomes involved at all in print media—the expectations of readers are as formative as the child's need for expression. Like any user of language, writers are members of particular speech communities (consisting of potential writers and readers [Nystrand, 1982a]), and to write is to traffic in the possibilities of text in terms of the expectations of readers. Skilled writers do not simply "express" themselves, nor do they simply "compose text." More fundamentally they manage elements of text that balance their own needs for expression with the expectations of their readers. Writers regularly stand or fall to the extent that they control shared, relevant terms of expression. For this reason writing skill reveals itself not as a set of arbitrarily, categorically weighted features of text but rather in the quality of interaction between writers and their readers in the medium of text (Millar and Nystrand, 1979).

As we struggled with these issues, we fortuitously discovered an alternative form of assessment, ultimately important in my thinking not so much for the solutions it offered for testing problems as for the insights about writing and reading that it generated. In confronting the difficulties of identifying and criterion referencing reading comprehension objectives, the New York group developed its Multiple-Choice Cloze Test of Literal Comprehension (the MCC: see O'Reilly, Schuder, Kidder, Salter, and Hayford, 1977), a test of comprehension requiring students to reconstruct systematically broken texts. Taylor (1953) first reported research on the **cloze technique** in a procedure he devised to test readability. To test readability the researcher deletes every nth (usually every fifth) word from a minimum of 220–250 words of running text. The reader's success in reconstructing these broken texts is taken as a measure of readability. Since reader comprehension is closely related to comprehensibility or meaningfulness of text, the procedure becomes an index of comprehension, in principle at least, once the difficulty of the text is established independently (O'Reilly, Schuder, and Kidder, 1976). O'Reilly et al. modified Taylor's criteria by deleting only lexical items (nouns, verbs, adjectives, adverbs) and presenting readers with multiple choices in a test format.

Kintsch and Vipond (1979) have recently challenged the validity of the cloze technique as a measure of readability, noting that the technique measures not comprehensibility but rather redundancy of text. By this score, Kintsch and Vipond write, "a high-order statistical approximation to English that nevertheless constitutes incomprehensible gibberish would be preferred to a well-organized text with less predictable local patterns [p. 337]." For example, a pseudotext merely repeating the same word 300 times might fare misleadingly well on a cloze test. Of course, no one writes such texts nor indeed any of the contrived "incomprehensible gibberish" that Kintsch and Vipond suggest, and though Kintsch and Vipond are no doubt correct when they assert that the statistical redundancy of a text inadequately defines comprehensibility, nonetheless no one denies that redundancies of all kinds are essential to the comprehensibility of any text. Indeed, Kintsch and Vipond propose **redundancy of argument repetition** as a categorical text variable in their own proposed model of readability (though in more recent work with van Dijk [van Dijk and Kintsch (1983)], Kintsch contends that it is still important though not categorical). In any event, I do not want to lose sight here of the important role that cloze and, above all, the related *gestalt concept of closure*—i.e., the tendency for people to complete an incomplete message or figure, to "find meaning" in events—ultimately played in the development of my own ideas about writing and written communication.

In the spring of 1976, the counties involved in the Trent Valley Project adopted multiple-choice cloze test procedures as well, modified some of the test specifications, and sampled Ontario materials, including Ministry-approved texts, Ontario newspapers, and commonly available consumer materials. The move to cloze affected the organization and management of the project in several ways. First, the project shrank dramatically (from the statement of many objectives to the articulation of one), only to expand again to a complexity of issues about discourse which we did not anticipate. In addition, geographic as well as conceptual divisions of language into such headings as *sentence* in one county, *paragraph* in another, and *prose* in still another were replaced by fundamental issues concerning the nature of writing and reading. Because the adopted format left only one objective with respect to reading (i.e., comprehension), we were better able to focus on the specific requirements for literacy relevant to individual districts and communities, including comprehension of the newspaper front page, the editorial page, warranties and leases, and other, particular kinds of texts. The adoption of cloze highlighted opportunities for school boards and communities to consider and articulate their own expectations regarding literacy while at the same time grounding this assessment in a psycholinguistic account of reading and comprehension.

The adoption of cloze, moreover, brought us face to face with considerations of construct validity. At the heart of this construct was the seminal importance of *relationships* among elements of language in use rather than focus on the elements abstracted from use and separated one from the other, an emphasis inherent in attempts to list and catalog behavioral objectives. On this point we were considerably influenced by then–Ontario Institute for Studies in Education Professor Frank Smith's work in reading. In learning to read, Smith (1971) contends, the reader develops an increasingly sophisticated sense of the regularities and significant differences of written text. For example, the beginner soon learns that there are important differences between *d* and *b* but no real differences between a and *a* even though a second glance might suggest that there are more differences between the graphic configurations of *a* and a than there are between *d* and *b* and *p* and q. Readers soon become adept at predicting many such things, e.g., how certain kinds of words can and cannot follow other words; how various conventions set up and introduce various genres; and so on. Reading is a continuous interaction between the reader's expectations and the actualities of text, and the import of text elements is largely defined by reader expectations in the process of reading.

This view of the reading process raises very serious issues about the uses of criterion-referenced testing in language instruction. If learning to read depends essentially on evaluating regularities and significant differences of text in context and use, then criterion referencing, which shatters the curriculum in the interests of "specificity," is at odds with the very process of learning to read. This was demonstrated in 1985 in Chicago, where, after 5 years and $8 million, the school board rejected its Mastery Learning Reading Program, concluding that the demands of mastering endless reading objectives essentially precluded students' reading from books (*NY Times*, October 8, 1985). By eschewing a definition of reading and writing processes, criterion referencing arbitrarily slices language into myriads of discrete objectives, lending a delineated, arbitrarily taxonomic character to curriculum. The specificity of criterion referencing is due not to the detail in which it depicts language processes but rather to its wholesale atomization of the curriculum. By adopting the cloze procedure, the Ontario counties voted to favor *reading for meaning* as a classroom focus and affirmed the central importance of comprehension in the process of learning at all ages.

While considering the usefulness of cloze in reading assessment, we wondered about its possibilities for examining writing. Could we not use cloze as a measure of writing ability, provided relevant readers were identified either by or for the writer before writing? We reasoned that the cloze scores of readers might bear on the success of the writer in making sense for intended readers. We hypothesized that competence in written communication requires awareness on the part of the writer, as reflected in performance, of the needs of the reader to make sense of the text. Specifically writers must not preclude their readers from making sense of the text. Readers require orthographic cues that are syntactic, graphemic, morphemic, and discourse-related, and an important test of the writer's ability is the extent to which intended and relevant readers can ascertain intended relations between and among words and sentences in the text. Writers will succeed or fail significantly to the extent that they control shared, relevant terms of expression, or rules of use.

TABLE 1

Clozed Writing Sample[a]

TOPIC: Does the government have the right to impose laws on us for our own protection?	
Yes, I_____	think
that the laws are_____.	okay
The people that puts_____	out
the laws are doing it_____	for
us to help us,_____	not
to hurt us. The_____	seatbelt
law, since they made us_____	use
it my sister_____	said
that there isn't so_____	many
head injuries on U-2_____	where
she is nursing. And the_____	laws
hasn't come out yet_____	about
the death penalty but I_____	think
they should, because I_____	think
there won't be so_____	much
crime. I also think the_____	OPP's
could be harder on the_____	people
that steal, kill and_____.	rapes
And the law for_____	going
over 60 on the _____	401
that is to_____	help
us to save_____.	gas
But I am just_____	one
person with my_____	ideas
and it might be_____	different
then my friends, family and_____	maybe
you judges. I believe_____	in
all laws, some even_____	sounds
crazy but, what there_____	doing
is for us.	

(FOLD BACK HERE)

[a]From Nystrand (1979). Copyright © 1979 by the National Council of Teachers of English. Reprinted by permission of the publisher.

In November 1976, 10 teachers from the project gathered to work 12 clozed writing samples, all written by eighth graders for a general adult audience. Table 1 shows an example; Table 2 shows the same sample with discrepant reader guesses in parentheses to the right. In addition to scoring the readabilities of these texts, we also examined the discrepancies between the writers' original words and the readers' wrong guesses. We assumed that in order to communicate, writers will constrain their readers, i.e., delimit the predictions they are likely to test as they read. We initially called the

TABLE 2

Adult Responses to Clozed Writing Sample[a, b]

Yes, I *think*
that the laws are *okay*. (2 *good*; 1 *right*; 3 *allright*)
The people that puts *out* (3 *down*; 2 *on*; 1 *together*; 1 *forth*)
the laws are doing *it for* (3 *use*)
us to help us, *not*
to hurt us. The *seatbelt*
law, since they made us *use* (6 *wear*; 1 *okay*; 1 *do*)
it my sister *said* (4 *says*; 1 *knows*; 1 *feels*)
that there isn't so *many*
head injuries on U-2 *where* (1 *because*)
she is nursing. And the *laws* (6 *law*; 1 *decision*; 1 *government*; 1 *police*)
hasn't come out yet *about* (1 *on*; 2 *for*)
the death penalty but I *think*
they should, because I *think* (1 *know*)
there won't be so *much* (1 *many*)
crime. I also think the *OPP's* (1 *police*; 4 *law*; 3 *laws*; 1 *courts*)
could be harder on the *people* (1 *criminals*; 1 *kids*)
that steal, kill and *rapes* . (6 *rapes*; 2 *rob*; 1 *speed*)
And the law for *going* (3 *driving*; 1 *speed*; 4 *speeding*)
over 60 on the *401* (6 *highway*; 1 *highways*)
that is to *help* (2 *make*)
us to save *gas*. (4 *lives*; 1 *ourselves*; 1 *money*)
But I am just *one*
person with my *ideas* (10 *opinions*)
and it might be *different* (1 *that*; 1 *wrong*; 1 *allright*; 1 *better*)
then my friends, family and *maybe* (1 *teachers*; 1 *others*; 1 *also*)
you judges. I believe *in* (5 *that*) (1 *police*; 1 *ale*; 1 *even*)
all laws, some even *sounds* (4 *are*; 1 *slightly*; 1 *so*; 1 *maybe*; 2 *is*; 2 *are*; 1 *for*)
crazy but, what there *doing*
is for us.

---

[a]From Nystrand (1979). Copyright © 1979 by the National Council of Teachers of English. Reprinted by permission of the publisher.

[b]Discrepant reader responses and numbers of subjects so responding are in parentheses to right. $n = 10$.

discrepancies "misconstraints," or elements of the text which result in miscue (cf. Goodman, 1967), i.e., erroneous predictions. Although useful, the concept of misconstraint failed to account adequately for all the discrepancies we found. More plausibly, when readers drew blanks, they seemed to be *inadequately* or *overly* constrained, not simply *mis*-constrained.

When writers inadequately explain or readers inadequately understand, the problem is not altogether explained by either the writers' or the readers' behavior alone. More fundamentally, these problems involve a mismatch between the respective needs and expectations of writer *and* reader. As Moffett (1968a) elegantly notes, writers never just write; they always write about something to someone. Analogously, readers never just read; they always read a text about something by someone. Moreover, the respective acts of expression and comprehension are fundamentally shaped by what the writer and reader assume about the intent and expectations of the other.

This important distinction underscores the configurational nature of written text, i.e., the role it plays in balancing the respective needs and expectations of the conversants. At the same time that the text encompasses the needs of the writer for expression, it also encompasses the expectations that readers bring to the text, and the balance that it strikes between these respective, interactive concerns shapes the text in very particular ways. Both readers and writers make sense—the one *of* print, the other *in* print. More fundamentally, each presupposes the sense-making capabilities of the other. Alfred Schutz describes this transcendental social fact as a condition of reciprocity which undergirds and organizes individual and social behavior at all levels: It is "assumed that the sector of the world taken for granted by me is also taken for granted by you, [and] even more, that it is taken for granted by 'Us' [1967, p. 12]." This principle is important to writing and reading research because it implicates writers and readers in a common social web.

Since 1970 writing and reading researchers have increasingly echoed each other. In his essay on "The Cognitive Base of Reading and Writing," Kucer (1985) summarizes their conclusions as follows:

1. "Readers and writers construct text world meanings through utilizing the prior knowledge which they bring to the literacy event";
2. "Discoveries of how the written language system operates feed into a common data pool from which the language user draws when constructing the text world";
3. "Readers and writers utilize common procedures for transforming prior knowledge into a text world"; and
4. "Readers and writers display common processing patterns or abilities when constructing text worlds [pp. 7–25]."

In other words, both writing and reading researchers have delineated writing and reading as cognitive processes in which the individual builds internal representations of experience and interprets subsequent encounters in light of expectations entailed by these representations. Composing process research has tended to see writing as the meaning-making act whereby the writer's thoughts are transformed into text, and reading research has tended to see reading as the interpretive act whereby readers test their expectations in terms of actualities of text. Curiously, as writing and reading researchers have drawn increasingly closer to each other in their common emphasis on the active, constructive nature of the language processes, the actual dynamics of writing as it relates to reading and reading as it relates to writing remain puzzling. What appears to be missing, Tierney, Leys, and Rogers (1984) note, is "a socio-cognitive examination of the various communicative contexts within which readers and writers reside [p. 7]."

A number of investigations have begun to address the interactive nature of writing and reading. Many researchers (e.g., Moffett, 1968a; Murray, 1968) have noted the effects of reader feedback on writing ability, and others have noted the socializing effects on children of the print media and the community of writer–readers that these media represent (e.g., Ferreiro & Teberosky, 1982; Heath, 1982). Elsewhere, Tierney (1983; Tierney, Leys, and Rogers, 1984) examines the mediating role of text in interaction between the intention of the author and the needs of the reader. Tierney and La Zansky (1980) persuasively elaborate the contractual nature of writing and reading, which, they contend, "defines what is allowable *vis-à-vis* the role of each in relation to the text [p. 2]." In "The Structure of Textual Space [1982c]," I argue that the motivation for discourse is not the author's intentions or goals so much as the need to reconcile a gap or discrepancy between the premises of the writer and those of the reader. It is the phenomenal tension occasioned by their respective concerns, I contend, that defines the **textual space** in which writers and readers function.

The principle of reciprocity is an essential key to understanding the interactions and negotiations of writers and readers. Most research on writer–reader interaction has focused on (a) the effects of reflection (for example, when writers reread what they have written; e.g., Tierney, 1983), (b) concrete response (including teachers' and peers'; e.g., Freedman, 1984, 1985; Gere and Stevens, 1985; Newkirk, 1984), and (c) projection (when readers speculate on the writer's intent and when writers speculate on the salient features of their audience; e.g., Steinmann, 1982). Much of this research works from the premise that writers and readers ultimately collaborate via the internal representation of meaning created in the process of writing and reading; i.e., that in interpreting the intent of the writer, readers seek to construe the writer's representation, and vice versa. The condition of reciprocity, however, penetrates more deeply into the fabric of discourse than this ostensible cooperation. Reciprocity has to do not with a commonality of representations but rather with a mutuality of expectations for certain qualities of discourse, namely elements of text that facilitate the sense-making requirements of both conversants. Reciprocity entails not the wholesale duplication of mindsets but rather the expectation for shared understandings, not as a precondition but as a continuous result of discourse. As a principle of discourse, reciprocity is transcendent, encompassing the activities of both writer and reader; it is constant, impinging on communication at every turn; and it is axiomatic, determining key aspects of text in terms of the balance that is struck between the needs and expectations of the conversants.

This book presents a series of inquiries exploring various aspects of writing and reading as they relate to each other and especially how their character as discourse processes is shaped by reciprocity between conversants.

Chapter 1 examines recent research on the composing process and notes a number of problems, chief among them the inadequate distinction of writing from other modes of discourse as well as the need for a fundamental, operating principle of discourse.

Chapter 2 sketches the general outlines of a theory of reciprocity in discourse, especially as treated in Rommetveit's (1974) analysis of message structure; analyses of conversation (especially Sacks and Schlegloff); studies of information structure (including given and new information; thematic progression, texture, and coherence–cohesion); and studies of adult–child discourse (especially as represented by Bates, 1976; Bruner, 1975a, 1975b, and 1978; Halliday, 1974, 1978; Corsaro, 1977; Garvey, 1977, 1979; and Cook-Gumperz, 1977, 1978). This chapter notes the "pact of discourse" whereby each participant agrees to maintain a balance of discourse, or communicative homeostasis, i.e., an equilibrium between what the one knows as producer and the other expects as receiver.

This equilibrium of discourse is by nature temporary and fragile—in need of constant repair. To counter the heteroglossic force of events and personal perceptions, which must inevitably render such negotiated categorizations precarious and temporary, conversants continuously engage in discourse: They make texts. This chapter reviews research on reciprocity and examines constraints of various media on resources, plus procedures whereby conversants establish, maintain, and restore as necessary communicative homeostasis, the fundamental principle of discourse functioning.

Chapter 3 examines implications of the reciprocity principle for written discourse and formalizes patterns and regularities of written discourse in a reciprocity-based text grammar consisting of one axiom and seven corollaries.

Chapter 4. The common claim that written texts are "autonomous" and explicit compared to speech, which is "context-bound" and fragmented, misses the main point of one aspect of writing. A text is explicit not because it says everything all by itself but rather because it strikes a careful balance between what needs to be said and what may be assumed. The writer's problem is not just being explicit. The writer's problem is *knowing what to be explicit about.*

The empirical work in this chapter, a collaboration of Nystrand, Doyle, and Himley, examines the well-established contention that, in the interests of comprehension, written texts must be "autonomous" and "self-contextualizing" compared to spoken utterances, which need not be as explicit since their meaning is largely in the interaction between the speakers. The study examines readers' and listeners' recall of written and spoken reports and speculations in terms of exophoric and endophoric cohesive ties, including reference, substitution, ellipsis, and lexis. The results show that explicitness of text (as defined by extent of endophoric cohesive ties) bears no significant relationship to recall. The written essays (speculations) examined were in fact more explicit than the oral speculations and also more explicit than the narratives, both written and oral. Nonetheless, readers recalled these written essays no better than the other genres despite their explicitness: Readers and listeners did not necessarily recall things better the more they were spelled out. This conclusion corroborates recent research reported by Tannen (1982) and Wells (1981): Writing and speech differ in the extent to which each is autonomous and self-contextualizing only if certain genres are compared, namely written speculation (i.e., expository prose) and spoken narrative (e.g., gossip).

Chapter 5. Texts are lucid to the extent that they maintain a balance of discourse between writers and readers. Texts are ambiguous or abstruse when they violate the pact of discourse. Chapter 5 not only develops this theme but also investigates the various roles of text elaborations in written discourse. There are two studies reported. The first study concerns the role of reciprocity in defining "choice points" which the writer must treat with available text options if communication is to be sustained. This study introduces the concept of text "buttressing" (or elaboration) and examines the relationship of text elaborations to "bridging" inference processes of readers. The second study examines the problem of writing for knowledge-able readers versus writing for unknowledgeable readers, in this case, expert and novice computer users, and shows how both choice points and options vary depending on the extent of shared knowledge between writer and reader.

Chapter 6, by Margaret Himley, examines the principle of reciprocity in written discourse from another point of view, that of the learner. In her case study of one first grader's path of entry into the community of writer–readers, Himley shows how this learner's development is characterized not only by awareness and use of more intricate text options but also by shifting notions of appropriate choice points. As the learner becomes more sophisticated and adventuresome in her social role as writer, she experiments with the options available to her, which in turn heighten her awareness of the possibilities for meaning entailed by this role. For the learner, choice points and text options shift continuously, with developments in either redefining the other. This learner "spirals" her way into the semiotic possibilities of the written medium.

Chapter 7 traces the development of word segmentation skills in one writer who learned to write before entering school. This study presents a new analysis of previously published research (Bissex, 1980), plus analysis of some unpublished data from the same research, and highlights the discourse function of spacing both between and within words. The beginning writer's use of dots to separate words in this case works as a "place holder" of sorts while he addresses other, more encompassing problems of orthography and composition. We examine this process as the learner's experiment with orthographic choice points and text options. As he learns to balance his own needs for written expression with the expectations of readers, a very opaque orthography becomes legible and transparent.

We note important similarities between the problem of the beginner of Chapter 7 in segmenting words and the problem of the expert of Chapter 5 in revising abstruse texts for an unknowledgeable audience—namely *managing the resources of the written language, not to transmit but to make meaning*. To become fluent, beginning writers must be "grammarians" of sorts—written-text experimenters whose tacit inquiry qua writer has less to do with organizing the contents of expression and mastering the aims of discourse than it does with systematizing the means of expression and synthesizing the resources of the written language. The learner's problem is how something can be said with pen and paper despite the fact that not one single stroke, word, or sentence corresponds natually to what we call thought. Much of the necessary experimentation takes the form of play and imitation, involving *assimilation* and *accommodation* in Piaget's terms. Hence, the invented spellings of young writers studied by Read (1975) and Bissex (1980) are a form of orthographic accommodation and assimilation, a way of mastering the system by experimenting with its possibilities. The principle of reciprocity in discourse undergirds not only the conduct of written discourse but also the task of learning to write.

Chapter 8 examines the learning process of adult writers. Specifically we look at college freshmen writing and discussing their writing with each other in a class devoted to peer conferencing. When peer groups work well and writers confront their readers regularly to review their papers, the groups tend to "gravitate" to unclear or troublesome parts of their writing. As long as groups do not engage in excessive "copy editing" but dwell instead on understanding the writer's purpose in terms of their own expectations, the discussions focus mainly on troublesources and uncertainties of text. More to the point, these groups have a keen sense of what problems need solving. They identify key troublesources (i.e., choice points) and deal concretely with how particular text structures (options) address these troublesources. These troublesources, which include ambiguities of purpose (What's the purpose of this?), genre (What sort of text is this?), topic (What's this about anyway?), and comment (What's the point?), constitute the subject matter of these sessions. In effect, the discussion examines a continuous set of rhetorical problems, which the group collaborates in solving.

In Vygotskyan terms, we may regard intensive peer review as a formative social arrangement (formative even for college writers) in which writers become consciously aware of the functional significance of composing behaviors, discourse strategies, and elements of text by managing them all in anticipation of continuous reader feedback. This is not to argue that writers in peer groups come to control their rhetorical problem-solving efforts by somehow conducting the same conversations "in their heads" that formerly were carried out in their groups. Rather, it means that the composing processes and discourse strategies that writers take from their groups largely emerge on the basis of reflective and regulative processes that can be observed to occur first in the social interaction of peer review.

In the final analysis, we see that empirical writing research has blossomed in the last few years. It has shown how writing, like other forms of behavior, is informed by intention and purpose. And it has isolated the major components of the composing process. But clearly this is not the whole story. As much as by thought and purpose, writing is shaped by audience, context, reader knowledge and expectations, as well as the idiosyncratic resources of the medium itself.

In all the studies presented here, we see that writing is not a straightforward skill like eating or swimming or typing. No one learns to write fluently once and for all in the way people drive cars and work lawnmowers routinely. If this were the case, accomplished writers would never suffer writers' block. Nor would they frequently need to renavigate the written language when addressing new topics and new audiences. Written discourse is not the well-oiled engine of written speech production nor the well-regulated cybernetic system of cognitive scripts and well-formed, permissible text types. It is the social process whereby literate individuals "writ[e] on the premises of the reader [and read] on the premises of the writer [Rommetveit, 1974, p. 63]."

Part I

Writing

Philosophical Assumptions Inherent in Current Cognitive Models of Writing

INTRODUCTION: THOUGHT AND LANGUAGE IN CURRENT COGNITIVE MODELS OF COMPOSING

Most cognitive models of writing highlight the central role of writer intention, purpose, plans, goals, world knowledge, and so on, in the composing process. These models are "meaning-" or "purpose-based," and by composing the writer is said to "translate" or "transcribe" these cognitive factors (or **metacomponents** [Sternberg, 1980]) into actual texts. This conception formalizes the commonsense and classical rhetorical notion that discourse consists of thoughts cloaked in words, or, to put it another way, that writing requires first finding something to say and then finding appropriate words and expressions for communicating these thoughts (cf. Cicero's stages of invention, arrangement, style, memory, and delivery). Put simply, composing starts with thought and ends with text.

The term *top down* is sometimes used to characterize the premises of these models regarding the organization of the psychological processes involved, referring to the primacy of the metacomponents: High-level plans (in the form of "scripts" and "schemas") govern and inform the "subprocesses of transcription," including the motor activity of handwriting and matters of orthography. Sternberg refers to these subprocesses as **perfor-**

mance components, and in the context of writing research, Scardamalia, Bereiter, and Goelman (1982) call them **production factors**. The performance components implement the decisions of the superordinate metacomponents.

For about a decade now, this emphasis on writing as process has affected both writing instruction and writing research. On the one hand, it has had a salutary effect on writing pedagogy, which has historically tended to treat products while generally ignoring what writers must continuously confront—the act of writing itself (cf. Emig, 1971). On the other hand, this emphasis on writing as process, which introduced methods of modern experimental psychology to issues of rhetoric (e.g., Gregg and Steinberg, 1980) and vice versa, has spawned the empirical investigation of writing. Like linguistics in the early 20th century, this development is noteworthy because it marks a shift in emphasis from *prescriptions derived from exemplary texts* to *descriptions derived from actual speakers/writers.*

There are, in fact, other conceptions of language–thought relationships available to psychologists and writing researchers in addition to the metacomponential paradigm. Rosenberg's (1977) survey includes (a) the hypothesis that linguistic form and cognitive structure are largely identical; and (b) the hypothesis that the resources of language precede thought in the sense that they constrain expression and so shape the conduct of discourse (for implications of each position for writing, see Gregg and Steinberg, 1980; and Nystrand, 1982a, respectively). Nonetheless, the idea that language comes "after the ideational fact" has become an axiom of much current American writing research. For this reason, it seems appropriate, as we start, to examine some of the premises and especially some of the difficulties of this characterization of writing.

WHY PURPOSE WILL NOT CHARACTERIZE WRITING AS A PARTICULAR MODE OF DISCOURSE

We note, first, that writing does not distinguish itself from other modes of discourse in terms of its metacomponents. That is, speaking is generally no less purposeful or meaningful than writing. Hence, metacomponential analysis is too general to capture the salient features of either speech or writing as a particular mode of discourse. Indeed, to contend that writing is "meaning-" or "purpose-based" is to claim no more than that writing is language, which is true, of course, but so too are speaking, painting, gesturing, and other sign systems.

Given this, it is not surprising to discover, as did Gould (1980) in experiments comparing dictating and writing letters, that analysis of discourse into the metacomponential phases of generating, organizing, and translating ideas into text shows no significant differences between writing and dictating: Effective composition shows more planning, for example, than ineffective composition *regardless of mode*. These results obviously do not mean that dictating and writing are identical—they obviously are not—merely that as discourse, they are alike in some fundamental ways, particularly as characterized by investigations controlling for purpose and context of use.

Speaking and writing simply cannot be differentiated as modes of discourse at the level of purpose since, as discourse, they are equally and essentially purposeful. This is the chief reason why metacomponential accounts work as general models of discourse but provide only rough descriptions of particular modes of discourse.

The issue here is analogous to biological characterization of *human being*, which at the level of genus requires going no further than *Homo* but which at the level of species requires examining the idiosyncracies of *Homo sapiens*. *Mutatis mutandis*, understanding the idiosyncratic functioning of writing requires going beyond generalities about purpose in discourse. As a minimum, we must distinguish the species from the genus, on the one hand showing how speaking and writing differ and, on the other hand, how writing and reading are related. We must examine how, by what is written, writers make something known to others.

LANGUAGE AFTER THE IDEATIONAL FACT

There is a strong Neoplatonic cast to cognitive models which seek to interpret the particulars of writing in terms of an underlying exemplar ambiguously defined as the composing process on the one hand and the writer's thoughts on the other. The **Composing Process Exemplar** is a set of "automatized routines, subroutines, and discourse scripts" which are mirrored in particular acts of writing. The **Writer's Thoughts Exemplar** is "an underlying semantic representation" or "cognitive map" "organized hierarchically in terms of propositions" and "networks of goals," which are mirrored in particular written texts. In the process of writers transcribing their thoughts, Flower and Hayes note, language impedes expression: There is "the inevitable truculence of language itself, which seems to resist our attempt to form a set of continuous sentences with forward and backward reference [1980b, p. 36]."

Figure 1.1 shows Flower and Hayes' model of the composing process; Figure 1.2 is Beaugrande's "text-world model" for Macbeth's thoughts as "transcribed" in the soliloquy of Act V, scene 5, lines 17–28.

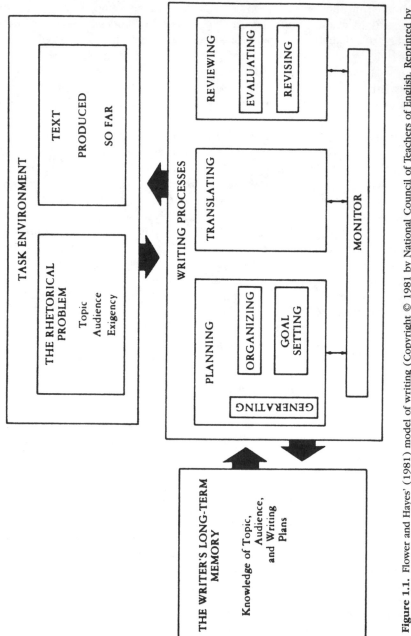

Figure 1.1. Flower and Hayes' (1981) model of writing (Copyright © 1981 by National Council of Teachers of English. Reprinted by permission of the publisher).

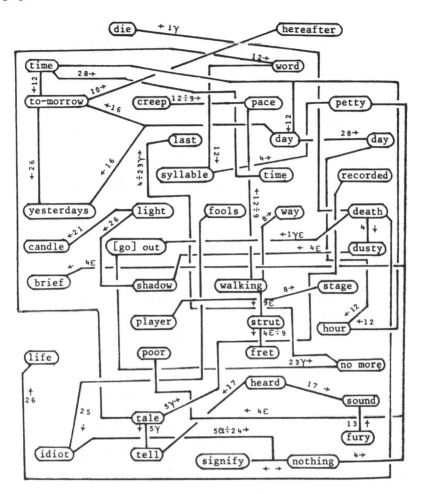

Key: 1=state of; 4=attribute of; 5=perception of; 8=location of; 9=motion of; 10=time of; 12=part of; 13=substance of; 16=specification of; 17=cause of; 21=instrument of; 23=modality of; 24=significance of; 25=equivalent to; 26=opposed to; 28=recurrence of; α = initiation; γ = entry; ε = proximity.

Figure 1.2. Beaugrande's (1979) text-world model of Macbeth's soliloquy (Reprinted with the permission of the University of Minnesota Center for Advanced Studies in Language, Style, and Literary Theory).

These research programs, which bifurcate writing into high-level cognitive processes and low-level behavioral elements, spatialize, detemporalize, and decontextualize writing. Writing is the translation of "complex networks of relationships...into linear pieces of written English [Flower and Hayes, 1981, p. 373]." The writer is assisted in this process by a cognitive editor-in-chief, or "monitor"—a "writing strategist which determines when the writer moves from one process to the next [Flower and Hayes, 1981, p. 374]." The principles which organize the strategies, plots, and assignations of this cognitive homunculus, however, remain unclear and unspecified.

These Neoplatonic accounts of writing, which seek to formalize "what writers know," are troublesome since writing is most essentially a use of language. Spoken and written language, for example, do not differ much in their syntactical and lexical resources (Wardhaugh, 1969; Miller, 1951) though writers and speakers deploy these resources very differently both in proportion and complexity (Joos, 1962). Compared to speech, writing generally has a higher lexical density (Ure, 1969) but a simpler sentential structure. As Halliday (in press) notes, writing tends to proceed syntactically by embedding, whereas speech tends to be **hypotactic** (one element is dependent on another but is not a constituent of it): "Spoken language tends to have more clauses in the syntagm (greater 'grammatical intricacy'), and fewer lexical items in the clause. Written language tends to have more lexical items in the clause (greater 'lexical density'), and fewer clauses in the syntagm." Because of these differences, the very character of writing as a language system is missed when its particulars are decontextualized in terms of the exemplar **Composing Process**.

Long ago, Aristotle charged that Plato failed to explain the particulars of experience in his theory of transcendental forms by claiming that they "mirror" underlying forms. Rather than explaining the particulars, Aristotle charged, Plato merely created something else to explain, namely the world of forms and the mechanism of imitation whereby the particulars "mirror" the exemplar. This criticism applies to metacomponential analyses of writing. Writing is not explained by postulating an intricate underlying cognitive world of knowledge and rules that are somehow "translated" or "transcribed" into concrete texts. Indeed, two new problems are created: the cognitive world and the mechanism of transcription (the mysterious homunculus monitor). Nor is the problem any less critical in "explaining" the species by appealing to the genus: Even the fullest account of **Composing Process** fails to explain the species' relationship to the genus and hence its salient features.

The importance of all this is largely to note that writing always takes place in a context. As Scribner and Cole (1981, p. 236) note after a 7-year cross-cultural study, literacy is "not simply knowing how to read and write a particular script but applying this knowledge for specific purposes in specific contexts of use." This is perhaps the most fundamental reason why writing is not adequately and simply explained as the externalization of thoughts or the practiced transcription of metacomponential content, whatever this might be. The particulars of writing relate less to the "transmission of meaning" and more to the set of management of the resources of written language available for making meaning in particular settings.

Moreover, the goal of identifying a set of universal, autonomous rules and a body of tacit knowledge (writer "competence") which might structure writing (writer "performance") is complicated by the fact that writing is culture-specific: The uses of writing vary from culture to culture, from one literate group to the next. Indeed, these uses and functions vary widely even in the same society over time (Vygotsky, 1978; Scribner and Cole, 1981; Phillips, 1975; Heath, 1982). For these reasons, Cicourel notes that accounts of discourse involving autonomous syntactic or macrolevel text or story-grammar rules "must be understood as aspects of a general processing system that reflects on and interacts with information from a local communicative context [1978, p. 26]." Walia (1983) notes that "Hayes and Flower find themselves heading down the rocky path TG grammarians have recently travelled of endless 'fix-up' rules ... to account for anomalous data [Walia, 1983, p. 10]." Hickmann concludes that "A model of linguistic or cognitive competence which not only describes a particular structure but also specifies why, when, where, and in what ways this structure might be used, becomes a performance model. It then becomes unclear how such a model would be theoretically consistent and would not lead to the postulation of a number of additions and qualifications which appear to be extraneous or ad hoc considering the very rationale motivating the use of a competence model" in the first place (Hickmann, 1980, p. xix).

The character of writing as language, moreover, is trivialized when the generation of language is presumed to be ancillary to the generation of ideas—that is, when words are seen as the garb of thought. In this view, thoughts take on written (rather than spoken, gestural, etc.) form only at the point of transcription. Kintsch's view is representative: "We assume that at this point [of translation] the writer has available both the macro- and microstructure of the text, that is, its complete semantic representation. . . . This is what the writer needs to put into words now [1980, p. 28]." In other words, in order to give thoughts written form, writers must encode them. After proceeding so far with the development of their thoughts, writers then must weigh constraints of audience, topic, and genre in order to find an appropriate form of expression. Kintsch explains: "Suppose, for example, that the writer decides on the over-all structure of an argument. We assume that he has internalized a series of strategies for organizing an argument. What these strategies are, we can take from rhetoric books. Thus, for instance, following Aristotle, a writer would immediately organize his material into three major subsections: statement of the issues, assembly of evidence, and conclusion [Kintsch, 1980, pp. 21–22]." In effect, the conventions of written text here are rather like particular typesetters' fonts (Palatino, say, rather than Baskerville): They are selected only in the final stages of text production, only after the real work is done.

Every writer knows, of course, that words do not always or only follow thought. Sometimes the words do themselves prompt thought, a phenomenon which Britton et al. (1975) describe as "shaping at the point of utterance" and which E. M. Forster noted when he quipped, "How do I know what I think till I see what I say?" Recognizing the fundamental role that language can play in the generation of thought, Flower and Hayes (1977) describe the composing process as potentially "recursive" and postulate a feedback loop in the production cycle which allows for idea generation *after* initial transcription (as in rewriting parts of a text after rereading what is already written; See Figure 1.1).

Beaugrande (1982), following Gould (1980), postulates multilevel processes or stages, proposing a "parallel-stage interaction model," whereby the dominance of any stage of writing can yield text. For Beaugrande, anything from reconsidered goals to an extended word search can prompt a writer to write more. Neither of these modifications, however—neither recursiveness nor parallel-stage interaction—fundamentally alters the status of language after the ideational fact in these models. Regardless of what prompts thought in the first place—whether something in memory, something just said, or some expression carefully reconsidered—the eventual expression of this thought requires the thought first and the expression second. In the case of recursive rules, the renewed generation of ideas after text production is still the precursor of additional text, and in the case of Beaugrande's parallel-stage interaction model, the linguistic shaping of thought (and the apparent identity of thought and expression) is a special case: Generally, Beaugrande notes, thought is formatted in the syntax of language.

If language production really works this way, then any writer's meaning (or gist) might presumably be reformatted as speech merely by recasting it in the conventions of the spoken language. And writing instruction might be treated as a kind of "revision training" whereby "the main ideas and the general direction of the discourse" might be considered "settled" but "the immediate formatting of phrases and clauses has to be navigated all over again [Beaugrande, 1982, pp. 258, 240]." With respect to expressing thoughts as either speech or writing, these models are neutral: There are no obligatory rules, for example, specifying writing for certain thoughts and speech for others.

But writing and speaking differ more fundamentally than in the conventions of their expression. And speech does not become writing merely by "swapping formats." First of all, as the culmination of expression, elements of text relate not only to speaker purpose and meaning but also to the situation which prompts the text in the first place. Hence, for every grocery list, essay, sermon, note to oneself, etc., there is a particular type of occasion that prompts it. These texts are not simply tacked onto the process that brings them into being; rather they are the very realizations of this process. They represent typical means for bringing about typical ends in typical situations (cf. Schutz, 1967). Regarding speech and writing as identical in their metacomponents and fundamentally different only in format fails to grasp the functional significance of elements of text, in effect trivializing these conventions rather than understanding them as essential elements in a very complicated psychosocial equation.

There are, in fact, many aspects of both speech and writing that have no easy, respective counterparts in the alternative mode. This is the major reason why, for example, conversation is so difficult to transcribe adequately and why certain forms of writing (e.g., library card catalogs; dictionaries; scholarly journals; grocery lists; technical reports with tables, charts, references, and notes) have no ready oral equivalents. Figure 1.3 arranges spoken and written modes of discourse along a continuum showing the relative ease and difficulty of "mode switching" or transposition (i.e., going from speech to writing and from writing to speech). Three main points should be noted. First, writing is never a simple transcription of speech. Second, those forms most difficult to transpose are most clearly distinguished by the medium-specific and nonoverlapping resources of each mode (e.g., intonation, pitch, stress, rhythm; paralinguistic features; and availability of physical and eye contact in speech versus spacing, layout, indentation, punctuation, typeface, capitalization, italics, graphics, margins, and availability of cotext in writing [cf. Stubbs, 1980, p. 117]). Third, those written and spoken forms intuitively most similar (e.g., casual conversation and dramatic dialog; essays and lectures) actually differ substantially. Conversation is typically marked by apparent non sequiturs, false starts, obscure allusions, anacolutha, and digressions whereas dramatic dialog is more explicitly cohesive, with pronouns and demonstratives typically having clear intext (or endophoric) references (Gregory and Carroll, 1978, p. 43). This is why transcripts of taped conversations seem fragmented and disjointed compared to drama scripts, which can usually be read as text. The difference is due to the fact that real conversation is only for the participants, whereas staged dialog is for nonparticipants and spectators.

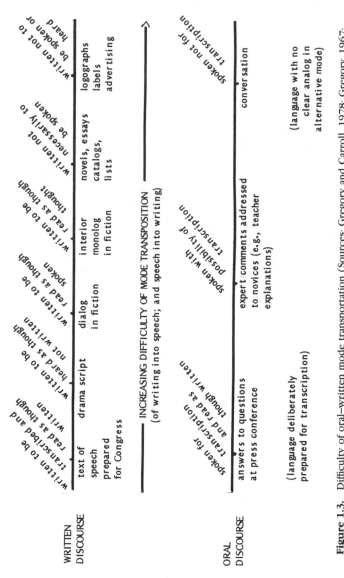

Figure 1.3. Difficulty of oral-written mode transportation (Sources: Gregory and Carroll, 1978; Gregory, 1967; Benson and Greaves, 1975).

The coherence of real talk, which need not be clear to strangers (e.g., eavesdroppers and readers of transcripts), derives largely from knowledge the participants share independently of actual talk. By contrast, the coherence of staged talk, which must be clear to an entire audience of strangers, eavesdroppers, and spectators, is largely due to the use of language itself to create a context for "talk." In many ways, transposing spoken and written forms is as complicated as any language translation (cf. Haas, 1970). Writing is never a simple transcription of speech: Written dialog and dialect (e.g., Huck and Jim in *The Adventures of Huckleberry Finn*) require skillful exploitation of the resources of written language to *suggest* speech by transposing it from one medium to another, not simply transcribing what someone says.

The decision to express oneself in writing rather than speech, or vice versa, is not usually free or neutral. Literate individuals typically choose one mode rather the other (Vachek, 1973) and do so appropriately (Nystrand, 1982a) because of the unique functional potential of each respective mode (Stubbs, 1980). Hence, people write essays, grocery lists, and novels, but they talk with their neighbors, the person at the door, and those with whom they dine. In principle, of course, we may speak an essay or epic (as Milton composed *Paradise Lost*), or, conversely, transpose one's thoughts during a conversation into written rather than oral form. However, no one ever does so except as a matter of exigency (e.g., Milton).

INDEXICALITY IN WRITING

The importance of all this is largely to note that writing, like any discourse, is more than a semantic–referential system. Writing is used not only for reference and predication but also for reflecting and shaping the social contexts of its use. In addition to working **symbolically**, i.e., in terms of references that work independently of any particular context, writing also works **indexically**, i.e., by virtue of existential, contextual connections between sign or text and its object. This is true in the trivial example of an EXIT sign, which works not only in terms of what the word *exit* refers to generally in any context but also, in any particular case, in terms of the proximity of the EXIT sign to a door, which the sign indexes or "points to." The indexical value or meaning in this case relates specifically to its copresence with some aspect of its context of use (Peirce, 1932).

The indexicality of written text is more subtly apparent in the example of the business executive reading a timely (say ominous) memo, which she interprets not only in terms of what it says about some topic (i.e., referential content) but rather in terms of certain facts in the context of use that this memo marks, namely who else has received it, who has not received it, who might have received it but is not indicated as having received it, and perhaps the very fact that this message is written; i.e., it arrives not as a telephone message but rather as a sealed memo (no doubt filed in triplicate in the author's file). And what of the troubling fact that this memo addresses the addressee formally as *Miss* or *Ms.,* not as in previous communications on a familiar first-name–no-last-name basis? Clearly, the memo is addressed to the same person; there is no shift here in reference. What is ominously different in the meaning of this memo is not so much "what it is about" or "what it says"—i.e., the denotational, referential meaning of the text—but rather information about the social context that this text **indexes**. Specifically the text indexes or marks a shift in the relative social status of the addresser and addressee (cf. Silverstein 1976, 1985).

Much has been made about the quintessentially referential character of written text, especially as compared to speech. Hirsch (1977) and Olson (1977), for example, argue that, whereas the meaning of an utterance is largely "in the context" shared by speaker and listener, the meaning of a written text must be fully contained and explicitly represented in the text itself because the writer and reader are unable to share any context in common. For many writing researchers this requirement for self-contextualization and referential autonomy is central to the character of exposition (though perhaps not "less quintessential" forms such as EXIT signs and timely memos to business executives). Yet even in the most elaborate academic prose, we find countless examples of indexicality at work, including **shifters,** or elements of text that depend for their reference on the context of use (including **deictics** such as *this* in *this point,* and other temporal or conceptual forms, e.g., *now* as in *We may now understand...*); **anaphora** (e.g., references such as *it,* which refer to previous parts of the text); and **cataphora** (e.g., references such as *the following:,* which refer to subsequent parts of the text). We also find the title, the author's name, and publication information; citations, footnotes, and bibliographies, each of which serves not so much to refer to something as to index some contextually relevant piece of information, typically to establish an existential contextual connection between one text and another. At a more fundamental level, we find genre markers ranging from tone to the use of a particular style sheet, from preferred patterns of organization to acceptable forms of argumentation and evidence—aspects of prose that index a particular text type or genre and consequently constrain the interpretation of the text itself.

We will examine these contentions closely in Chapter 4, but for now we merely note that writing is far more indexical than usually thought, and that as a result of undue emphasis on the meaning of written text as abstract and ascertainable apart from context, writing has recently been thoroughly "semanticized" in recent research.

DIALOGIC SEMIOTICS

This view of "language after the ideational fact" echoes the premises of Wundt, Vossler, Croce, and Husserl, who, for example, saw language as essentially a secondary activity requiring the speaker to find adequate words and expressions to describe and report inner states and fixed meanings. Yet writing clearly involves more than simply externalizing, transcribing, or inscribing thoughts with all due respect for convention and context. And the salient features of written text are not just so many arbitrary conventions somehow to be taken into account while writing.

The Russian philosopher and semiotician Mikhail Bakhtin (1973, 1981, 1983) was keenly aware of these issues, and a careful examination of his ideas on language and discourse offers many useful insights here. For Bakhtin, language is inherently **dialogic:** Not only are the material resources of the medium social in origin, but also the choices speakers make at every turn are shaped by the balance their utterances must strike between what they have to say and the context in which the text must function. This is true not only of speaking but also ostensibly monologic forms of discourse such as writing. "[E]very . . . prose discourse—in any of its forms, quotidian, rhetorical, scholarly—cannot fail to be oriented toward the 'already uttered,' the 'already known,' the 'common opinion' and so forth. The dialogic orientation of discourse is a phenomenon that is . . . a property of *any* discourse. It is the natural orientation of any living discourse [Bakhtin, 1981, p. 279]." Hence:

> [T]he word is always oriented toward an addressee, toward who that addressee might be . . . each person's inner world, and thought has its stabilized *social audience* that comprises the environments in which reasons, motives, values and so on are fashioned . . . the word is a two-sided act. It is determined equally by whose word it is and for whom it is meant. . . . Each and every word expresses the one relation to the other. I give myself verbal shape from another's point of view, ultimately from the point of view of the community to which I belong. A word is territory *shared* by both addresser and addressee, by the speaker and his interlocutor [1973, pp. 85–86].

In this view, a text is never the simple result of language production— something the individual simply does—but always what the individual does *vis-à-vis* a conversant: It is "the product of the reciprocal relationship between speaker and listener, addresser and addressee. . . . [1973, pp.

85–86]." Nor is language essentially put in motion by the speaker in the act of speaking. More fundamentally, discourse is something that is perpetually in motion in any given speech community, and the speaker's problem is not how to format ideas in a semantically adequate representation but rather how to enter and sustain the flow of discourse that is "always already" there.

Bakhtin was reacting to the abstract linguistics of Saussure, whose main focus was not on speaking (or **la parole**) but on the systematic, normative properties of **la langue**. Whereas the individual "speech facts" of **la parole** are "heterogenous" and unsystematic and therefore unanalyzable per se, Saussure argued, together "some sort of average will be set up [Saussure, 1959, p. 9]." It is this average, abstracted from the evidence of individual speech events, that constitutes **la langue**. For example, in children's tendency to regularize strong verbs (*runned*, *doed*) and irregular plurals (*mouses*, *fishes*), we may observe a consistency that contributes to our understanding of the developing language systems of English-speaking children. In effect, Saussure's radical distinction conceptualized individual speech events as evidence or data for articulating language as system: "As soon as we give language first place among the facts of speech," Saussure said, "we introduce a natural order into a mass that lends itself to no other classification [1959, p. 9]."

Not surprisingly, this approach to linguistics, while tilling fertile land in the investigation of **langue**, has not yielded great insights about **parole** per se except insofar as the latter randomly manifests the systematic properties of the former. Generally, language researchers have approached the problem of **parole** (or pragmatics, language use in particular situations), by asking how the abstract system "informs" or "underlies" the particular instance of use, quite literally how "language" is "used." This approach to language not only views researching the normative, systematic properties of language as an essential procedural prerequisite to addressing problems of use but also and more fundamentally posits the character of language as ontologically prior to use itself. That is, language is first a "something" (e.g., grammatical rules) and only secondarily a use. In this view, language is used in the way money is spent or rockets are launched, and it makes no sense to inquire about spending or launching without first understanding the nature of money or rockets.

Bakhtin reacted against this abstraction of speech events and focused instead on the dynamics of expression and communication in discrete social contexts. What Saussure saw as "heterogeneous" and therefore intractable Bakhtin saw as **heteroglossic**—involving "stratification, diversity and randomness," which "is not only a static invariant of linguistic life, but also what insures its dynamics [Bakhtin, 1981, p. 272]." In his investigations of these dynamics, Bakhtin sought an account of language as neither intention-driven expression nor abstract system but rather "the product of the reciprocal relationship between speaker and listener, addresser and addressee [1973, pp. 85]." This emphasis on the inherently dialogic character of discourse lends a distinctly rhetorical tone to Bakhtin's distinctions: All discourse—even ostensibly monologic discourse (e.g., novels and essays)— orients its producers towards the "specific conceptual horizons" of its receivers.

Bakhtin believed that a fundamental fact of human existence was "the relation between the 'I' and 'the other,' an irreducible duality conceived in terms of the need to *share* being [Holquist, 1983, p. 5]." On the one hand, there are the individual's values and goals, which represent a "behavioral ideology" that is never completely formulated, not "finished off." On the other hand, there are society's values and goals—"the achieved, stable quality of official ideologies that are shared by the group as a whole [Holquist, 1983, p. 7]" that are "finished off" and "always already there." It is this latter "pre-located discourse of authority" that defines the possibilities of meaningful discourse for any individual in any particular situation, and it is the inevitable gap between ideologies—i.e., between the inner speech of the individual and the outer speech of the group—that shapes and constrains discourse at every turn. Discourse and communication are possible when this breach between inner and outer speech is not overwhelming. Discourse and communication "acquire formulation, clarity and vigor [Bakhtin, 1976, p. 86]" when inner speech is "fixed in terms of the shared values of the group." This insight is important because it suggests an operating principle for discourse: In any given situation, the speaker anticipates the premises of the listener and counts on the listener to interpret the premises of the speaker. "Understanding and response are dialectically merged and mutually condition each other," Bakhtin notes; "one is impossible without the other [1981, p. 282]."

If any text is significantly shaped by the reciprocal relationship of speaker and interlocutor, it follows that the meaning of the text is not irrevocably fixed by the speaker's intentions; rather it is reciprocally configured by the speaker's intentions and the interlocutor's interests as they relate in the context of use. "In essence, meaning belongs to a word in its position between speakers; that is, meaning is realized only in the process of active, responsive understanding [Bakhtin, 1973, p. 102]." The "actual meaning" of an utterance, Bakhtin notes, "is understood against the background of other concrete utterances on the same theme, a background made up of contradictory opinions, points of view and value judgments [1981, 281]." Since different interlocutors on different occasions (or even the same interlocutor on different occasions) may well have different interests, the precise meaning of the text will vary accordingly.

Reconsider, now, Kintsch's Aristotlesque essayist, who (a) states issues, (b) assembles evidence, and then (c) concludes. What determines the issues to be examined? How much evidence is enough? Which evidence is essential? What is a suitable conclusion? To say that it is the writer who determines each of these in accordance with his or her purpose does not adequately explain the principles involved in the behavior. Nor does postulating a black-box monitor as the key element of the composing process do more than beg questions about the organization of discourse: What criteria are relevant to the writer's making these evaluations? What principles bear on the writer's regulation of discourse? How do the character and possibilities of written text shape the writer's options? What criteria govern the production of discourse? How shall we characterize these principles?

For Kintsch's essayist, as for any skilled writer, the very points he makes, the examples he chooses, the form of his conclusion—each of these will vary substantially depending on whom he addresses as well as the context of the argument. And note that it is not just the presentation of some presumably intact semantic textbase that is reinterpreted for particular readers on particular occasions. Rather, it is the very substance of the argument which is shaped by such exigencies. Just whom one addresses, just which points need elaboration, just which need not be mentioned, etc., are all considerations that shape discourse not just in its presentation, but at the most fundamental levels of planning and organization.

Writing, though clearly monologic as an activity, is nonetheless dialogic in its communicative structure: Each point at which the skilled writer chooses one example rather than another, one term rather than another, certain comparisons rather than others, etc., is ultimately arbitrated not only by what the writer has to say but also by the needs of his or her readers to understand. As a factor in production, writer purpose addresses each of these issues only in part.

WRITING AS A SOCIAL PROCESS

Clearly, texts do not take the shape they do merely because the writer wants to say something or has something to accomplish. One does not merely "will" a text. And writers do not merely "act on readers." It is more accurate to say that the shape and direction of discourse are configured by the communicative need of writers to balance their own purposes and intentions with the expectations and needs of readers. If the aim of writing research is to account for writer behavior, then the claim that writing is shaped chiefly by writers acting on readers (by saying x, the writer intends to accomplish y) fails to do justice to the multiplicity of interacting variables operative during the act of composing, including readers' expectations as the writer interprets them, the impact of any previous communication with the reader, the effect of the text as the writer composes it on whatever remains to be written, any reader feedback which the writer anticipates, and many characteristics of the context which gave rise to the communication in the first place. Hence, writer purpose per se tells us nothing about the way in which *what writers do* is synchronized with *what readers do* when readers finally read the text. This is the central reason why writing is inadequately characterized as a particular mode of discourse when its form is viewed principally as a function of the writer's purpose. Text is not just the result of composing, it is also the medium of communication.

The very information structure of written communication, for example, depends not just on the writer's meaning or purpose but rather on the extent of match between what the writer has to say and what the reader needs to know, i.e., the extent to which writer and reader share knowledge. This knowledge may be shared independently of the text, in which case linguists say it is "contextually recoverable," or it may be shared because of what the writer actually writes, in which case it is "textually recoverable." In either case, this mutual or shared knowledge is **given information,** and what is not shared is **new information.** Writers cannot choose what is given and new though they can fashion texts that carefully counterpoint and effectively juxtapose the two.

Some theorists (e.g., Bach and Harnish, 1979; Johnson-Laird, 1982) argue that mutual knowledge is impossible and therefore useless as a concept in discourse analysis. By definition, mutual knowledge requires speakers not only to know everything their conversant knows but also to know that their conversant knows that they know it, to know that their conversant knows that they know that their conversant knows it, and so on *ad infinitum*. Since this infinite regress quickly leads to cognitive overload, these theorists argue, true mutual knowledge is a psychological impossibility. But this line of reasoning misses the essential point that although successful communication involves shared knowledge, it does so *as a result of communication, not as a precondition* (cf. Sperber and Wilson, 1982, p. 62). Or to put it another way, each conversant works from the assumption that whatever the one says is relevant to the needs of the other. It is not mutual knowledge but rather the premise of mutuality that underlies discourse and communication.

The dyadic nature of discourse has been emphasized in studies of conversation and language acquisition. Conversation researchers now agree, for example, that many apparently erratic and dysfunctional "performance errors," including restarts and repairs, are really functional in the terms of conversational interaction (cf. Goodwin, 1982). This is true, for example, of conversational beginnings, where, in the absence of her conversant's gaze, the speaker will pause and restart until mutual gaze has been established. In this instance, the restart serves to elicit mutual gaze, thereby synchronizing the conversants and initiating the talk. In other studies of language acquisition (e.g., Ninio and Bruner, 1978; Wertsch and Hickmann, 1985), researchers explain that key aspects of language development are explained by making special reference to the joint activity of child and caregiver. Findings such as these underscore the need to examine key aspects of discourse as interactions in their own right "with properties that cannot be deduced from an examination of the characteristics of individual partici-pants [Schaffer, 1984, p.8]."

The set of studies in this volume extends this line of research by demonstrating the central importance of reciprocity as a principle of written discourse. It shows that all aspects of writing—from the formation of individual letters and words to the composition of whole texts—are subject to the requirement for common categorizations and mutual under-standings between writer and reader and can therefore be considered within the powerful conceptual framework of reciprocity theory, which is more typically applied to the give and take of talk and language acquisition than to the sustained expression of writing.

2

Reciprocity as a Principle of Discourse

INTRODUCTION

In the previous chapter I argued that contemporary views of the composing process as recursive, goal-oriented language production interpret ancient themes of rhetoric in terms of the concepts and methods of modern experimental cognitive psychology. I noted many problems with this characterization of writing, including inadequate distinction of writing from other modes of discourse and trivialization of the linguistic aspects of writing. As we have seen, the crux of these problems is a confusion of competence and performance which results from seeing writing as the surface encoding of "deep" elements such as propositional content, genre rules, and so on. In this chapter, I will take the position that an adequate account of performance is indeed the chief challenge of a principled account of writing, but that such an account requires a radically different and far more social approach to language production. In particular, we must view the text not as a "natural" result of expression—the "garb of thought"—but rather as an integral part of a communicative process involving the writer and some readers. When we examine writing and texts in this way, we find striking patterns and regularities in the way people write. This chapter and the next formalize these patterns and regularities in one axiom and seven corollaries.

LANGUAGE AS INTERACTION

Communication requires the interaction of two participants, usually called a *producer* and a *receiver*. This interaction is obvious enough in the give and take of talk. But it is true of writing too. When readers understand a text, an exchange of meaning has taken place. The writer has spoken to the readers.

Writers and readers obviously do not interact in the sense that they take turns as do speakers and listeners. But then speaking and listening are not interactive simply because the conversants conspicuously take turns. Turn taking is merely one of the many ways speakers exchange meanings and understand one another. Other ways include furtive glances, quizzical looks, and so on. On occasion, it is a conspicuously absent turn that provides critical information to the listener. This is why turn taking is not interaction per se but merely the way conversants *accomplish interaction*. The interaction of interest is what the turn taking accomplishes, namely *an exchange of meaning or a transformation of shared knowledge*. In this sense, writers and readers interact everytime the readers understand a written text. Conversely, the failure to comprehend means an absence of interaction.

Throughout this chapter, in my discussion of "meaning" and "exchange of meaning," I shall mainly be concerned with the problem of reference and predication, what Rommetveit (1974) calls the speaker's problem of "making things known," and what Halliday (1978) calls the "ideational function of language."

Statisticians have a technical definition of "interaction" that is useful in this discussion. In statistics, **interaction** refers to the particular manner in which two independent variables combine to influence behavior, not one another. For example, in studying the effects of combined alcohol and coffee consumption on driving, the interaction has to do not with what the alcohol and coffee do to each other, but rather how the combination uniquely and adversely affects driving. Also, because of their significant interaction in this case, the effects of coffee and alcohol on driving manifest themselves not simply in terms of the main effects of each one. Each contributes to a joint effect. In other words, interaction refers not to the influence of two independent factors on each other but rather on the result of their combination, or "interaction," to produce something different from the respective contributions of each.

Discourse is interactive in just this way. When each conversant does certain things (e.g., takes turns), the result is intelligible, meaningful communication. Similarly, when writers do certain things and readers do certain other things, the result is lucid, comprehensible text. Writing is no less interactive than speech in either principle or practice. As discourse, writing is nonetheless an interactive medium even if the reader does not know the writer and indeed even though the writer may be long deceased when the reader finds the text. As long as writers and readers collaborate in their complementary and reciprocal tasks of composing and comprehending, or as Rommetveit (1974, p. 63) puts it, as long as writers write on the premises of readers and readers read on the premises of writers, the result is coherent communication.

THE PACT OF DISCOURSE

The interactive character of language has been characterized in a number of important papers representing a variety of theoretical orientations. The fundamental premise in this literature is that discourse presumes a joint "contract" between producer and receiver. For some, this contract specifically obligates speakers to use language structures appropriate to effective social action. An important example here is Grice's (1975) communicative maxims, especially his **Cooperative Principle** ("Make your conversational contribution such as is required, at the stage at which it occurs, by the accepted purpose or direction of the talk exchange in which you are engaged [p. 45]"). From the point of view of this means-end view of language production, successful communication requires speakers' finding expressions that appropriately effect their purposes. This interpretation of language as social action in terms of the effects that speakers have on listeners reflects ancient concerns of rhetoric (cf. Nystrand, 1982a) and is represented in contemporary work in the philosophy of language of Austin, Searle, Grice; the psycholinguistic research of H. Clark; and the artificial intelligence research of Schank and Abelson. It has recently been the dominant paradigm for research on the writing process. This work, surveyed in Gregg and Steinberg (1980), is best represented by the work of Flower and Hayes (1981) and Steinmann (1982).

In contrast to this view of language production is a social interactive position in which the text is interesting less as the means whereby speakers act on listeners and more as the functional, interpretive link between what writers have to say and readers need to know. In this view, communication is less a matter of speakers' transmitting their intentions to listeners and more a matter of operating on and transforming a shared knowledge base. Hence, discourse involves "negotiating" understandings and meanings, and the mutual expectations the conversants bring to the exchange define the terms of the "contract" by which they may negotiate. Psychologist R. Rommetveit (1974) argues that any given text or utterance has meaning only with respect to what is tacitly and jointly assumed by the conversants, assumptions normally established in previous discourse. Linguist M. A. K. Halliday defines both spoken and written texts as

> a sociological event, a semiotic encounter through which the meanings that constitute the social system are *exchanged*. The individual member [both speaker

and listener, writer and reader] is, by virtue of his membership, a 'meaner', one who means. By his acts of meaning, and those of other individual members, the social reality is created, maintained in good order, and continuously shaped and modified [1978, p. 139].

Russian psychologist Lev Vygotsky (1962; 1978) views language as internalized dialog and social, group behavior. For Vygotsky, the power of speaking and writing lies in their capabilities to mediate and transform shared definitions of experience.

As often as not, of course, discussion leads to different rather than common perspectives. Given this fact, what sense does it make to argue categorically that discourse is a negotiation of meaning? This important issue, raised by Bennett (1976) and Stubbs (1983), hinges on how *negotiation* and *meaning* are defined. If negotiation is viewed as a kind of bartering or debate over issues, then clearly all discourse is not negotiation. And if meaning is defined in terms of signification (i.e., signification to external or conceptual realities), then not all discourse is a negotiation of meaning since conversants are not categorically required to construe the things signified in discourse the same way, or indeed even at all, as a goal of the discourse.

However, if we examine discourse, not in terms of conversants' goals and not in terms of the content of any particular discourse, but rather in terms of the rules and constraints that bear on the conduct of discourse, then discourse clearly involves a negotiation of meanings. Discourse involves negotiating meaning in the sense that, to begin, the conversants must first establish a mutual frame of reference. They must furthermore sustain this mutual frame of reference, and where it is weakened by new or unclear contributions, they must restore it through renegotiation ("Whadya mean?" "Hmm?"). The function and importance of such negotiating is nowhere more apparent than on occasions when conversants hurriedly begin talking only to realize after several unproblematic turns that they are talking about altogether different things. Realizing this, the conversants quickly and explicitly reestablish the topic of their discourse, which is to say, they renegotiate the start of the talk.

What then determines the meaning of such talk? Following Wittgenstein (1968), Rommetveit (1974; 1983) argues that the meaning of any text ultimately depends on its interpretive context. Wittgenstein argues that reality is not fully determinate (i.e., just waiting for us to describe and refer to it) but has meaning only to the extent that we construe it, especially in language. Hence, language has meaning, Wittgenstein argues, not because it refers to a fully determined present-tense reality but rather *its very use constitutes the meanings we assign*. Any word typically has a multitude of potential meanings, and precisely the one or ones that speakers actualize in discourse (i.e., bring into focus), Rommetveit contends, will depend on "what at the moment of utterance is taken for granted by both conversation partners [1983, p. 18]." The interpretive context of any text is the necessary, tacit ground upon which the figure of meaning is finally cut and known.

Tierney (cited in Guthrie, 1985) notes, moreover, that context of use is essential not only to meaning in conversation but also in written communication. Two different readers (or indeed the same reader on different occasions) may approach the same text with different purposes. The meaning derived from the text in each case (or on each occasion) will largely be determined by the particular needs of the reader. If we consider the ways in which texts mediate the intentions of the author and the needs and expectations of the reader, Tierney argues, then we see that stable singular meanings of texts are not easily established. As we shall see in Chapter 3, the speaker's/writer's role in these negotiations is to set in motion certain possibilities of meaning, possibilities which are fully realized only by the reader. Texts are like electric circuits in this respect: There is potential but no arc of meaning till some reader completes the circuit.

The negotiation of meaning is also especially obvious in exchanges between individuals who have very different understandings of the discourse topic. Rommetveit, for example, gives the example of teaching modern French history in a culture, e.g., rural Africa, where the concept of "president" is utterly meaningless. For the purposes of such instruction, the teacher may explain this concept with a compromised yet functional reference to Charles de Gaulle as a "powerful king of France." Rommetveit explains: "And the teacher's reason for employing that particular expression may be by no means malevolent or cynical: The fact may simply be that in that particular situation he can hit upon no better means of bridging the gap between what the students already know of relevance to the topic and what at such a stage of pre-knowledge can be made known to them about de Gaulle and his political role in France [1974, p. 34]." Hence, though "powerful king of France" is not a valid definition of de Gaulle's role, it nonetheless "anchors" the topic by establishing a mutual frame of reference in terms which allow discussion to proceed so that teacher and students can discuss modern French history in this setting.

Bruner (1981) describes a similar kind of negotiation of meaning in adult–child discourse. He gives the following example (p. 170) of book reading between one mother (M) and her child (C) at age 23 months:

M. What's that?

C. Ouse.

M. Mouse, yes that's a mouse.

C. More mouse (*pointing to another picture*).

M. No, those are squirrels. They're like mice but with long tails. Sort of.

C. Mouse, mouse, mouse.

M. Yes, all right, they're mice.

C. Mice, mice.

One day, of course, the mice will be "mice" and the squirrels will be "squirrels," but the significance of this negotiated settlement in which squirrels shall be called "mice" is that, like Rommetveit's example of de Gaulle as "a powerful king of France," it establishes a mutual frame of reference from which meaningful discourse may proceed.

The idea of negotiating such compromised linguistic references might seem extraordinary—limited to such extraordinary circumstances as extreme cross-cultural communication and adult–child discourse as a communication strategy of last resort. However, philosopher H. Putnam (1975) argues that it is the normal method of reference in discourse. As a joint enterprise between producer and receiver, he notes, reference is established not so much by signifying an unequivocal aspect of reality as "by tracking back how the term was used in the historical chain whose last link is the present speaker [Bruner, 1981, p. 170]." Hence, "a speaker may 'have' a word in the sense of possessing normal ability to use it in discourse, and not know the mechanism of reference of that term, explicitly or even implicitly [p. 278]." For example, we regularly and successfully use "gold," "language," "God"—literally thousands of words—without knowing the criteria for their valid definitions. The point is that what we know about gold is one thing, and what we know about using "gold" in discourse about gold is quite another. From this analysis, it follows that discourse is not so much the encoding and transmission of what the speaker knows as it is a set of procedures whereby the conversants focus jointly on various aspects of what they know for the purpose of examining and perhaps transforming this knowledge. Bickard (1980) makes this important distinction when he notes that "the objects of communicative interaction constitute representations, and thus have truth values, but the communicative interactions themselves are operators on, functions on, such representations. They are not representations themselves, and, thus, have no truth values themselves [p. 118]."

We shall look more closely at just how producers interact with receivers when we examine the structure of discourse. I shall show that there are discrepancies between what the producer has to say and what the receiver needs to understand that can be resolved only if the producer carefully balances these respective interests. But there is one example that can be given without technical detail to illustrate the interactive skills of the speaker in producing discourse. The problem is this: In conversation when the listener interrupts the speaker and says "What?" how does the speaker know exactly which part of the previous statement to repeat or rephrase? In this situation, the speaker never starts at the beginning of the conversation, nor does the speaker ever rephrase a complete assertion unless it is called for. More typically the speaker replies precisely with the single word or phrase that the listener needs. How does the speaker know what this expression is? The listener obviously cannot explain what he or she missed, and the speaker certainly cannot read the listener's mind to find out (even if this might help). This puzzle can be solved only if the speaker has a keen sense of what needs to be said in terms of what the listener understands, i.e., *if the speaker knows what to say in relation to what is already known.*

CONTEXT OF PRODUCTION VERSUS CONTEXT OF USE

In both speaking and writing, communicative interaction takes place in a context of use, i.e., the situation in which the utterance or text functions and has meaning. It is important to note, however, that context of use (or **context of situation** [cf. Firth, 1957]) is not the same as context of production (or **context of utterance** [cf. Lyons, 1977]). **Context of production** refers to the occasion of the text's creation by speaker or writer whereas **context of use** refers to the occasion on which the text is actually processed by the hearer or reader. In speech, this distinction typically has no practical meaning since the context of production and the context of use are inevitably identical. Hence, when I shout, "Watch out, it's going to fall!" the context of production and the context of use are one and the same, in this case the dangerous situation of a wobbly ladder which my addressee is obliviously climbing.

The failure to distinguish context of production from context of use has led many (e.g., Olson, 1977; Dillon, 1981; Hirsch, 1977) to conclude wrongly that writing is a "decontextualized" mode of discourse, necessarily more explicit than speech. For example, psychologist David Olson argues in a much-cited passage that speakers can circumvent the ever-present possibility of ambiguity in speech "by means of such prosodic and para-linguistic cues as gestures, intonation, stress, quizzical looks, and restate-ment [Olson, 1977, p. 272]." Since writers have no recourse to linguistic and paralinguistic means, Olson argues, written texts must stand on their own and far more explicit than spoken utterances. Olson concludes by asserting that because meaning must be "preserved in sentences which have to be understood in contexts other than those in which they were written," writers "must guard against possible ambiguity with only the resources of the text [p. 272]."

The fact that writers do not converse with readers face to face or that their texts speak independently of their actual physical presence does not mean that the texts are work independently of context. Rather, it means that unlike speech, written texts are composed for a **context of eventual use** (cf. Nystrand, 1982a). Similarly, the fact that writers cannot express themselves through intonation and gesture does not mean that written language is devoid of expressive, nonlinguistic resources. Rather, it means that writers show emphasis and mark boundaries, as well as suggest tone and attitudinal color and so on through paragraphing, punctuation, genre conventions, and other devices which work in conjunction with the actual words of the text to produce a coherent communication. But unlike intonation and gesture in speech, these devices of written language do not fully function at the time they are produced. Rather, the writer builds them into the text as it were so that they will function appropriately in a context of eventual use.

The context of use impinges as much upon the writer as the reader. As they write, writers pause often to review and frequently to repair what they have already composed. When done, they sometimes survey the results from the vantage point of their intended reader or readers. In so doing, the writer momentarily becomes a reader, and the context of production temporarily becomes a context of use. As the writer "tries out the text" in this way, the text comes to have meaning and import. The writer decides that she has used enough examples or needs more reasons or a different reason or another paragraph or another beginning, and so forth and so on. Making the appropriate revisions and repairs, the writer, of course, returns to work in the context of production. Hence, we see that even during the composing process, ostensibly solitary and private, the writer is continuously negotiating and balancing what she wants to say with her own expectations as a reader, either real or imagined. Throughout the process, the context of use is the key factor in arbitrating these negotiations and regulates production at every turn.

Clearly, explicitness bears no relation to how long the text is: A long text is not necessarily more explicit than a short text. A STOP sign is utterly unambiguous and explicit despite its brevity whereas legal contracts, despite their comprehensiveness of text, are notoriously ambiguous to many readers. A text is explicit not because it says everything all by itself but rather because it strikes a careful balance between what needs to be said and what may be assumed.

Writers are no more at expressive loss because they are unable to resort to intonation and quizzical looks than speakers are at expressive loss because they are unable to resort to italics, paragraphing, quotation marks, and parentheses. Intonation, gesture, and gaze resemble turntaking in this regard: They are the ways speakers accomplish interaction, but they are not the interaction itself. This book is largely about contexts of eventual use and specifically about writers' involvement with them.

In the remainder of this chapter, I argue that writing and reading are collaborative, social acts which obligate writers and readers to particular kinds of tasks. More specifically, I argue, and seek to show in subsequent chapters, that all elements of text—from the segmentation of individual words to the adequate development of paragraphs—are in large measure structured by the essential requirement that the text must strike a balance between the expressive needs of the writer and the comprehension needs of the reader. This is not to say, of course, that the aim of discourse is always substantive agreement, only that the character and conduct of discourse are governed by the expectations of the conversants that they should understand one another.

THE RECIPROCITY PRINCIPLE

Social phenomenologist Alfred Schutz (1967) analyzes mailing a letter as the quintessential example of a social act. Although mailing a letter is ostensibly a simple individual act, it is nonetheless premised on a host of assumptions about what other people—none of whom the writer need ever meet—will do. Suppose, for example, that I deposit into my corner mailbox a letter along with a check written to purchase a book. In so doing, I assume that some uniformed stranger will pick up the mail and do whatever such uniformed strangers typically do to forward it to my addressee, most likely another stranger. I furthermore assume that this addressee will read my letter as a particular sort of letter (as a mail order and not some peculiar act of trivial philanthropy) and will respond in a particular way (i.e., will not rob me blind but will indeed send me the book I have ordered).

Clearly, mailing a letter is not a simple individual act. It is a highly contextualized act requiring, indeed *assuming*, considerable social knowledge on the part of the letter writer. By dropping my letter irretrievably into these public boxes—even into one I have never seen before—I take for granted a complicated set of actions by other people.

The tools and artifacts involved in my correspondence—the letter itself plus the envelope, the mailbox, the mail truck, and so on—are ultimately social in nature too. We experience these tools and artifacts not as mere things in the world but rather "in terms of the purpose for which [they were] designed by more or less anonymous fellow-men and [their] possible use by others [1967, p. 55]." We need only find in an attic some obscure widget from a bygone generation to appreciate this insight. We understand such widgets only when we learn about their purpose and use, i.e., when we can situate the widget in its appropriate context of use. This is why blue metal boxes with painted eagles found on corners are not just any boxes in the USA and why my letter and enclosed check are not mere scribbled pieces of paper tucked inside other pieces of paper. Like all of the many complicated things I take for granted when I drop my letter into a mailbox, each of these artifacts is implicated in an intricate social web involving many people and their relationships to one another. In all these affairs, as Schutz puts it, it is "assumed that the sector of the world taken for granted by me is also taken for granted by you, [and] even more, that it is taken for granted by 'Us' [1967, p. 12]."

This key assumption is the **Reciprocity Principle**, which is the foundation of all social acts, including discourse: *In any collaborative activity the participants orient their actions on certain standards which are taken for granted as rules of conduct by the social group to which they belong.* In learning to collaborate in this way, the collaborators develop a *mutual co-awareness* "not only of what the other is doing, saying and so on, and of what I am doing, but also of how what I am doing appears to the other, and even what I must do to communicate more clearly [Cox, 1978, p. 21]."

The expectation for reciprocity in discourse is important because it means that the shape and conduct of discourse is determined not only by what the speaker or writer has to say (speaker/writer **meaning**) or accomplish (speaker/writer **purpose**) but also by the joint expectations of the conversants that they should understand one another (producer-receiver **contract**). Of these three forces that shape discourse, moreover, the contract is most fundamental: Without a contract between writer and reader, both meaning and purpose are unfathomable at best and untenable at worst. We may consequently view discourse generally as a social act based on the premise of common categorizations and mutual knowledge (cf. Sperber and Wilson, 1982). Both speakers and writers must fashion texts that will establish and maintain this mutual knowledge and so effect an exchange of meaning. In talk this negotiation is comparatively conspicuous, manifesting itself in turn taking, querulous glances plus rephrasings, etc. In writing, however, this process is more subtle. The writer must skillfully treat potential troublesources such as the start of a text or the introduction of complicated terms or ideas which might threaten reciprocity in a context of eventual use such as future reference, personal communication, etc. This is not to say, of course, that the aim of discourse is always substantive agreement, but only that the character and conduct of discourse are governed by the expectations of the conversants that they should understand one another. To repeat Rommetveit, we write on the premises of the reader and read on the premises of the writer (1974, p. 63). In making this point, I am making a distinction between the *practical purposes* of discourse and the *principles* which govern its functioning.

THE ORIGINS OF RECIPROCITY IN DISCOURSE

One area of language research that has investigated reciprocity as a fundamental principle of discourse is language acquisition. Collaboration between parent and child is important first because it provides the setting in which children experiment with and discover the significant differences and regularities of their language (cf. Smith and Miller, 1966). But the more important contention of this research is the conjecture that this collaboration lays an essential foundation for language long before actual words and sentences emerge.

There is some research to suggest that the expectation for reciprocity may be present from birth. Indeed, Condon and Sander (1974) report that "the movements of 1-day-old infants is precisely synchronized with the articulatory segments of human speech (whether English or Chinese, live or taped) but not with disconnected vowels or tapping sounds [Goodwin, 1981, p. 28]." Parents, moreover, begin attributing intention to their children's gestures well before the infants are 2 months old (Stern, 1974). Whether these gestures are actually intentional is not nearly so important in terms of the infants' development as the parents' *attribution of intention.* By 3 to 4 months, infants' cooing and gazing show clear elements of turn taking (Stern, 1977; Brazelton, Koslowski, and Main, 1974; Trevarthen & Hubley, 1978). By 4 to 6 months infants follow their parents' gaze when the parents look away from the child to another place or person (Scaife & Bruner, 1975), a clear suggestion that, contrary to Piaget's research on egocentrism, children learn very early on to take the point of view of the other (Donaldson, 1978). By 6 to 7 months they respond to their parents and regularly show them things by picking up things themselves and bringing these things to their parents' attention (Clark and Clark, 1977, p. 312). And before 1 year, they master indicating by pointing in return to show things to their parents (Bruner, 1981; M. Lewis and Freedle, 1973).

Many researchers view infants' pointing as a prelinguistic form of reference because in so gesturing the child draws into focus selected objects for comment. As Bruner (1978) notes, such acts mark the child's entry into "transactional dialog"—necessarily nonverbal, of course, but communicative nonetheless. Parents and their children understand each other by means of such elementary social interactions. The important role of the adult in this social interaction is to "orchestrate" these encounters, systematically albeit unconsciously providing a "scaffolding" of increasingly mature dialog with carefully structured "privileges of occurence" for the child's participation. The child not only learns to participate appropriately but also to initiate procedures—including gesture, utterance, and gaze—that the parent will interpret appropriately (Bruner, 1981).

Gradually, as these routines become established, the relationships between the two partners become predicable ("scripted [Nelson, 1978]") for both, and the communicative procedures themselves become conventional. The character of the utterances the child learns is significantly shaped by their potential use in the established social order of the family. Much of this research on the prelinguistic roots of language has been influenced by the work of Vygotsky and his followers, who argue that "once a child develops the social uses of language, he becomes able to turn them back to his own private, or reflexive, use—he learns to use language to regulate his own behavior . . . [Gundlach, 1982a, p. 2]." Language acquisition is an important step—though hardly the first—in the progressive "integration of the child into a social world [Richards, 1974]."

Clearly, the collaboration of parent and child is important to this development. For example, Bruner argues that, in learning reference, the child's task is as much socially interactive as it is cognitive, i.e., in addition to matching the semantic features of signs with critical features of objects, the child faces the problem of "developing a set of procedures for constructing a very limited taxonomy to deal with a limited set of extralinguistic objects with which he traffics jointly with adult members of the linguistic community [Bruner, 1978]." Similarly, Weinrich (1963) argues that in learning predication, the child's task is as much semiotic as it is syntactic. That is, predication involves the differentiation of given and new information, which, in turn, develops out of an increasingly astute sense on the part of the child of what in dialog can reasonably be taken for granted as known (and hence is shared and given information) and what is not known (and hence is unshared and new information). This distinction is consistent with research reported by Wall (1968, 1974), who found that children quickly learn to elaborate more for strangers than for parents with whom the extent of shared knowledge allows for comparable abbreviation "with little or no loss of information [Wall, 1974, p. 233]." The general significance of parent–child collaboration as a prerequisite to actual dialog and talk is, in Bruner's terms, that it allows participants in discourse "habitually to find each other [p. 22]." As important a milestone in language development as the first word spoken is another, much earlier one—the shared word.

RECIPROCITY AS A PRINCIPLE OF CONVERSATION

Other research that has examined the role of reciprocity in discourse is the study of conversation. A fundamental fact of conversation, as Sacks, Schegloff, and Jefferson (1974) point out, is that neither the content nor the conversational turns of a conversation can be specified in advance by either conversant. These things can be negotiated only in the process of talking; they result from the conversants' mutual needs respectively to express themselves and understand one another. This is why conversation researchers determine the structure of conversation by focusing not on the behavior of either the speaker or the listener alone but rather on that of the conversants *vis-à-vis* each other. For example, considerable empirical evidence (e.g., Goodwin, 1981) shows that many of the pauses and hesitations of speakers engaged in conversation are inadequately explained either as performance errors (Chomsky, 1965) or as complications due to the demands of cognitive processing (Goldman-Eisler, 1961, 1972). Rather they have to do with the competence of the speaker in synchronizing her talk with the needs of her conversant. To be more specific, the speaker's restarts often function to request the joint attention of the listener. Once this gaze is secured, the speaker typically completes her turn quite fluently.

In effect, these initial pauses, hesitations, and start-up queries ("Do you remember that note I received last week?") function to "calibrate" the discourse. They do this by establishing a mutual frame of reference in terms of which subsequent comments are made and interpreted. This functional aspect of restarts is not apparent, of course, in research focusing solely on the speaker's behavior. Rather, it is an interactive phenomenon which implicates the participation of each conversant in an underlying social order.

Sometimes after securing the gaze of their conversants, speakers nonetheless hesitate and rephrase something they have said. Some of these rephrasings involve recycling segments of talk that the speaker senses the other conversant has not understood (Erickson, 1979). Sometimes the listener makes the speaker aware that there is a problem by asking "What?" or "Hmm?" But in many instances the listener doesn't say anything; the speaker just seems to know. Even when a listener does say "What?" the speaker must still solve the puzzle of determining just what word, phrase, or term is the troublesource. As with restarts, the critical mechanism here is gaze, specifically the use of mutual gaze to synchronize what the speaker has to say with what the listener needs to know. The speaker knows what the troublesource is because the listener actually precedes "What?" with a glance that pinpoints the problem for the speaker quite precisely. But because competent conversants carefully synchronize utterance and gaze—which are the behavioral manifestations of reciprocity in talk and which the conversants use in managing their coparticipation—the speaker may often know that rephrasing is appropriate without the listeners verbally saying anything.

Sometimes speakers "repair" their utterances even when there has been no breakdown in communication or any apparent error (Schlegloff, Jefferson, and Sacks, 1977; Jefferson, 1978). The most obvious example is a word search on the part of the speaker. When this occurs—in contrast to most phrasal breaks (e.g., restarts which listeners usually interpret as requests for gaze)—the listener typically does *not* glance at the speaker. Mutual gaze is restored only when the speaker completes the repair and is ready to continue the conversation.

To summarize: Speakers request the gaze of their conversants by restarting. They recycle material to clarify points that the gaze of their conversants marks as troublesome. But when they initiate repairs to refine a point they want to express (rather than to clarify a point the listener did not understand), the listener normally suspends gaze until the speaker has completed the repair. On the surface, this behavior might seem inconsistent, e.g., with restarts, phrasal breaks secure the gaze and joint attention of the listener whereas with repairs, phrasal breaks result in suspended gaze. But this inconsistency is only apparent. The structure of conversation has to do with the synchronization of what the speaker wants to say in terms of what the listener needs to know. Mutual gaze marks joint focus for both conversants; and restarts, recycling, and repairs respectively are essential ways in which conversants establish, maintain, and reestablish this focus and mutual orientation, which is the foundation of all communication.

MUTUAL KNOWLEDGE VERSUS MUTUAL FRAMES OF REFERENCE

Clearly, reciprocity involves mutual, shared knowledge. For example, along with all other users of the postal system, I have a common and mutual knowledge of how to write and mail a letter. Everything I take for granted in these activities is by definition mutual knowledge. I shall define these key terms as follows:

(a) **Mutual knowledge** is knowledge that two or more individuals possess in common. When such individuals communicate, of course, the extent of their mutual knowledge is an important factor because it defines the possibilities for establishing a mutual frame of reference. For example, to the extent that conversants are mutually knowledgeable, they are able to take for granted much that they would otherwise need to explain to someone else not privy to the same knowledge. Nonetheless, whether or not such mutually knowledgeable individuals ever communicate with each other does not in itself affect the status of their knowledge as mutual. Experts in the same field (e.g., optometrists) or witnesses to the same event (e.g., all people who watched television coverage of the Kennedy assassination) have a high degree of mutual knowledge even if they never discuss it.

(b) **Shared knowledge** is the result of people exchanging whatever knowledge they have, mutual or not. Individuals need not be mutually knowledgeable, of course, to share knowledge. It is a mutual frame of reference, not mutual knowledge, that is the precondition for communication. Hence, parents who vividly remember the Kennedy assassination (and thus have a high degree of mutual knowledge about the event) may nonetheless share this knowledge with their children (who are not privy to the same mutual knowledge as their parents). Once knowledge has been shared, of course, it becomes part of the common stock of knowledge between or among the conversants. That is, knowledge once shared becomes mutual knowledge.

(c) **Reciprocity** is not knowledge at all. Rather, it is *the principle that governs how people share knowledge*, specifically their determination of *what* knowledge they shall exchange when they communicate, plus how they choose to present it in discourse. As long as the terms of reciprocity are upheld, communication and texts are coherent. Conversants do not typically share everything they know with each other; mutual knowledge is not a goal of communication. Rather, they share only that knowledge which is relevant to the purpose of the discourse and to their needs as conversants. In so doing each conversant speaks and listens, writes and reads in terms of what he or she expects the other to know. Hence, parents will discuss the impact of Kennedy's assassination differently with each other than they will with their children and grandchildren. In particular, they will elaborate certain details for children and grandchildren that they may take for granted with each other. In any case, the reciprocity principle governs the participation of the conversants. Whether speaking to each other or to their children or grandchildren, reciprocity guarantees only that speakers will share relevant knowledge at the same time that it warrants the relevance of each conversant's contribution.

A number of scholars have argued that true mutual knowledge is impossible. In particular, Bach and Harnish (1979), Harder and Kock

(1976), and Johnson-Laird (1982) note that, as a psychological reality, mutual knowledge introduces a problem of infinite regress. If A and B are individuals having mutual knowledge of C, then it must follow that A knows that B knows about C, that B knows that A knows about C, that A knows that B knows that A knows about C, that B knows that A knows that B knows about C, et cetera ad infinitum. Since this state of affairs introduces an endless subroutine into cognitive processes, many psychologists and linguists conclude that true mutual knowledge is impossible.

No doubt mutual knowledge in this sense is impossible; no two individuals ever have completely identical, mutual knowledge. But there is no practical reason why they must; communication does not depend on it. As we have seen, mutual knowledge is neither prerequisite to nor necessary for communication or social acts. Mutual knowledge affects *what* knowledge conversants can share and *how* they can share it, not *whether* they can share knowledge. In order to communicate, it is essential not that knowledge be identical but only that the conversants find a frame of reference which encompasses and relates their respective perspectives. As Sperber and Wilson (1982) note, "The fact that some knowledge is considered mutual is generally a result of comprehension rather than a precondition for it [p. 62]."

Reciprocity, unlike mutual knowledge, implies a clear and specific social relationship with other knowers. For example, people distinguished by substantial mutual knowledge, e.g., experts such as optometrists or baseball fans, are not bound by reciprocity until they actually collaborate in some joint activity, such as the physicians' attending a medical convention or the baseball fans' attending a game or both mailing a letter. Conversely, individuals who share little or no expert knowledge (e.g., doctors and patients) are nonetheless bound by the terms of reciprocity as soon as they become partners to some particular act (such as doctor–patient consultation). Mutual knowledge alone is neither necessary to nor sufficient for communication though appropriate knowledge is inevitably shared as the conversants uphold their respective ends of the reciprocity principle through communication and comprehension.

In discourse, conversants work from the assumption that they should understand one another. For example, speakers take for granted that their conversants will attempt to make sense of what they say. Indeed conversants depend on each other to do just this. Conversation would be impossible, for example, if the conversants could not depend on each other to mean what they say and interpret each other's comments in the same spirit. This expectation for mutual sense is so fundamental to discourse that, whenever conversants sense it is in jeopardy, they take appropriate actions to restore balance to the exchange: They ask for clarification, they rephrase troublesome comments, they pause regularly to monitor their conversant's understanding, and so on. Conversants continue attributing sense to each other's comments only so long as it remains uncontradicted. In this sense, reciprocity is a fundamental principle underlying discourse—not just because it initially prompts the discourse but also and especially because it regulates the discourse once the conversants begin talking. For comprehensive reviews of reciprocity as a principle of discourse from various threoretical points of view, the reader is referred to Grice (1975), Haviland and Clark (1974), Sperber and Wilson (1982).

The concept of equilibrium or homeostasis has relevance to discourse in much the same way that Piaget has shown that it has relevance to cognitive development. Piaget argues that intelligence is a process of cognitive adaptation to the environment in which the individual constructs a series of cognitive representations, or schemata, which, through experience, the individual tests for fit. The individual continues to use these cognitive representations to interpret experience so long as they do so adequately and are not confounded by new experience which challenges their validity and usefulness. In the event that a cognitive representation does prove inadequate, the individual then adapts by revising the representation in such a way as to accommodate the anomalous event, seeking once again to make sense of the world. In this way, the individual achieves equilibrium between reality and her construction of it.

Reciprocity operates in a similar way in discourse. Each conversant assumes, until evidence to the contrary, that the other conversant's comments will sustain a balance of shared knowledge, i.e., will clearly relate to an established frame of reference. As Sperber and Wilson (1982) argue, "In ordinary circumstances, the hearer assumes that the speaker has not only tried to be as relevant as possible, but has also succeeded. The hearer therefore selects, from all the propositions ... that the utterance could express, the most relevant one, and assumes that it is the one intended by the speaker [p. 75]." I shall call this expected balance in discourse **communicative homeostasis**, which is the normal condition of coherent discourse. Whenever this balance is threatened or upset, the conversants will take corrective measures to restore it. As long as conversants' comments make sense in terms of an established frame of reference, these comments will be meaningful ("uh huh ...") and the discourse will proceed smoothly. But if anyone should introduce anything anomalous or problematic ("huh?"), the conversants must accommodate this information by discussing it and in so doing establish a new mutual frame of reference.

READING AS A PROCESS OF ELIMINATION

In the office where I work there are two kinds of mailboxes. One kind is private and locked, and the other kind—a sort of pigeonhole—is public and open. All correspondence that is actually mailed (via either the U.S. Post Office or campus interoffice mail) is delivered to the locked box, and everything else—dittos, miscellaneous papers, general announcements, etc.—ends up in the pigeonhole. Knowing this, I know quite a bit about my mail even as I collect it. I know, by where it ends up, quite generally what sort of text to expect. Very rarely will anything important end up in the pigeonhole. The locked box, by contrast, is more complicated. It includes personal and professional correspondence, mass computerized mailings, and sealed campus memos. The sealed campus envelopes are always more important than fat packages with cheap postage and computer mailing labels; the latter inevitably contain unsolicited textbooks—the junk mail of the academic world.

The point of all this is that even before I open my mail I know something about it. Once the envelope is open, the trail of clues which precedes the text continues. My expectations are progressively set and fine-tuned by such details as logos, letterheads, typeface, and mode of production (handwritten, typed, or dittoed); the identity of the correspondent, what I know about the subject, previous correspondence (if any), who if anyone is copied (*cc:*), and on occasion even why the communication was done in writing rather than by telephone or in person. I know quite a bit about my mail even before I get to the text. These many layers of context which envelop the text provide important clues to the text's meaning. The skilled reader uses these clues systematically to eliminate what the text might be about. In the jargon of information theory, these clues are essential to reader comprehension because they reduce the reader's uncertainty about the text's meaning (cf. Smith, 1971).

With experience, readers learn to use these clues to set a course through the text as surely and skillfully as any yacht captain reads the tides and winds and currents to set his sail. And indeed as the reader narrows the semantic field, each new level of understanding constrains the interpretation of the next.

When the reader actually begins reading the text, this process of elimination continues. Each statement, every bit of information narrows the field of semantic possibilities further and further to the point where the reader has no uncertainties about the meaning of the communication. From reaching for one mailbox rather than the other, noting one sort of envelope rather than another, one letterhead rather than another, one typeface rather than another, one topic rather than another, one comment rather than

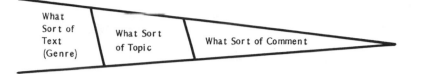

Figure 2.1. The wedge: Hierarchic constraints on the comprehension process.

another, the reader systematically works his way through the many layers of context in which the text itself is embedded to the point where he understands what the writer says. The act of reading is a great wedge which the reader drives through the text in opening up and probing its possibilities for meaning (see Figure 2.1).

Discourse analysts often discuss this organization of the comprehension process in terms of "top-down effects." That is to say, instead of first processing letters in order to understand words, and instead of processing words in order to understand sentences, and so on up to the very text itself, readers proceed in just the opposite direction. Texts make sense in terms of cotext and the nonverbal context in which they are situated, sentences take on meaning in the context of adjacent sentences, words take on meaning in the context of sentences, and letters have value in the context of words. Parts have meaning with respect to wholes.

The effects of context on comprehension of various text elements have been much studied. Cattell (1886) first observed experimentally that subjects tend to remember letters better when they are presented in words than when they are presented randomly. Huey (1908), Miller (1956), and others have replicated these results in various ways. More recently, Rommetveit and his associates report research using stereotachistoscopic techniques to test the effects of context on word perception. Each of the experiments introduces a binocular rivalry of letters, which involves presenting two different words or strings of letters separately and simultaneously to the left and right eyes. Because the words are presented so quickly (a matter of microseconds), only the dominant member of the pair is perceived. The technique has been used to test a number of hypotheses about comprehension. For example, Kleiven and Rommetveit (1970) found that when subjects are presented simultaneously with a meaningful string of letters and a competing nonword string, they invariably see only the meaningful string. This is true even when the meaningful string occurs less frequently in the language than the nonword string (e.g., as part of another word). Rommetveit, Berkley, and Brøgger (1968) found that when subjects are presented with two nonword strings (e.g., *shap* and *shar*), they often perceive a real word that results from combining the two (e.g., *sharp*).

Rommetveit and Kleiven (1968) found that when rival pairs of words are presented (e.g., *soup* and *soap*), subjects will see the word more closely related in meaning to the word which immediately precedes it (e.g., *towel* or *spoon*). The conclusions in all these studies and many others (e.g., Reicher, 1969; Tulving & Gold, 1963; Wittrock, Marks, and Doctrow, 1975; Bransford and Johnson, 1972) are the same: Comprehension is always affected by previous text and expected text, as well as the nonverbal context in which the text is situated. Comprehension is the process whereby words emerge as meaningful constructs from otherwise empty perceptual forms.

From such research, we have learned that reading is a process whereby, ironically, the reader gains information by eliminating possible meanings (cf. Smith, 1971). Readers gain knowledge by discarding possibilities, not adding them. Any term out of context (*war, cousin Matilda, winter*) has numerous if not infinite possible meanings and interpretations. But rarely, of course, do readers and listeners encounter such terms in isolation. Instead they find them associated with other words in some context of use. And their comprehension of the terms is quite literally loaded in terms of other terms. Readers comprehend texts largely by finding out what topics they are *not* about, using sufficient context to eliminate spurious interpretations and retain only the most salient. In this process, readers work their way into and through the text, processing each layer of context in terms of expectations set up by the previous layer. Hence, as I reach into my locked box rather than the pigeonhole, I eliminate some possibilities; as I note how the envelope is addressed, I eliminate yet more possibilities; and so on and so forth as I work my way through the text itself.

As each layer of text and context is processed, it constrains or **frames** the possibilities for interpretation of the next layer. Readers' expectations are increasingly "fine tuned" as they work their way into the text. In effect, everything understood defines new horizons of expectations as previous text becomes context for interpreting text yet to be read. Through the cognitive transformation of comprehension, each layer of understanding becomes the ground against which the figure of subsequent text takes shape and has meaning.

What Writers Do

INITIATING DISCOURSE

If reading is a process of eliminating alternative meanings and interpretive possibilities, then writing is the complementary and reciprocal process of elaborating these possibilities, associative paths, and interpretive contexts. The writer gets the reader off and running by setting the text in one particular direction rather than another, i.e., by loading the communication in favor of certain possibilities and interpretive contexts rather than others.

The start of a text performs this function quite directly. A professional journal article titled "The Effects of Text Editing on the Cognitive Processes of First Graders" announces a different kind of text than a newspaper article in the Modern Living Section titled "Byting Bits in First Grade." These titles indicate to readers just how they should proceed to read what they find there. Among other things, readers must have some insight about the relative importance of understanding details. In reading the newspaper piece, "Byting Bits in First Grade," all the reader really needs to get is the main idea whereas with the research article on "The Effects of Text Editing on the Cognitive Processes of First Graders," far more than just the main idea is at stake. To fully understand this latter piece, the reader must know about computers, text editing, and cognitive psychology. But note that to understand these respective texts, knowledge of the topic is not sufficient. Comprehension requires not just understanding what a writer says about a topic; comprehension also requires understanding what sort of text the writer has chosen to write and being able to evaluate the relevance of details in terms of the purpose of the genre. Hence, to properly understand "Byting Bits" and "The Effects of Text Editing," readers not only need to have

some understanding of computers; they also need to know how to read
articles about computers.

As we have seen, however, the skilled reader begins deducing the meaning
of the text prior to reading the text itself, using a myriad of "pretextual"
clues for this purpose. Knowing this, the skilled writer is able to exploit the
entire range of such possibilities to advantage. In business communications,
for example, skilled memo writers (and their secretaries) give due attention
to such things as the formality of the communication; the signature of the
author (first name only?); type of stationery (with or without logo); manner
mailed (first class, overnight express, special delivery with return request
for time of delivery); and who is indicated (and who is not indicated) as
receiving carbon copies. Skilled business writers know full well that each of
these factors is potentially important in indicating to readers just how they
are to interpret the text. Each of the factors, especially when used in
conjunction with others, is available to the writer for elaborating just what
sort of communication is under way.

It is important to note that the many factors that contribute to what
writers have to say and what they say about it are meaningful in different
ways. For example, "Sincerely yours" is *meaningful but nonreferential.* In
addition, some of these "meanings" are *indexical* (e.g., "Cordially" versus
"Sincerely yours," my locked mailbox versus open pigeonhole are indexes
since their meaning depends not on their referential content per se but
rather on some significant aspect of the context they bring to bear on the
interpretation of the text). The reader uses all of these factors of text and
context, including referential and nonreferential elements, various indexes,
etc., to gauge just what the text is about (i.e., **discourse topic**) and exactly
what the writer has to say about it (i.e., **discourse comment**). In return,
writers depend on their readers' predictable uses of such factors to make
things known with the idiosyncratic resources of written text.

The skilled business writer also knows that each of these elements has
interpretive value with respect to other, previous uses, which set interpretive precedents for the reader. Hence, in an office where formal memos are
the norm, the informality of a note from an employer to an employee will
carry meaning in and of itself. The reverse is true, too: In an office where the
norm is informal communication, the sudden appearance of a sealed memo
will also have meaning.

Of course, the text itself is the chief vehicle for written communication
and the *raison d'être* for all the pretextual clues. In addition to genre
conventions which indicate *what sort of communication* is under way
(e.g., essay rather than memo; memo rather than note; an important note
rather than obligatory note), the writer also has access to various resources
of text which allow for message construction in no uncertain terms. It is in

the text proper, of course, that the writer proceeds to indicate just *what sort of topic* he has in mind and *what sort of comment* he wishes to make about the topic. This is not to say, of course, that composing always proceeds linearly in terms of genre, topic, and comment, but rather that writers are constrained in their composing by these factors which figure prominently in the ultimate meaning of the text.

TEXT ELABORATIONS: GENRE, TOPIC, AND COMMENT

Very generally, we may summarize the communicative options and strategies of the writer by noting that the skilled writer establishes (a) what sort of text is under way, (b) what sort of topic is under discussion, and (c) exactly what he wishes to say about it. In other words, the writer proceeds by elaborating at the levels of (a) genre, (b) topic, and (c) comment. Elaboration at each of these levels progressively constrains the interpretive possibilities of the subsequent level, and when elaboration at each level is sufficient, the writer leaves the reader with no uncertainty about the meaning (the point or gist) of the communication.

To examine these concepts in more detail, consider Thomas S. Szasz's essay, "The Myth of Mental Illness," originally published in *The American Psychologist* in 1960.

The Myth of Mental Illness
THOMAS S. SZASZ

My aim in this essay is to raise the question "Is there such a thing as mental illness?" and to argue that there is not. Since the notion of mental illness is extremely widely used nowadays, inquiry into the ways in which this term is employed would seem to be especially indicated. Mental illness, of course, is not literally a "thing" — or physical object — and hence it can "exist" only in the same sort of way in which other theoretical concepts exist. Yet, familiar theories are in the habit of posing, sooner or later — at least to those who come to believe in them — as "objective truths" (or "facts"). During certain historical periods, explanatory conceptions such as deities, witches, and microorganisms appeared not only as theories but as self-evident *causes* of a vast number of events. I submit that today mental

From "The Myth of Mental Illness" by Thomas Szasz, *The American Psychologist,* Vol. 15, pp. 113–118. Copyright 1960 by the American Psychological Association. Reprinted by permission of the American Psychological Association and Dr. Thomas Szasz.

illness is widely regarded in a somewhat similar fashion, that is, as the cause of innumerable diverse happenings. As an antidote to the complacent use of the notion of mental illness — whether as a self-evident phenomenon, theory, or cause — let us ask this question: What is meant when it is asserted that someone is mentally ill?

In what follows I shall describe briefly the main uses to which the concept of mental illness has been put. I shall argue that this notion has outlived whatever usefulness it might have had and that it now functions merely as a convenient myth.

Mental Illness as a Sign of Brain Disease

The notion of mental illness derives its main support from such phenomena as syphilis of the brain or delirious conditions — intoxications, for instance — in which persons are known to manifest various peculiarities or disorders of thinking and behavior. Correctly speaking, however, these are diseases of the brain, not of the mind. According to one school of thought, *all* so-called mental illness is of this type. The assumption is made that some neurological defect, perhaps a very subtle one, will ultimately be found for all the disorders of thinking and behavior. Many contemporary psychiatrists, physicians, and other scientists hold this view. This position implies that people *cannot* have troubles — expressed in what are *now called* "mental illnesses" — because of differences in personal needs, opinions, social aspirations, values, and so on. *All problems in living* are attributed to physicochemical processes which in due time will be discovered by medical research.

"Mental illnesses" are thus regarded as basically no different than all other diseases (that is, of the body). The only difference, in this view, between mental and bodily diseases is that the former, affecting the brain, manifest themselves by means of mental symptoms; whereas the latter, affecting other organ systems (for example, the skin, liver, etc.), manifest themselves by means of symptoms referable to those parts of the body. This view rests on and expresses what are, in my opinion, two fundamental errors.

In the first place, what central nervous system symptoms would correspond to a skin eruption or a fracture? It would *not* be some emotion or complex bit of behavior. Rather, it would be blindness or a paralysis of some part of the body. The crux of the matter is that a disease of the brain, analogous to a disease of the skin or bone, is a neurological defect, and not a problem in living. For example, a *defect* in a person's visual field may be satisfactorily explained by correlating it with certain definite lesions in the nervous system. On the other hand, a person's *belief* — whether this be a belief in Christianity, in Communism, or in the idea that his internal organs are "rotting" and that his body is, in fact, already "dead" — cannot be explained by a defect or disease of the nervous system. Explanations of this sort of occurrence — assuming that one is interested in the belief itself and does not regard it simply as a "symptom" or expression of something else that is *more interesting* — must be sought along different lines.

The second error in regarding complex psychosocial behavior, consisting of communications about ourselves and the world about us, as mere symptoms of neurological functioning is *epistemological*. In other words, it is an error pertaining not to any mistakes in observation or reasoning, as such, but rather to the way in which we organize and express our knowledge. In the present case, the error lies in making a symmetrical dualism between mental and physical (or bodily) symptoms, a dualism which is merely a habit of speech and to which no known observations can be found to correspond. Let us see if this is so. In medical practice, when we speak of physical disturbances, we mean either signs (for example, a fever) or symptoms (for example, pain). We speak of mental symptoms, on the other hand, when we refer to a patient's *communications about himself, others, and the world about him.* He might state that he is Napoleon or that he is being persecuted by the Communists. These would be considered mental symptoms *only* if the observer believed that the patient was *not* Napoleon or that he was *not* being persecuted by the Communists. This makes it apparent that the statement that "X is a mental symptom" involves rendering a judgment. The judgment entails, moreover, a covert comparison or matching of the patient's ideas, concepts, or beliefs with those of the observer and the society in which they live. The notion of mental symptom is therefore inextricably tied to the *social* (including *ethical*) *context* in which it is made in much the same way as the notion of bodily symptom is tied to an *anatomical* and *genetic context* (Szasz, 1957a, 1957b).

To sum up what has been said thus far: I have tried to show that for those who regard mental symptoms as signs of brain disease, the concept of mental illness is unnecessary and misleading. For what they mean is that people so labeled suffer from diseases of the brain; and, if that is what they mean, it would seem better for the sake of clarity to say that and not something else.

Mental Illness as a Name for Problems in Living

The term "mental illness" is widely used to describe something which is very different than a disease of the brain. Many people today take it for granted that living is an arduous process. Its hardship for modern man, moreover, derives not so much from a struggle for biological survival as from the stresses and strains inherent in the social intercourse of complex human personalities. In this context, the notion of mental illness is used to identify or describe some feature of an individual's so-called personality.

It is the context of this essay, specifically the scholarly forum of the professional journal, that largely sets the tone and indicates to readers just what sort of communication is under way. Readers know even as they open the cover that this will not be satire, fiction, or irony. The text is precisely the serious discussion of the idea announced in the title and restated explicitly in the first sentence: "My aim in this essay is to raise the question 'Is there such a thing as mental illness?' and to argue that there is not." As with most academic journal articles, the type of text, which is principally established by the context of the journal, is never at issue. Hence, the author need not establish in the text itself just what sort of text he is writing.

By the end of the first sentence, we know not only (a) what sort of text we are reading (serious academic essay) but also (b) the general topic, i.e., what the author mainly wants to discuss (the concept of mental illness) and (c) his general comment about this topic, i.e., what he mainly wants to say about it (it's a myth). But the essay continues beyond the first sentence, of course, and the author explains the many reasons why he believes mental illness is a myth. The general topic has many subtopics, and the author has many comments about each one of them.

In this particular essay, **topical elaboration** proceeds systematically and explicitly in separate subsections, each one with its own subheading, introduction, development and summary. For example, the topic of the first subdivision, like the one that follows it, is announced by a subheading ("Mental Illness as a Sign of Brain Disease"), and the author's comment about this topic is clear within the first two sentences (organic neurological disorders are diseases of the brain, not of the mind). The section is explicitly summarized in the last paragraph of the section ("To sum up: . . ."). The next section ("Mental Illness as a Name for Problems in Living") is similarly structured.

In contrast to these topical elaborations, the author elaborates the text "locally" when he treats technical terms and complicated concepts and terms with definitions, examples, and illustrations. For example, upon the mention of "neurological defect," he quickly explains the term by writing, "For example, a *defect* in a person's visual field may be satisfactorily explained by correlating it with certain definite lesions in the nervous system." Similarly, when he argues that the tendency to regard complex psychosocial behavior . . . as mere symptoms of neurological functioning" is an "*epistemological*" error, he not only defines the term but he does so with a contrast: "In other words, it is an error pertaining not to any mistakes in observation or reasoning, as such, but rather to the way in which we organize and express our knowledge." Many of these elaborations are parenthetical clarifications, e.g., "In medical practice, when we speak of physical disturbances, we mean either signs (for example, a fever) or symptoms (for example, pain)" and "The notion of mental symptom is therefore inextricably tied to the *social* (including *ethical*) *context* in which it is made in much the same way as the notion of bodily symptom is tied to an *anatomical* and *genetic context.*" All of these **lexical elaborations** address potential **troublesources** throughout the text.

Figure 3.1 shows lexical elaborations in paragraph 6 of Szasz's essay. At each point, the author proceeds by elaboration of text. The large-scale elaborations are more topical in nature than the "local" elaborations, which are more lexical. The author uses the former elaborations to stake out the topic, which is to say, by means of these topical elaborations, the writer establishes a mutual frame of reference, focusing the readers' attention on the topic in certain ways rather than others. By contrast, the lexical elaborations treat potential troublesources (e.g., they define technical terms or explain obscure concepts).

The title and initial thesis statement in this particular essay put the writer and reader on the same footing; they "anchor" the discourse by tapping a mutual frame of reference. In elaborating the particular topical possibilities that he does, Szasz "pushes" the discourse to the edges of the mutual frame of reference. That is to say, he introduces information that is sufficiently new so as to be potentially troublesome and require clarification. Such clarification is appropriate in several places and takes several forms. It is appropriate at the start of each new section and takes the form of explicit subtitles and introductory remarks. It is appropriate periodically with the lesser shifts in the topic that coincide with the starts of paragraphs and are so marked by indenting. And it is appropriate with the introduction of technical terms and is achieved by use of definitions, contrasts, illustrations, and parenthetical explanations.

TOPIC AND COMMENT

The relation of topic and comment has been the subject of considerable research by Prague School linguists, in the work of Mathesius, Firbas, and Daneš, as well as in other, more recent work by Halliday and psychologists interested in discourse processes. While most of this research has been at

CORE TEXT

The second error in regarding complex psychosocial behavior, → consisting of communications about ourselves and the world about us,

as mere symptoms of neurological functioning is epistemological. → In other words, it is an error pertaining not to any mistakes in observation or reasoning, as such, but rather to the way in which we organize and express our knowledge.

In the present case, the error lies in making a symmetrical dualism between mental and physical → (or bodily)

symptoms, → a dualism which is merely a habit of speech and to which no known observations can be found to correspond.

Let us see if this is so. In medical practice, when we speak of physical disturbances, we mean either signs → (for example, a fever)

or symptoms, → (for example, pain). We speak of mental symptoms, on the other hand, when we refer to a patient's communications about himself, others, and the world about him. He might state that he is Napoleon or that he is being persecuted by the Communists. These would be considered mental symptoms only if the observer believed that the patient was not Napoleon or that he was not being persecuted by the Communists.

This makes it apparent that the statement "X is a mental symptom" involves rendering a judgment. The judgment entails, moreover, a covert comparison or matching of the patients ideas, concepts, or beliefs with those of the observer and the society in which they live. The notion of mental symptom is therefore inextricably tied to the social → (including ethical)

context in which it is made in much the same way as the notion of bodily symptom is tied to an anatomical and genetic context.

LEXICAL ELABORATIONS

Figure 3.1. Text elaborations in paragraph of Szasz's "The Myth of Mental Illness."

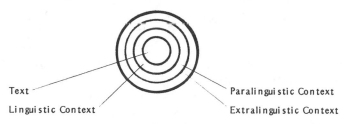

Figure 3.2. The concentric organization of text and context.

the level of the sentence, there are many important concepts in this literature that are germane to the study of extended texts.

From the time of its first congress in 1929 [Prague School 1978], Prague School linguists have focused their efforts on studying language in use, i.e., language in communicative contexts. This has been true even at the level of sentence analysis, which, in contrast to American studies of syntactic structure (e.g., Chomsky, 1957) and semantic structure (e.g., Fillmore, 1968; Kintsch, 1974), has been directly concerned with characterizing the organization of utterances and ultimately articulating a theory of utterance (Daneš, 1966). Unlike linguists in the tradition of Bloomfield, Prague linguists have not viewed linguistic performance as a set of confounding variables, nor have they viewed issues of pragmatics and language use as ripe for investigation only after securing advances in syntax and semantics. Rather, they have sought—in principle, theory, and method—to investigate language at the level of use and interpret the significance of language variables accordingly.

For the Prague School, the communicative value and function of words is in terms of other words, and the communicative value and function of texts is in relation to other texts (e.g., preceding text) and context (e.g., the setting in which the communication takes place). In these functional terms, communication and discourse always involve hierarchies of embedded elements (see Figure 3.2).

FUNCTIONAL SENTENCE PERSPECTIVE

This emphasis on understanding language in context is apparent especially in Prague approaches to sentences, a school of thought known as *Functional Sentence Perspective* (FSP). Mathesius (1939), for example, contrasted (a) "the starting point of the utterance" or "that which is known or at least obvious in the given situation and from which the speaker proceeds" with (b) "the core of the utterance" which is "what the speaker states about,

or in regard to, the starting point of the utterance [cited in Daneš, 1974]."
Mathesius called this starting point the **theme** of the sentence and the
latter, remaining portion the **enunciation**. In the first sentence of this
paragraph, for example, the theme is *This emphasis on understanding
language in context* and the enunciation is *is apparent especially in
Prague approaches to sentences, a school of thought known as Functional
Sentence Perspective (FSP)*. Normally, Mathesius argued, theme precedes
the enunciation, which is to say given information normally precedes new
information. In later discussions by others, including Firbas (1964) and
Daneš (1974), these concepts are called **theme** and **rheme**. In other
treatments of these concepts by non-Prague linguists, they are called **topic**
and **comment**.

Mathesius' twin criteria for *theme*—namely (a) that the theme identifies
something that is known by speaker and listener and (b) that the theme is
that part of the sentence from which the speaker proceeds—are potentially
at odds with each other as Trávníček (1962) and Firbas (1966) point out.
The difficulty is especially obvious at the start of a communication in which
the speaker asserts something that is *not* known but which the speaker
means to explain. Indeed, an important distinction between the first
sentence and subsequent sentences of any text is that the first sentence
must situate the reader, usually by *inititating* a common frame of reference
whereas the subsequent text must *sustain* this frame of reference (cf.
Benes, 1959). In Szasz's essay, for example, the theme of his first sentence
(*My aim in this essay*) is in fact not known until we complete the sentence
(My aim in this essay *is to raise the question "Is there such a thing as
mental illness?" and to argue that there is not*) and continue the essay.

As an alternative to Mathesius' definition of theme as known information,
Firbas proposed his concept of **communicative dynamism** (CD). Communicative dynamism refers to "the extent to which any sentence element
contributes to the development of the communication, to which it 'pushes
the communication forward,' as it were [1966, p. 270.]" For example,
imagine that I mention to you that I've heard that your father is visiting next
week. If you were to ask me how I learned this and I replied *Your father
wrote me a letter*, then *Your father* would be the theme of the sentence not
(a) because it is the first element in the sentence and not just (b) because
it expresses known information but rather (c) because, compared to the
remainder of the sentence (the rheme: *wrote me a letter*), it contributes less
to the overall movement of the communication. Hence, as in the above
example, it is entirely possible for the theme of a sentence to express new
information "although any element conveying known information has to be
regarded as thematic [Firbas, 1966, p. 255]." The expression of known
information is thematic because it contributes less information than the

remainder of the sentence, the rheme. But just as "thematic" cannot be equated with "known" information, Firbas argues, " 'rhematic' cannot be equated with 'unknown,' [or] 'new' . . . although rhematic elements always convey new information [Firbas, 1966, p. 255]." This definition of theme and rheme in terms of their relative contribution to the communicative dynamism of the text is important because it avoids the problems of approaches that define theme and rheme (as well as given and new information) in terms of particular syntactic structures, namely aligning theme and given information with syntactic subject, and rheme and new information with syntactic predicate.

THEMATIC PROGRESSIONS AND GRAMMATICALITY OF TEXT

It was František Daneš (1964, 1974) who showed how the dynamics of given–new information, as it is expressed in the theme–rheme relationships of individual sentences, can be applied to the structure of extended texts. He did this by showing that in well-formed texts, the theme–rheme relationships of individual sentences build on each other in sequences which he called **progressions**. For example, in the sentence pair, *I'm studying physics this term. It's hard*, the theme of the second sentence (*It*) reiterates the rheme of the first sentence (*physics*). In so doing the second sentence continues in effect to comment upon the assertion begun in the first sentence. That is to say, the second sentence elaborates upon the first. This particular thematic progression, which Daneš called a **simple linear progression**, is one of three types he identified. Altogether the three kinds are as follows:

1. **Simple linear progression**, where the thematic information of a sentence is the same as the rhematic information of the preceding sentence;
2. **Constant theme**, or **run-through progression**, where the thematic information of a sentence is the same as the thematic information of the preceding sentence; and
3. **Derived theme progression**, where the thematic information is the same for a sequence of sentences but this information is implied, not stated.

Daneš's classification of the ways in which sentences build upon each other is important because it demonstrates the viability of the given–new distinction in the analysis of extended texts and provides a vocabulary for discussing the patterning of information in any given text. It also separates the issue of information from orthographic boundaries, as Witte (1983) points out. Nonetheless, the classification does not in and of itself provide a grammar, which is to say, whereas it allows the description of texts in terms of particular thematic progressions, it offers no general principles with respect to permissible and nonpermissible text sequences. For example, each of the following sequences is an example of a run-through progression: The thematic information is identical in each sentence pair. Yet the second sequence, if read as a complete text, I submit, is ungrammatical and would be rejected as it stands by most readers:

> **Text 3.1.** *The tree is living. It is in bloom.*
>
> **Text 3.2.** *The tree is living. It is dead.*

While there are many possible grounds, including both logic and grammar, for discarding the second text as unacceptable, thematic progression is not one of them. What principles determine particular progressions in well-formed texts? What characterizes a grammatical rheme? Is there any way to characterize the constraints on the enunciation of one theme rather than another especially in terms of sentences as they relate to each other? When are particular thematic progressions preferable to others? What criteria might be used to characterize preferred progressions?

For a text linguist, identifying thematic progressions without specifying how they typically relate to each other is comparable to linguists' identifying nouns and verbs without specifying how nouns and verbs typically relate: Such description is pretheoretical. Daneš (1974) notes this limitation in applying Functional Sentence Perspective to the analysis of whole texts when he notes the need "to find out the principles exactly according to which this and not another portion of the mass of known information has been selected. In other words, we have to inquire into the principles underlying thematic choice and thematic progression [p. 112]." Without such principles, a theory of utterance—Saussure's long elusive account of *la parole*—is, of course, impossible.

In Daneš's third progression type, the sentences of some texts are related to a derived theme or **hypertheme**, Daneš's term for the central idea of any text in which this idea is not stated explicitly. An example is a paragraph with a thesis but no explicit thesis statement. In what sort of text may the writer merely imply the thesis, i.e., proceed hyperthematically? By contrast, when is an implied thesis inadequate? When is it important to state a thesis explicitly? What principles of discourse are relevant to this distinction? In an insightful analysis of expository writing, Witte (1983) shows that these hyperthemes, or **discourse topics** as he calls them, are derived not from the text alone "but from the interaction of the text with the reader's prior knowledge [p. 316]." Whereas knowledgeable readers might find the explicit statement of the main idea in such text unnecessary or even superfluous, unknowledgeable readers are obviously at a loss without an explicit statement since they have no way to find out what is only implied.

This conclusion is consistent with my analysis of lexical elaborations (Nystrand, 1981). I note that skilled writers elaborate potentially trouble-some parts of texts according to the terms of the given–new contract and the general requirements for semantic coherence. These elaborations are carefully keyed to those terms and concepts which are critical to reader comprehension; their purpose is to "buttress" the text in precisely those spots which threaten common categorizations and reciprocity between writer and reader, in effect providing explicit bridges (cf. Haviland and Clark, 1974) between precisely those propositions and assertions whose relations readers might otherwise miss.

NOTES TOWARD A RECIPROCITY-BASED
TEXT GRAMMAR

Fundamental Axiom: A given text is functional to the extent that it balances the reciprocal needs of the writer for expression and of the reader for comprehension. Communicative homeostasis is the normal condition of grammatical texts.

It might seem that, aside from certain essential prescriptions for "correct prose," there are no rules determining what such prose might be; that certainly there are no descriptive rules or principles which might be said to characterize, if not govern, the matter of generating and elaborating text; that indeed composing is a new enterprise every time, always requiring the writer to find appropriate forms to fit given occasions, subjects, and individual purposes. As Michael Stubbs puts it, "It is easy to get the impression that discourse analysis is at least a foolhardy, if not a quite impossible undertaking, and that expanding the narrow range of phenom-ena that linguists study to include natural language in use causes all hell to break loose [1983, p. 15]."

But every written text is not wholly idiosyncratic. And it is my purpose, like Stubbs', to show that "the chaos can be contained," that "in fact, only some hell breaks loose [p. 15]." The constant in the equation of discourse is reciprocity, the underlying premise that the text generated must result in shared knowledge between writer and reader. Hence, what counts is not simply what the text says but how what is said relates to what is already shared by writer and reader. In effect, a coherent text secures a balance between the needs of the writer on the one hand to say something and the expectations of the reader on the other hand for a certain kind of text. This is merely another way of saying that writers must initiate and sustain conditions of reciprocity between themselves and their readers if their communication is to be coherent. Texts function and are lucid to the extent that this balance is maintained; they are unclear and dysfunctional to the extent that it is not. And this is precisely why writers are obliged to be explicit about their topics with unknowledgeable readers in a way that they are not with knowledgeable readers.

The text is obviously central to the interaction between writer and reader. It is the bridge between the producer and receiver in both spoken and written communication. When writers strike a careful balance between their own expressive needs and the expectations of their readers, the result is clear communication and lucid text. This comes about when the writer's elaboration of text meaning matches readers' requirements for eliminating potential meanings. It is essential that what the writer says complements what readers bring to the text.

Choice Point Corollary: Potential troublesources which threaten reciprocity define choice points for the writer. Options Corollary: Text options at each choice point are text elaborations.

Whenever the terms of reciprocity are threatened or jeopardized by the introduction of new information, the writer may restore the balance by elaborating. E. Ochs (in press) recently argues that speakers will vary in the extent to which they assume the burden of making sense of each other and that this variation is largely related to the respective social rank or status of the speakers. Hence, some writers and speakers (e.g., assistant professors and children) may be more obliged to explain troublesources than others (e.g., full professors and parents). Nonetheless, to the extent that writers deal with potential troublesources, their options consist of various text elaborations. For example, explicit statement of the discourse topic—for example a title or a thesis statement or a suitable introduction—serves exactly this function for unknowledgeable readers. So too do definitions and illustrations of technical terms and troublesome concepts.

How much and what sorts of elaboration are needed? And what determines which text structures to generate? Which one should come first, which next, and so on? How should a writer proceed? In the interests of communication, the writer will elaborate or "buttress" precisely those parts of the text where reciprocity is threatened. This is why close colleagues can identify themselves unambiguously with only initials (or less, e.g., handwriting alone) whereas other situations require more elaborate identification. In either case, of course, the writer's purpose is the same: to provide unambiguous identification. But this purpose does not translate directly into any particular text structure. This is why *more text* is not categorically more adequate than *less text*. This is also why skilled technical writers carefully treat the points they do for nontechnical readers with definitions, examples, and illustrations. And it is one important reason why children's literature is so heavily illustrated. In all of these instances the text is the way it is because it effectively strikes a balance between the purposes of the writer and the expectations of the reader.

Often writers do not strike such a balance. For example, when a writer misjudges how much more he knows about a topic than the readers, the readers may be unable to follow him. The text is too dense, and either the reader feels the writer is "speeding" through the material without due consideration for the reader, or the reader feels he has chosen a text that is too advanced. There are other cases in which a text that might have been functional in its original time and place ceases to be for extraordinary reasons. For example, in the case of Chaucer's tales and Shakespeare's plays, where each writer masterfully matched his texts to his contemporary reader's expectations, the texts have outlived the readers for whom they were written. In such cases, readers may need to take a course in Chaucer or Shakespeare, and/or an editor may need to provide marginal glosses in order to revitalize the texts, making them function once again in terms of the author's original purpose and new readers' needs.

Misconstraint Corollary: Inadequate elaboration results in miscon- straint, i.e., mismatch between the writer's expression and the reader's comprehension. Inadequate elaboration at the level of topic results in abstruse text. Inadequate elaboration at the level of comment results in ambiguous text. Inadequate elaboration at the level of genre results in misreading.

It is easy, of course, to blame everything on the writer and especially to point to certain text characteristics (such as complicated syntax and big words) as the source of the problem, and to the extent that the writer is responsible for initiating and sustaining the communication, this blame is well placed. But while the writer can rightly be held responsible for all manner of sins (of both omission and deed), the failure is not adequately explained in terms of the writer alone. Nor can readability be explained simply in terms of syntax and lexis. At its core, readability has to do with how the text works in terms of both the writer and its readers. Readability has to do with how the text functions as a medium of exchange between writer and reader. Hence, the extent to which a text is lucid or turgid has less to do with a particular writer's expression in any categorical sense (or a particular reader's comprehension, for that matter) than it does with the presence or absence of interaction between the production skills of the one and the processing resources of the other. In terms of communication, writers and readers are not so much right or wrong in their expression and interpretations as they are *in or out of tune with each other*. When writers and readers are out of tune in this way, the result is mismatch, or **misconstraint** (cf. Nystrand, 1979; 1982b).

In the case of **ambiguous text**, which is *a text that says too little about too many points*, the reader finds the text inadequately developed and its terms inadequately defined ("Tell me more"). Writers can revise ambiguous texts effectively by being *more specific* about points of ambiguity. In the case of **abstruse text**, which is *a text that says too much about too few points*, the reader finds the topic inadequately defined ("What is this about anyway?"). Writers can revise abstruse texts by effectively clarifying the topic, particularly at the start of the text. In a third kind of mismatch, the reader understands the topic of the text and each of the points made about the topic, but nonetheless misreads the writer's purpose. Examples include misperceived irony, e.g., concluding that the author of "A Modest Proposal" must have been pathologically insane or that *Animal Farm* is merely an innocent children's story.

In the first sort of mismatch, which results in ambiguity (and which I have elsewhere [1979, 1982b] called **rarefaction**), the problem is inadequate elaboration at the level of comment. In the second sort of mismatch, which results in abstruseness (and which I have elsewhere [1979, 1982b] called **impaction**), the problem is inadequate elaboration at the level of topic. Finally, in the third sort of mismatch, which results in misreading, the problem is inadequate elaboration at the level of genre: In not seeing the irony, in reading humor seriously, the reader understands what the writer says but doesn't understand what sort of text is "going on."

Masters of irony such as Swift and Orwell exploit readers' expectations for certain sorts of text. Consider Jonathan Swift's "A Modest Proposal." On the one hand, we may wonder how readers detect the irony at all; it cannot be due to anything that Swift actually writes, certainly not in the first few pages. For Swift says virtually nothing to actually indicate that he is not serious about his proposal to control the population of Ireland by eating children. Perhaps most readers finally read the text as irony because proposals to eat children make sense only if the writer doesn't really mean it. But without knowing something beyond the text—about Swift and his times—there is no real way to know whether the author is brilliant because he is a lunatic or a satirist.

A more interesting issue is why readers invariably take Swift's proposals seriously at all. Why do naive readers not question the piece from the very start? (No one ever begins by asking, "How am I to read this?") The answer has to do with the fact that "A Modest Proposal" is exposition and that one of the fundamental expectations set up by the genre is the straightforward intent of the author—that is, as Olson (1977) puts it, essayists say what they mean and mean what they say. This aspect of exposition has nothing to do with anything the writer actually states; rather it is a fundamental characteristic of the genre. Readers read exposition on the premise that the writer is serious, and writers compose it on the premise that readers will so interpret it. Hence, genre is a way of elaborating not the text itself but rather the communicative event. Swift exploits his readers' expectations for exposition by framing a preposterous proposal in terms of this serious genre which sets reader expectations for measured, rational analysis. By the time readers detect the irony, they have experienced exactly what Swift wants—a penetrating revulsion toward certain forces in Irish society which he opposes.

From this analysis, we understand why nothing categorical can be said about the communicative function of any particular text structure per se. Long sentences are not categorically worse than short. Short words are not categorically better than long. And long sentences are not necessarily made better by making them short. The very examples and definitions that help some readers will confuse others. For example, the same explanations and court decision that might help attorneys understand current Supreme Court interpretations of tax shelters will overwhelm the general taxpayer. To understand tax shelters, general taxpayers need not greater detail but rather a general definition of terms, starting with the term "tax shelter." These readers need to "step back from the picture," not move more deeply into the frame.

Not all new information is equally new, of course. The newness of information is entirely related to what the reader knows *vis-à-vis* what the writer wants to say. Hence, some information, e.g., highly specialized and unfamiliar technical knowledge, is not just new; it is *extremely new*. If the writer introduces such highly new information without preparing or helping the reader upon introducing it, the reader is simply run over by the communicative dynamism of the text. Instead of pushing the communication forward, the writer pushes the reader over. In other words, any point in the communication which endangers or disrupts the established frame of reference is a **choice point** for the writer.

At each such choice point, which is a potential troublesource for readers, the writer has a variety of options, all of which involve a text elaboration of some sort. The most common sort of elaboration includes those mentioned previously—glosses, definitions, examples, illustrations, and diagrams. Typically these "local" elaborations are introduced precisely at those points of text which are potential troublesources. The function of these constructions is to "buttress" the text at these points where the writer's purpose and the readers' needs may not be balance, i.e., where the terms of reciprocity are threatened.

Situation Corollary: The beginning of a text functions to situate the reader in terms of a mutual frame of reference.

In order for a text to function, the writer and reader must start on the same footing. Most fundamentally, the text establishes genre and consequently mode of interpretation, and if the text is informative, the beginning will normally situate the reader in terms of topic and comment quite directly. In some texts, this will be accomplished quite explicitly (e.g., Szasz's *My aim in this essay is to raise the question "Is there such a thing as mental illness?" and to argue that there is not*). Interoffice memos typically establish this mutual frame of reference by identifying when (DATE:), who (TO: and FROM:), and what (RE:). Sometimes context plays an essential factor in situating the reader: Readers know what sort of text Szasz' essay is, for example, largely because they find it published in *The American Psychologist*. And just what refrigerator-door notewriters write about and just how much they need say about it is largely determined by the fact that they may leave it on the refrigerator door and as a consequence can reasonably anticipate the expectations of the reader.

Elaboration Construction Corollary: Writers may elaborate texts at the level of genre, topic, and comment. Text elaborations in English include words, phrases, clauses, sentences, and paragraphs. Elaborations must be consistent with expectations initiated by the writer. Constructions which might fundamentally threaten reciprocity (i.e., complicate rather than clarify) may not be used.

A consequence of the fundamental axiom is that elaborations must be consistent with the expectations of the reader. Hence, elaborations must not complicate the text for the reader. That is, if the writer introduces a technical term for an audience of general readers, the lexical elaboration which treats the term may not be comparably technical. Rather, the elaboration must be an example, definition, or illustration which appropriately contextualizes the term or concept in terms of what the reader already knows or has come to understand from previous text.

Elaborating text, then, is not just a matter of saying more. In the case of genre, for example, writers typically clarify text type by saying things one way rather than another (e.g., "The Effects of Text Editing on Cognitive Processes" versus "Byting Bits in First Grade"). Elaborations may vary a great deal in construction and length. Sometimes an appropriate elaboration is nothing more than a qualifying adjective or phrase. Alternatively, elaborations may be clauses, sentences, whole paragraphs, even chapters, and, in extraordinary circumstances whole volumes (e.g., scholarly bibliographies which gloss historic texts).

Elaboration Episode Corollary: Elaborations which approach the limit of the reader's capacity for processing information mark elaboration episodes which define new choice points for the writer and result in text segmentations (such as new paragraphs, sections, chapters, volumes, etc.).

A further consequence of the fundamental axiom is that the particular form of any coherent text will directly reflect a functional balance of given and new information. The degrees of communicative dynamism, of newness and givenness, moreover, are relative, and depend on the extent to which the speaker and listener share common understandings and the extent to which what the speaker says pushes the limits of this common understanding. " 'Givenness,' " Daneš writes, "depends on the length of the portion of preceding text in relation to which the evaluation is being carried out" and should be "empirically ascertained. . . . We may tentatively assume that these portions of 'intervals' are in a way correlated with the segmentation of text into paragraphs, groups of paragraphs, chapters, etc. [Daneš, 1974, p. 109]." That is, when a given–new cycle is completed, the writer encounters a choice point and, in order to continue appropriately, marks the introduction of the subsequent cycle of new information by indentation or some other appropriate device. "We may even expect a kind of hierarchy or stratification of the feature 'given': taking for granted that not only particular utterances but also the sections of text, as paragraphs, etc., and the whole text have 'themes' of their own ('hyperthemes'), we can expect that, e.g., the theme of a chapter will be evaluated as 'given' throughout the chapter, so that the 'interval of givenness' in respect to the information carried by this 'hypertheme' will be the whole chapter [Daneš, 1974, p. 109-110]."

In other words, to the extent that an elaboration is substantial, it may well result in text which approaches the limits of the reader's capacity for processing information. The inevitable result of such substantial elaboration therefore defines a choice point, which the skilled writer appropriately treats with a new text elaboration. For example, the writer starts a new paragraph, section, or chapter. This corollary is important because it underscores the character of text segments (e.g., paragraphs) as text episodes, structured largely as they are because of the need of the writer to maintain the terms of the reciprocity principle.

Elaboration Type Corollary: Three basic elaboration types are available to writers. (a) Genre elaborations clarify the character of the communication and the text type. (b) Topical elaborations clarify discourse topics. (c) Local elaborations, or commentary, clarify discourse comments.

Many of these elaborations clarify concepts and terms—potential trouble-sources that otherwise might be unclear. That is, they "buttress" the text locally. In this category are definitions, examples, illustrations (including pictures, maps, diagrams, and other graphic material), parenthetical expressions, footnotes, restrictive and nonrestrictive clauses, appositives, glosses, and circumscriptions.

But writers buttress not just the text; writers also buttress the communicative event itself. Elaborations of this sort include genre-related characteristics, openings, logos and letterheads, titles, elements of tone (sort of title, level of formality, diction [e.g., the Victorian "we"], and typeface). These elaborations clarify just what sort of a text is underway and provide an interpretive context for the text itself. The net effect of these is to "frame" the text, to serve notice to the reader what sort of text it is and suggest how to read it.

Texts are specially elaborated at their starts in the form of titles, introductions, and explicit statement of discourse topic (e.g., thesis statement in expository prose and various metastatements). The purpose of these special elaborations is not so much to sustain reciprocity, however, as to initiate it. In beginning a text, the writer must take appropriate measures to make sure that the writer and reader start off on a common footing. Their frames of reference must be the same; it is from this mutual knowledge base, this common frame of reference that writers contextualize their expression and introduce the new information which follows.

Do the fundamental axiom and corollaries have relevance for **fictive texts** as well as informational texts? In reading fiction, the reader will normally be situated in terms of genre but often not immediately in terms of topic and comment. Stories often begin *in medias res*, for example, and, as a result, characters, places, and plots may well be introduced in a way that, while initially complicating the *who, what,* and *when* of *topic* and *comment,* nonetheless—and largely because of such complicating—maintains reciprocity at the level of genre. Hence, one of the things that "There was no hope for him this time: it was the third stroke" confirms as we begin Joyce's "The Sisters" is that this is a fictive type of text. The writer of fiction is not obligated, as is the writer of exposition, to restore reciprocity whenever and wherever it may be threatened; indeed, the novelist's options include complicating the text at just those points the essayist might clarify. But this does not mean that reciprocity is irrelevant to fiction. What is unique about fiction is the temporary suspension and promise of reciprocity; in the end things will come together. Hence, when Melville begins *Moby Dick* by writing, "Call me Ishmael," he does in fact enunciate that part of the text from which the narrator proceeds, but he does not allude to anything that is jointly known by both the writer and reader. And significantly, the reader does not object, thinking that Melville might have written 'a better introduction to his book about whales.' It is precisely by beginning in the middle of things and alluding to unknown characters and settings that novelists induce readers' suspension of disbelief and engage readers in a particular kind of text and reading experience. That is to say, whereas the identity of "me" is unknown at the start of *Moby Dick*, it is precisely Melville's treatment of new information as known that functions to make the world of the narrative plausible. Whereas the beginning of exposition situates the reader directly in terms of genre, topic, and comment, the beginning of literature situates readers to a kind of text that gains comparable clarity only as readers work their way through. No doubt the unique engagement of literature is largely due the suspended and protracted nature of the reciprocity or closure that the writer promises and the reader finally finds.

A RECIPROCITY-BASED GRAMMAR OF WRITTEN TEXT

Axiom and Corollaries

Fundamental Axiom: A given text is functional to the extent that it balances the reciprocal needs of the writer for expression and of the reader for comprehension. Communicative homeostasis is the normal condition of grammatical texts.

Choice Point Corollary: Potential troublesources which threaten reciprocity define choice points for the writer.

Options Corollary: Text options at each choice point are text elaborations.

Misconstraint Corollary: Inadequate elaboration results in misconstraint, i.e., mismatch between the writer's expression and the reader's comprehension. Inadequate elaboration at the level of topic results in abstruse text. Inadequate elaboration at the level of comment results in ambiguous text. Inadequate elaboration at the level of genre results in misreading.

Situation Corollary: The beginning of a text functions to situate the reader in terms of a mutual frame of reference.

Elaboration Construction Corollary: Writers may elaborate texts at the level of genre, topic, and comment. Text elaborations in English include words, phrases, clauses, sentences, and paragraphs. Elaborations must be consistent with expectations initiated by the writer. Constructions which might fundamentally threaten reciprocity (i.e., complicate rather than clarify) may not be used.

Elaboration Episode Corollary: Elaborations which approach the reader's capacity for processing information mark elaboration episodes, which define new choice points for the writer and result in text segmentations (such as new paragraphs, sections, chapters, volumes, etc).

Elaboration Type Corollary: Three basic elaboration types are available to writers. (a) Genre elaborations clarify the character of the communication and the text type. (b) Topical elaborations clarify discourse topics. (c) Local elaborations, or commentary, clarify discourse comments.

4

A Critical Examination
of the Doctrine
# of Autonomous Texts

MARTIN NYSTRAND, ANNE DOYLE, AND MARGARET HIMLEY

INTRODUCTION

The common claim that written texts are "autonomous" and explicit compared to speech, which is "context-bound" and "fragmentary," is an oversimplification that misses the main point of one aspect of writing. A text is explicit not because it says everything all by itself but rather because it strikes a careful balance between what needs to be said and what may be assumed. The writer's problem is not just being explicit; the writer's problem is knowing what to be explicit about.

In this chapter, we examine the fallacies of the doctrine of autonomous texts, showing how even the most formal of essays works *not apart from but in terms of its context of use*. These issues are relevant to psychologists and linguists concerned about the nature of text and discourse processes. These issues also concern educators, who typically work from the premise that formal prose ought to work independently of its context and who accomplish this objective by teaching writing as a matter for preferred form rather than effective use.

THE DOCTRINE OF AUTONOMOUS TEXTS

A substantial body of thought, from Plato to the present, supports the notion that written and spoken language differ most with respect to the contexts in which each is created and must function. The essential argument is as follows: Writers, unlike speakers, do not produce language in the company of a language receiver. And written texts, unlike spoken, must function apart from the context of their production. Therefore, writing must differ fundamentally from speech. Specifically, written texts must be "autonomous" and "explicit" in order to function "acontextually."

Plato was perhaps the first philosopher to examine the context of oral language. He especially distrusted the performances of bards and poets who he believed appealed to the emotions rather than reason. Following this line of reasoning, classicist Eric Havelock (1963, 1977) supports Plato's suspicions about oral language by arguing that the requirements for memorizing Homeric epics, as well as the conditions of their recitations, promoted the use of such oral mnemomic devices as prosodic organization, personal reference, concrete images, and narrative style. Goody and Watt (1968) contend that such logical language forms as syllogisms, propositions, and the elaboration of premises became possible only with the advent of writing and the availability of permanent text for inspection and review. In this view, writing made possible historical and literary criticism as well as modern systems of logic: The former enabled Herodotus to compare past and present claims whereas the latter enabled Plato and Aristotle to compare propositions. Sociolinguist M. Stubbs (1980) discusses written language in this regard when he notes the special role it plays in Sir Karl Popper's (1972) *Theory of World 3:* Writing makes possible objective knowledge which lies beyond the world of of physical events (Popper's World 1) and beyond the world of experience and consciousness (Popper's World 2). Writing is that essential and ultimate path of language that leads its users to the archives of a knowledge which exists independently of the knowers (for example in libraries).

These notions of written and spoken language have been amplified more recently by psychologists. For example, Luria (1982) and Vygotsky (1962) both note how the basic cognitive processes of abstraction, generalization, and inference are favored by the propensity of written language for reflection and analysis: Writing, Vygotsky states, is "the deliberate structuring of the web of meaning [p. 100]" and so enhances the analytic requirements of "scientific concepts." Patricia Greenfield, a developmental psychologist whose work has been influential among educators, concludes (1972) that schooling and literacy are the primary factors involved in the development of context-free, abstract thought mainly because of the impact of written language on cognitive processes. By learning to write, she notes, students learn skills of critical analysis because of the requirements of written language for autonomous text. More recently, C. Snow (1983) outlines important similarities in the development of both oral and written language development. Both, she concludes, require learning how to understand and produce decontextualized language, i.e., "growth in their ability to discuss the remote and the abstract [1983, p. 175]." In this view, language development is the progressive separation of speech from dependence on context for meaning. Language starts as telegraphic and context-embedded and becomes elaborated and explicit.

This view of language development obviously oversimplifies actual development. After all, mature writers and speakers are not always elaborate and explicit even though they are able to be: They still write notes to themselves and the person who delivers the milk. Speakers and writers do not simply become more elaborate and explicit with age; they also develop a subtle sense of the relation between text and context, knowing *how and when to be explicit about what.*

Even though this view of language development from telegraphic utterance to explicit text oversimplifies the actual course of development, it nonetheless usefully characterizes the pedagogical rationale for literacy activities and objectives in schools. In her excellent analysis of sharing-time (or show-and-tell) activities, for example, S. Michaels (1981) shows how teachers promote this very kind of language development, beginning as early as first grade. Indeed, recent composition research distinguishes composition from writing a priori in precisely these terms (e.g., Bereiter & Scardamalia, 1981; Dillon, 1981; Hirsch, 1977; Kroll, 1981; Olson, 1977). Bereiter and Scardamalia's distinction is typical:

> Writing is use of the written medium and entails such skills as handwriting, spelling, and punctuation. People who could converse by passing notes back and forth to one another would be said to know how to write. If that were all they could do, however, they could not be said to know how to compose.... [Composition] involves producing ... "autonomous text" ... a coherent piece of language that can accomplish its rhetorical purpose without depending on context or on interaction between sender and receiver. One does not, in principle, need to know how to write in order to compose. Composing can be done by dictation [1981, pp. 3–4].

From its historic emphasis on sentences as units of complete thought to its persistent rationale for essays as autonomous embodiments of thought, schooling has sought to give pedagogical force to the contention that *written text is the culminating stage of language development* [cf. Scinto, 1986]. We may note, too, in this regard, that the doctrine of autonomous texts juxtaposes normative and prescriptive rules: Oral language "is" context-bound, but written text "must be" autonomous.

By far the best known statement of this distinction between spoken and written language is to be found in the work of Canadian psychologist David

Olson (e.g., 1975, 1977, 1981, 1983; Hildyard and Olson, 1982; Watson and Olson, in press), who has done extensive comparisons of preschool and preliterate children with schooled children and adults on a variety of cognitive tasks. The following tenets, derived from Olson's work, summarize the key points of the distinction we have been examining between written text as autonomous and context-independent and spoken utterance as concrete and context-bound:

1. Speakers are able to circumvent the ever-present possibility of ambiguity in speech "by means of such prosodic and paralinguistic cues as gestures, intonation, stress, quizzical looks, and restatement [p. 272]." Since writers have no access to these linguistic and paralinguistic devices, *writers must take special care to make their texts more explicit* than they might if they were otherwise speaking. Writers "must guard against possible ambiguity with only the resources of the text [p. 272]." Meaning must be "preserved in sentences which have to be understood in contexts other than those in which they were written [p. 272]." For this reason, writer intentions must be fully realized in written texts: *What is said* must be carefully aligned with *what is meant*.

2. Because written language potentially represents speaker meaning more fully than oral language can, written language plays an important archival role in our culture (e.g., libraries, books, and written records).

3. *Fullness of meaning is explicitness of text.* Working from Grice's (1957) distinction between *what is meant* (speaker–writer intention) and *what is said* (speaker–writer expression), Hildyard and Olson (1982) show that readers, unlike listeners, make clean distinctions between the two. And it is precisely because readers work more from *what is said* than *what is meant*, Olson argues, that writers, unlike speakers, are especially obliged to be explicit, i.e., to represent fully *what they mean* by *what they say* in texts "which, like Popeye, *say* what they *mean* and *mean* precisely, neither more nor less than, what they *say* [1981, p. 108]."

4. Writing fosters critical reasoning skills by requiring learners to master the logical or ideational functions of language and to distinguish these functions from the interpersonal functions of spoken language. Because written texts are "biased" in favor of fuller semantic representations than spoken utterances, learning to write and read enhances thinking as well as language skills. Specifically, learning to read school texts requires coping with the demands of an objective, universal, and analytic medium (Watson and Olson, in press).

5. Because of its demands for utterly explicit, unambiguous language,

expository prose is the epitome of text development. "Within this genre of literature, if unconventionalized or nonlinguistic knowledge is permitted to intrude, we charge the writer with reasoning via unspecified inferences and assumptions or the reader with misreading the text [p. 272]."

Carefully considered, the doctrine of autonomous texts, which contends that writing is the mode of language par excellence for reasoning, is not altogether persuasive. That writing will necessarily (or even probably) yield logic is clearly not true (as any teacher of composition will readily testify). That logic is better conducted in writing than speech is not true either, as Socrates first noted in *The Phaedrus*. In a recent seminal study of the cognitive consequences of literacy, Scribner and Cole (1981) conclude that literacy per se contributes only marginally to cognitive development. They argue that literacy is not adequately understood as proficiency in decontextualized language. "Literacy is not simply knowing how to read and write a particular script but applying this knowledge for specific purposes in specific contexts of use [1981, p. 236]."

The precise relation between writing and reasoning in Olson's distinctions is unclear. Is the language of essays explicit because it is written, or is the language of essays explicit because essays are the chief forum for the discussion of abstract issues? Are written language and reason related necessarily (by cause and effect) or accidentally (by correlation)?

Similar questions can be asked about the relationship between explicitness and mode of discourse. It is certainly true that some texts are more self-sufficient than others in the sense that situational factors relevant to their meaning are derivable from the text itself. There is clearly a difference, for example, between an essay or a legal contract and quarterback talk in a football huddle. Essays and contracts permit readers to entertain text meaning per se; quarterback instructions merely provide salient cues to the meaning entertained by the quarterback. In principle anyway, this difference is a chief reason why legal contracts are usually written documents rather than oral agreements. Nonetheless, the fact of endless legal disputes over the precise meaning of legal documents raises many questions about the extent to which any written text can be truly autonomous.

The doctrine of autonomous texts is muddled, moreover, by readily available counterexamples from spoken and written language. Tannen (1982), for example, shows that features which are typically associated with each mode (for example, prosody and alliteration in written language and rementions and assonance in oral language) are as likely to be found in one mode as the other. R. Lakoff (1982), moreover, shows that in any given culture, oral and written language "crossfertilize" each other so the particular features which distinguish each are in a constant state of flux. For example, at the same time that writers of fiction have increasingly used quotation marks to personalize their writing and bring an emotional directness to their prose, she notes, many speakers have learned to indicate quotation marks with their fingers as a paralinguistic gesture.

In short, formal speeches, lectures, and seminar discussions are all good oral examples of the "autonomous text register" which Olson (1977) characterizes as **written text.** And public signs, kit instructions, and notes left on refrigerator doors are all good written examples of the "context-dependent register" Olson characterizes as **spoken utterance.** One might object that formal speeches, lectures, and seminar discussions are not typical of spoken language and, similarly, that public signs, kit instructions, and notes left on the refrigerator door are not typical of written language. However, essays and Homeric performances are probably even less typical. We must remember that the issue here is quite general and regards not the bias of language in essays and casual conversation but rather "the bias of language in speech and writing." Are the differences that Olson and others note real differences between speech and writing, or are they *differences in selected uses of speaking and written language*? If they are the latter, just how representative are these uses of speech and writing? How valid is the distinction?

AN EXPERIMENT

To examine these many issues, we elicited and analyzed four discourse types in terms of cohesion, endophoric and exophoric references, and recall. The four discourse types we examined were reports and speculations in both writing and speaking.

Subjects, Materials, Procedures

Subjects were 23 college juniors and seniors in an advanced expository writing course at the University of Wisconsin-Madison. On the first day of data collection, half the class wrote reports based on personal experience, and the other half wrote speculations on contemporary social and political issues. Subjects were randomly assigned to these two writing tasks. The oral samples were elicited on two different days in the subsequent week. Tasks and subjects were counterbalanced so that subjects who wrote speculative pieces during the first week did oral reports the following week, and vice versa. The subjects were split into two groups during this second round of data collection so that those who had written reports were not present to

TABLE 4.1

Length (Number of Words) of Elicited Text Samples

Text type	Mean	Standard deviation	N
Oral report	371.8	117.6	5
Oral speculation	262.8	66.9	6
Written report	433.0	63.7	6
Written speculation	362.2	141.7	6
Grand mean	356.8		

hear the oral reports, and vice versa. The average number of words per sample was 356.82 (see Table 4.1). There were no significant differences among discourse types in length [ANOVA $F(3, 19) = 2.72; p = .07$].

Comprehension of all language samples was measured by written free recall. After listening to each oral report and speculation and performing a distractor task, students wrote recalls. Recall data related to the written samples were collected two weeks after the samples were collected. Each written report or speculation was read by seven other subjects. Subjects who originally wrote reports read only speculations, and vice versa.

All taped samples were transcribed, and all written samples were typed whereupon each was analyzed by two readers for explicitness. Following Halliday and Hasan (1976), we defined an explicit text as one where relevant situational factors are derivable from the text or utterance itself. Specifically, we operationalized the distinction between "autonomous text" and "context-bound utterance" in terms of proportions of **endophoric** and **exophoric** cohesive ties, including reference, substitution, ellipsis (including deixis), and lexical cohesion (e.g., reiteration). For definitions of each type of cohesive tie, the reader is referred to Halliday and Hasan, but here is one example: **Exophoric references** "point outside" a text either to things in the speaking environment (e.g., the *it* in *Put it here*); or to ideas which exist as presumed, shared knowledge and require no elaboration (e.g., the *it* in *I don't believe it*). By contrast, endophoric references "point within" to other parts of the text where they are specifically elaborated, illustrated, or defined by other words. Consider the following example:

(4.1)   *What we really need in our field is articulation of a comprehensive theory. This effort is complicated by the fact that so many researchers operate out of different and frequently incompatible assumptions.*

In the second sentence of this example, *This effort* is an endophoric reference to something identified in the text itself, namely *articulation of a comprehensive theory* in the previous sentence. Endophoric referencing is the chief way writers and speakers explain what they mean; and when editors and teachers ask a writer to be "clear" and "explicit," they are typically requesting a more endophoric and less exophoric text.

To assess recall, all samples were segmented into and listed by clauses. Two raters compared these lists with the written recalls, giving 1 point for each clausal unit fully recalled and 1/2 point for each clausal unit partially recalled. Paraphrases and allusions were accepted. Recall of each text was scored as the average of each individual recall score. Recall of each individual respondent was scored as the proportion of clausal units recognized by readers in the protocols. The interrater reliability of the readers, computed as a Pearson product-moment correlation, was $r = .91; F = 27.9; p = .0025$.

Results

If writing is necessarily more explicit than speech, then we expected to find the two written modes collectively more explicit than the two oral modes. If a writer's meaning is more fully embodied in explicit texts, then we expected to find reader/listener recall enhanced by endophoric referencing regardless of mode. Alternatively, if explicitness results from the expression of complicated, abstract ideas, then we expected to find the extent of endophoric references associated not with mode of discourse but rather level of abstraction regardless of mode. Table 4.2 summarizes the results in terms of all dependent variable means by treatment.

A quick comparison of these means shows that there is virtually no difference between the writing and speech here in proportion of endophoric references at the level of report (.18 versus .20). It is only as we move on to examine the means of the speculative samples and the written

TABLE 4.2

Dependent Variable Means by Treatment

	ENDOPHORIC PROPORTION			ENDOPHORIC:EXOPHORIC RATIO	
	Report	Speculation		Report	Speculation
Oral	.18	.16	Oral	1.56	2.18
Written	.20	.27	Written	1.72	7.17
	EXOPHORIC PROPORTION			RECALL	
	Report	Speculation		Report	Speculation
Oral	.12	.08	Oral	.37	.46
Written	.12	.04	Written	.35	.36

samples that we begin to notice some differences: The written speculations are nearly twice as endophoric as the oral speculations (.27 versus .16 respectively), and a third more endophoric than the written reports (.27 versus .20 respectively). These particular comparisons tend to support the contention that the endophoric character of writing involves more than just modal differences between written and oral language.

Looking more closely at means before proceeding with the analysis, we find as much movement among the exophoric references as among the endophoric: As the endophoric references increase, the exophoric references decrease. Comparing oral and written speculations, for example, we note that the mean proportion of endophoric references in the latter is nearly twice that of the former whereas just the reverse is true for exophoric references: In the case of exophoric references, there are on average twice as many in the oral speculations as in the written speculations. This inverse relationship between the two types of references holds for all text categories except the oral samples where we find virtually no difference between the endophoric references but nonetheless a striking drop in exophoric references as we move from report to speculation (.12 versus .08).

To test the significance of these differences, the data were analyzed in a 2 × 2 MANOVA, treating MODE of production (written and oral) and LEVEL of abstraction (reports and speculations) in terms of proportions of endophoric and exophoric references, as well as the ratio of endophoric to exophoric references. In this analysis, we find that neither MODE nor LEVEL significantly affects endophoric references per se. That is, writing is not significantly more endophoric than speech [univariate $F(1, 18) = 1.108$; $p = .306$], and speculations are not significantly more endophoric than reports [univariate $F(1, 18) = .93$; $p = .348$]. Nor is there a significant interaction between MODE and LEVEL in terms of endophoric references. Tables 4.3 and 4.4 summarize these results.

It is not in fact the extent of endophoric references that accounts for the significant overall differences between the two modes of production [multivariate $F(3, 16) = 8.93$; $p = .001$] nor for the significant differences between the two levels of abstraction [multivariate $F(3, 16) = 13.35$; $p < .001$]. Rather it is the ratio of endophoric to exophoric references. That is, as our speakers shifted over to writing and as they became increasingly abstract, the "endophoric effect" commonly noted in the research literature was really two effects, an increase in endophoric references accompanied by a decrease in exophoric references.

More specifically, we find that LEVEL of abstraction, but not MODE of production, significantly affects the proportion of exophoric references. Overall the speculations were far less exophoric than the reports

TABLE 4.3

MODE × LEVEL Multivariate Analysis of Variance on Endophoric Proportions,
Exophoric Proportions, and Endophoric to Exophoric Ratios

	Endophoric proportion	Exophoric proportion	Endophoric:Exophoric ratio
Means:			
Oral			
Report	.18	.12	1.56
Speculation	.16	.08	2.18
Written			
Report	.20	.12	1.72
Speculation	.27	.04	7.17
$N = 22$			
MANOVA			
MODE effect ($F = 8.93$; $df = 3, 16$; $p = .001$)			
Dependent variable canonical coefficients:			
	1.647	.507	1.909
Univariate:			
$F(df = 1, 18)$	1.108	3.121	5.939
$p =$ less than	.306	.094	.025
LEVEL effect ($F = 13.25$; $df = 3, 16$; $p = < .001$)			
Dependent variable canonical coefficients:			
	.586	−.69	.594
Univariate:			
$F(df = 1, 18)$	.93	40.513	8.766
p less than	.348	.001	.008
MODE × LEVEL interaction ($F = 7.353$; $df = 3, 16$; $p < .003$)			
Dependent variable canonical coefficients:			
	1.612	.415	1.851
Univariate:			
$F(df = 1, 18)$	1.011	3.761	5.063
p less than	.328	.068	.037

TABLE 4.4

MODE × LEVEL Multivariate Analysis of Variance on Recall

Source	S.S.	df	M.S.	F Ratio	$p <$
MODE	.02	1	.02	3.56	.075
LEVEL	.013	1	.013	2.374	.141
MODE × LEVEL	.008	1	.008	1.488	.238
Error	.1	18	.006		

[$F(1, 18) = 40.513$; $p < .001$]. Hence, unlike differences in endophoric references, which reflect both MODE of production and LEVEL of abstraction, the decrease in exophoric references in our samples was significantly affected by abstraction but not mode of production.

Significantly we find no relationship here between explicitness of text and comprehension as measured by recall. For example, the written speculations were no better recalled than the oral reports [univariate $F(1, 18) = .059$; $p > .05$] even though the written speculations were overwhelmingly more endophoric than the oral reports [univariate $F(1, 18) = 19.52$; $p < .0001$)]. Overall subjects recalled no one discourse type significantly better than any other [univariate $F(3, 18) = 2.47$; $p = .09$]. Speculations as a group were not recalled significantly differently from the reports [univariate $F(1, 18) = 2.37$; $p = .14$], and the written samples were not recalled significantly differently from the oral [univariate $F(1,18) = 3.56$; $p = .075$]. If anything, there was an overall negative (though insignificant) correlation between recall and proportion of endophoric references ($r = -.143$; $p > .05$) among the samples. If explicitness has to do with lack of ambiguity and clarity of expression, clearly these texts were not necessarily meaningful to the extent that they were endophoric. We find no support here for the contention that fullness of meaning and categorical elaboration of text go hand in hand.

Overall variation in endophoric references among our four text types is much greater than variation in recall of the four types. There are significant differences among the proportions of endophoric references among the four types [univariate $F(3, 18) = 10.96$; $p = .0004$]. However, as noted, recall shows no significant difference in the same comparison of types [univariate $F(3,18) = 2.47$; $p = .09$]. For whatever reason, the respective audiences understood spoken and written messages at both levels of abstraction comparably well. This means that balance of understanding and overall coherence were generally maintained, but that several language samples achieved this coherence by means other than text cohesion and endophoric referencing.

Discussion

We see, first, that the doctrine of autonomous texts, which juxtaposes writing and speaking in terms of explicitness of text, conflates two significant effects. On the one hand, our speakers became more endophoric as they shifted over to writing; on the other hand, they became less exophoric as they became more abstract. The overall differences among the samples, however, was due not to either of these factors alone but rather to their combined effect. The endophoric character of our written speculations was affected as much by level of abstraction (which tends to suppress exophoric references) as it was by idiosyncratic differences between oral and written modes of production. Clearly, the "endophoric effect" of formal written prose here is not an *exclusively endophoric* effect. Nor indeed is it a single effect at all. Rather, the explicit character of formal written prose is the result of two effects, level of abstraction and mode of production, which together manifest themselves in increases in endophoric references accompanied by decreases in exophoric references. No doubt researchers have conflated these effects to the extent that they have compared the formal language of essays with the informal language of conversation rather than more representative samples of writing and speech.

How might we explain the effects of abstraction on referencing systems? It is important to note that as speakers–writers move from concrete to abstract topics, they increasingly distance themselves from the here and now (Britton, 1975; Moffett, 1968a) and presumably, too, from the deictic forms entailed by such discussions. In speculation, for example, "I think" — at least used more than once—becomes an intrusion; therefore it is used less. Theorists distinguish themselves from reporters not by making more references than the reporters. Rather it is what they omit—what they *don't* reference—that distinguishes the theorists from the reporters.

No doubt the coherence of the spoken samples we examined was maintained largely by the use of nonverbal, paralinguistic gestures and gaze behavior. No doubt, too, the coherence of many language samples—both written and spoken—was due to knowledge shared by producers and receivers independently of and prior to comprehension. Coherence and cohesion are not the same (Nystrand, 1981): Communication is coherent when conversants agree on the meaning of *what is said*, but this adequacy of message by no means depends categorically on the use of explicit text references and cohesive ties. Cohesive ties and endophoric referencing are only two means by which coherence can be achieved; these means are two of the resources of language whereby speakers and writers maintain reciprocity and so communicate successfully.

SOME IMPLICATIONS FOR DISCOURSE ANALYSIS

Whether or not the reader does in fact make the critical relations required for comprehension depends not on whether each part of the text clearly references some other part but only on the extent to which readers do in fact find the communication adequate and comprehensible. A text is meaningful not when *what is said* matches *what is meant* but rather when *what is said* strikes a balance between *what needs to be said* and *what may be assumed*.

Writers and readers, like speakers and hearers, may share knowledge independently of the text, in which case writers need say little; texts and utterances may be very cryptic (e.g., EXIT, STOP, *None today, thanks* stuffed into an empty milk bottle left on the door stoop for the milkman who will visit tomorrow morning) and still be fully meaningful. On the other hand, knowledge shared by writers and readers, by speakers and listeners may be lacking or weak in which case writers and speakers must be more explicit if readers are to bridge this gap (see discussion of "text buttressing" in Chapter 5). It is important to note that the resulting coherence and message adequacy is the same in either case and that no analysis of text (e.g., cohesive ties and endophoric references) can reveal this equivalence.

There is, in short, no definitive way to determine just how much *what is said* embodies *what is meant* merely by scrutinizing *what is said*. Presumably there is a continuum of semantic possibilities at one end of which *what is said* embodies *what is meant* entirely (e.g., a true logical proposition) and at the other end of which *what is said* embodies *what is meant* not at all (e.g., lies, irony). But without independent access to *what is meant* (e.g., corroborating texts, evidence, statements), there is no positive way to gauge *what is meant* merely from *what is said*. Hence, even in situations such as contract law that rigorously assume that meaning is in the text, that intentions are irrelevant, and that only *what is said* counts — even in such situations as this, extrinsic evidence such as testimony from the plaintiff, the defendant, and even experts is regularly evaluated to determine just *what is meant* by *what is said*. Legal scholar Arthur L. Corbin explains:

> No man can determine the meaning of written words by merely gluing his eyes within the four corners of a square paper. . . . When a judge refuses to consider relevant extrinsic evidence on the ground that the meaning of the words is to him plain and clear, his decision is formed by and wholly based upon the completely extrinsic evidence of his own personal education and experience [1965, p. 164].

In effect, to accept *what is said* as prima facie evidence of *what is meant* is to commit an intentional fallacy (cf. Michaels, 1980).

John Lyons (1977, p. 591) makes this same point in different terms: He notes that one can perhaps study the meaning of propositions without alluding to the context of their utterance, but one "cannot get from sentences to the propositions expressed by them . . . without taking account of certain contextual features [cf. Stalnaker, 1972, p. 383]" such as previous text, further text, cotext, other relevant texts, or circumstances pertinent to the communication. The important thing about expository prose is not that the writer's meaning is clear because it is fully represented and "decontextualized" in "autonomous texts" but rather that indexical features of the genre exposition (including tone, organization, indigenous patterns of organizations, certain sorts of titles) prompt the reader to interpret what is said as indeed what is meant.

We see, then, that the difference between our written and oral samples has as much to do with abstraction as mode of discussion. No doubt the discussion of abstract issues—whether spoken or written, formal or informal—will always enhance the "endophoric effect" more than spoken or written accounts of immediate events, e.g., televised sportscasts and chatty letters. The contention of Dillon (1981), Olson (1977), Hirsch (1977), Kay (1977), Collins and Williamson (1981), and many others that written language is self-contextualizing and autonomous compared to spoken utterances, which are context-bound and fragmented, is true only if, as Tannen (1982) notes, the analysis compares certain genres of writing with certain kinds of oral language, namely formal expository prose with unplanned casual conversation. Such biased sampling excludes all speech that is monologic and/or abstract, apparently assuming that abstract monolog is solely a written language phenomenon. Indeed, the contention that written texts are autonomous and context-free associates the discussion of abstract issues solely with writing. Clearly, this is not the case: We do indeed all know individuals who can talk as well as write in paragraphs.

THE DOCTRINE OF AUTONOMOUS TEXTS IN RETROSPECT: THREE FALLACIES

In reconsidering the Olson tenets, we may now make the following observations.

1. *All language functioning—both oral and written—is governed by context of use.* It is true that written texts typically function in contexts other than those in which they were written. It does not follow from this premise, however, that in order to function, written texts must be "autonomous," "acontextual," and "explicit." Nor does it follow that those which are abbreviated, e.g., notes, are poorly composed, fragmented, or "semantically abbreviated [Collins and Williamson, 1981]." There are three fallacies in such deductions. The first fallacy confuses **situation of expression** with **context of use.** It is true that writers do not typically converse with readers face to face, that writers' texts speak independently of them, that indeed the writer may even die long before the text is read. However, none of this means that these texts are therefore "acontextual" and "autonomous," i.e., that written texts must work apart from context. Rather, it means that

unlike speech, where situation of expression and context of use are concurrent, written texts are composed for a **context of eventual or potential use,** for example, consideration by the busy executive (memo), future reference (diary, log, technical report), and later prompting (grocery list). Context of eventual use is determined by *time* of eventual use ("By the time you read this . . ."), *place* of eventual use ("Will be back in 5 min. Please wait" is best left outside the office door, not locked inside on the desk), and *purpose* of eventual use (reference, prompting, legal record, etc.).

In speech, planning processes and generated text are largely simultaneous and inseparable whereas in writing, they always separate as soon as the composing is complete. As public behavior, speech presents itself not only as words spoken but also as a sequence of starts and restarts and pauses. By contrast, writing, which is private behavior, conceals hesitations and restarts, and presents itself only as the tidied up result, altogether detached from the process. As a result, it is very easy to get the impression that oral language is "fragmented" compared to written discourse, which is "integrated" and "compact" (cf. Chafe, 1982). But this difference is not merely one between writing and speaking per se but also one between covert and overt processes of language production.

It should surprise no one that written *texts* seem "integrated" by comparison to written *transcripts*, which seem "fragmented." Nor should anyone be surprised that what sounds "coherent" to a listener might, when transcribed, seem "cryptic," "elliptical," and even "defective" to a reader. Speech is indeed fragmented by the very process of transcription, a process which written texts never undergo.

2. *Fullness of meaning is not the same as explicitness of text.* The second fallacy confuses **fullness of meaning** with **explicitness of text.** Although it is true that difficult texts often benefit from revisions which clarify and elaborate key points, it does not follow that texts become categorically more meaningful as more of their references are elaborated. This is why legal documents do not necessarily mean more for all their explicitness and why EXIT signs and grocery lists do not necessarily mean less for all their crypticness. Moreover, the kind of effective elaboration which characterizes, say, well written technical manuals with ample explanations, illustrations, and definitions is neither random nor ubiquitous. Rather, it is planned and selective, dealing only with points requiring emphasis or clarification.

A text is explicit not to the extent that it says everything (which is impossible [cf. Stubbs, 1984]) but rather to the extent that it balances the respective concerns of the writer for expression and the reader for comprehension. Ambiguity and clarity are not intrinsic qualities of text but rather aspects of *agreement* on meaning between conversants.

W. B. Michaels (1980) makes this essential point when he compares the interpretation of difficult terms in contract law and literary criticism. In both fields, Michaels shows that "explicitness is a function not of language but of agreement. . . . The process of adjudication . . . depends not on words which have plain meanings and can be used as touchstones against which to measure words whose meanings are not so plain. It depends instead on . . . 'undisputed contexts,' agreement on the meaning of one piece of language which can then compel agreement on the meaning of another. . . . To read is always already to have invoked the category of the extrinsic, an invocation that is denied . . . not only by avowedly formalist critics but by all those who think of textual meaning as in any sense intrinsic [pp. 418–419]." An explicit text is not a text whose meaning is completely embodied in the text but rather a text about which relevant contextual evidence is not in dispute.

We shall see in Chapter 5 that there is a subtle and important difference between an **elaboration** and a **complication of text.** For example, a particular passage of computer documentation that might be ambiguous and consequently troublesome for knowledgeable users of computers may well be abstruse and hard in a very different way for the computer novice. That a given text can be ambiguous for some readers and abstruse for others can easily be demonstrated by showing that high- and low-knowledge readers require qualitatively different revisions: Knowledgeable users of computers, for example, require more details—elaborations of key points— whereas computer novices need the main idea to relate all the details. The same endophoric text which works to clarify things for the experienced user works just the opposite to complicate things for novices.

A well-written text communicates not because it says everything all by itself but rather because it strikes a careful balance between what needs to be said and what may be assumed. Clearly, what counts in effective composition is knowing how and when to be explicit, not simply being explicit.

3. *Comparing exposition and conversation is not a valid comparison of writing and speech.* The third fallacy is distinguishing written and spoken language in terms of autonomy of text. The doctrine of autonomous texts juxtaposes not spoken and written language but rather certain highly specialized *uses* of language, namely literary composition and casual chatter. It is a skewed comparison, overlooking such examples of spoken language as lectures, seminar discussions, and college rap sessions; and such examples of writing as kit instructions and notes. **Cohesion** results not when language is written but rather when language—both written and spoken—is put to particular uses, especially those uses which bridge discrepancies in writer-reader knowledge, as in expert-layman communi-

cation. Language is not composed *because* it is internally cohesive; language takes particular form when it is put to particular uses. To characterize written composition in terms of textstructure is to put the structural cart before the functional horse.

The extent to which people need to be explicit—and precisely those points they need to be explicit about—has less to do with the idiosyncracies of medium or topic (i.e., writing rather than speaking, discussing abstract issues rather than concrete events) and more to do with the mutual demands that conversants collectively make on language to speak and be understood, i.e., maintaining the terms of the reciprocity principle.

Not only is the doctrine of the autonomous text specious. By excluding a priori important examples of written communication, this doctrine has fostered a number of misconceptions about the composing process, especially among educators. For example, it has perpetrated the idea that certain uses of written language (*viz.*, essays) not only can *but ought to* function rhetorically without any relationship to their context of use. As a corollary to this point, it has justified teaching writing as a matter of correct form rather than effective use. It has furthermore perpetrated the idea that there are some uses of written language (e.g., notes) that are acompositional. And it has promoted a categorical explicitness of text as an appropriate instructional objective.

In order to examine the many problems with these sundry contentions, we now consider the composition of notes.

HOW NOTES ARE COMPOSED

If composition is a deliberate process of organizing language and thoughts in order to achieve a particular purpose or effect, then writing notes clearly qualifies. It certainly involves far more than "the mere basic skills" of handwriting, spelling, and punctuation. Composing notes requires the writer to make a great number of correct assumptions about context. Notes are no less composed because they are abbreviated. As with all composition, the writer must carefully *balance what is said, against what need not be said*. And what need not be said, of course, depends on the actual context of use, i.e., who's reading, what they know, when they read it, what they want to find out, and so on.

Notes and signs are typically informational (e.g., EXIT or "Gone to store—be home for dinner"); and their composition requires keeping in mind a number of critical informational factors having to do with who, what, when, where, and how: *Who* the readers will be and what they will know at the time they discover the text; *when* the readers will read and, in the case of signs, how much time they will have to read; and *where* the readers are most likely to find the information (notes), or where the readers are most likely to be when they discover the information (signs). These situational variables are critical to text meaning, defining a window of semantic opportunity as it were: EXIT signs have no meaning except in relation to doors, and notes which are addressed to the person who delivers the milk must be placed next to empty bottles, etc. Children's notes are often amusing and uncommunicative because of their failure to take these factors into account (e.g., "Mom, I'll be home in a few minutes")(Gundlach, 1982a).

In the margin of the paragraph which I am presently drafting, I have made several miscellaneous notes to myself. They will complete their mission as it were and fulfill their function within the next paragraph or two, and so it is altogether irrelevant that I will not understand them beyond that point. By contrast, I have other notes that I have made from readings and lectures which I have carefully filed in folders. These notes are far more explicit since I made them on the assumption that I might use them but did not know when or exactly how. In many cases, I photocopied the articles in their entirety exactly for this purpose. The "half-life" and explicitness of my notes relates roughly to the context in which I anticipate their use.

I compose notes differently depending on who will read them. For example, if I make a note to myself to buy groceries later in the day, for example, I typically write a cryptic, highly abbreviated note (Applebee, 1982), which I will consider semantically adequate merely if it helps me remember what I want to buy when I get to the store. The same note, of course, might well be inadequate for someone else, like my spouse, who might require further specificity.

I also write notes differently depending on when and where they will be read. For example, if I leave a note on my office door indicating to anyone who might come looking for me that I have left my office for a half hour, I will be careful to leave the note in a context (such as on my door) where visitors are most likely to read the note. I will also indicate the time I expect to return and not merely state that I will be back "in a half hour" since I do not know when people may be reading the note. (Of course, I may deliberately write "in a half hour" if I do not want to be specific but want instead to give the impression that I'll be back soon.) This note is somewhat different from one I know will be read tomorrow or next week or next year. The point is that the note I write must function on the occasion for which it was written, and what I actually say must take this context of eventual use into account.

We may now observe that the demand for reciprocity potentially involves both writers and readers of notes, like writers and readers of any text, in three different kinds of demands on language. First, notes will vary in their **degree of specificity**: The note I write myself, for example, is not nearly as elaborate or specific as the note I write for someone less knowledgeable. Notes will also vary in their degree of **category definition**. Hence, if I write a complicated note detailing a great many specifics (e.g., a shopping list involving more than one store, or a memo regarding a series of discrete events), I may need to categorize the details and not just list them: Specificity alone may not be sufficient. Finally, if there is the possibility of ambiguity about how my message is to be interpreted—Is this a request or a complaint? a polite complaint or a formal complaint?—I may need to elaborate not just the text but variables related to the text type or genre.

In these examples, we see some essential outlines of how written texts work and how writers are implicated in these transactions. In each case, the writer assumes reciprocity exists between himself or herself and the reader. This is true even of notes to oneself since the writer becomes the reader when the note is read: The writer prepares a text for specifically that situation when he or she will consult it as a reader. In each case, the writer takes for granted a particular set of concerns that are common to writer and reader at the time the reader reads the note. Hence, the writer prepares the text for a specific context of eventual use, and the text is structured precisely in terms of this context of use. This is why the shopping list I give to someone else is more explicit than the one I write for myself, this is why an invoice listing more than one kind of goods not only specifies items fully but categorizes them as well, and this is why the marginal notes I make while writing one paragraph for use in the next need not be as explicit as notes I make while reading for some use I cannot anticipate as precisely.

HOW ESSAYS COMMUNICATE

If notes are no less composed because they are cryptic and contextualized, essays are no more composed and "autonomous" because they are elaborately explicit. The composition of an essay is as much constrained by its context of eventual use as is the briefest grocery note. A good example of this point is Canadian psychologist David Olson's seminal essay "From Utterance to Text: The Bias of Language in Speech and Writing" (1977), which, we have noted, argues the case for autonomous texts and is typically cited as the source of the doctrine. Olson wrote this essay for a very particular context of use, namely the forum of *The Harvard Educational Review*, a research journal for scholars with multidisciplinary interests in educational issues. So that the essay might function in this context of scholarly dialog, argument, and reference, it is paginated; it is prefaced by an abstract; it is replete with footnotes, reference notes, and references; and it is appropriately formatted in such a way that the author's name and the title of the journal, along with volume, number, and date, appear on the title page of the essay. The publisher has made sure that these essential contextual factors accompany all future photocopies of the text.

The author himself, moreover, contextualizes his argument by starting with an extensive literature review, reciting not only historical but also contemporary evidence from research in the structure of language, the nature of comprehension, the nature of logical reasoning, the acquisition of language, and the psychology of reading. The **argumentative purpose** of this review is obvious: The author hopes to show compelling reasons for his thesis. The **communicative function** is different, however: The review serves to establish a **footing**—shared knowledge or common ground with readers from which the author sallies forth with his main points. In this sense, the review functions like the question that begins a conversation, "You know that box I'm always talking about? Well . . ." or the "re:" of business correspondence or, indeed, the effective introduction to any essay: It works thematically by establishing a communicative footing and so initiates the communication.

THE STRUCTURE OF ARGUMENT VERSUS THE STRUCTURE OF COMMUNICATION

It is generally true that the British essayists Olson discusses proceed by explicating the many implications entailed by their premises in the manner of Locke's *An Essay Concerning Human Understanding*, and that, for this reason, essays tend to be highly explicit. Yet if essays are more explicit than grocery lists, this explicitness is due to more than requirements of genre to state propositions. Reasoning by inference, deduction, demonstrations, and proof—particularly on topics new to readers—makes special demands on language as well as logic. These two kinds of demands require careful distinction if we are to understand what essayists do qua thinker compared to what essayists do qua writer.

It is the essayist qua thinker whom we "charge with reasoning via unspecified inference and assumptions" "if unconventionalized or non-linguistic knowledge is permitted to intrude" into the argument (Olson, 1977, p. 272). But it is the essayist qua writer whom we charge with incomprehensibility if complex new ideas and terms are inadequately contextualized in terms of shared, nonlinguistic knowledge. Indeed, any text which might succeed in eliminating all dependence on presupposed, world knowledge would be a very ambiguous and nonexplicit text—as unclear as any image which is all figure and no ground. The essayist qua thinker formulates "a small set of connected statements of great generality that may occur as topic sentences or paragraphs or as premises of extended scientific or philosophical treatise [Olson, p. 269]." By contrast, the essayist qua writer makes appropriate text segmentations, this "indentation functioning, as does all punctuation, as a gloss upon the overall literary process underway at that point [Rodgers, 1966, p. 6]." Endophoric referencing is important in terms of **exposition** because it is the way essayists spell out the implications entailed in their premises. Endophoric referencing is important in terms of **communication** because it is the major way writers contextualize new information and so maintain a balance of understanding between themselves and their readers.

In short, effective text analysis requires careful distinction between the **structure of argument** and the **structure of communication**. As argument, Olson's essay works by stating explicit points and propositions. As communication, however, it works by juxtaposing these propositions with knowledge readers bring to the text. This reader knowledge is unstated, mutual, given, and not necessarily propositional in nature. Hence, as important as the many explicit points that Olson makes are the many that are never stated. And this omission is surely no sin. To the contrary: Olson's thesis is clear because he strikes an effective balance between what needs to be said and what may remain unsaid. Were he elaborate in his treatment of the latter, his essay would be turgid, wordy, unclear, and we might rightly hold him in violation of the "contract" that underlies all communication from the briefest note to the longest treatise.

The contract which writers have with their readers requires them to attend to three different kinds of compositional tasks. First, they must establish a footing by identifying common ground, as noted above. In addition, they must contextualize new information—buttressing those points of text which, if not treated, would threaten the established balance of discourse between writers and their readers. And finally (though not necessarily last), they must carefully mark relevant text boundaries to indicate conceptual, narrative, and other shifts, and to break the text into manageable information units.

Olson's essay is clearly not just an autonomous text explicating all the implications entailed by his general premise. We understand Olson's thesis largely as we do (a) because it appears in the context of a research journal and (b) because the argument concerns an idea which has a history (dating back at least to Plato), and which has been researched by scholars in many diverse fields of inquiry. The text of Olson's essay, like all well-written compositions, functions not because it is independent of its context of use but because it is so carefully attuned to this context.

THE ROLE OF CONTEXT IN WRITTEN COMMUNICATION

What, then, is the role of context in written communication? To begin, context of use in written communication is eventual, not concurrent with the production of discourse as with spoken language. For the most part, the writer's situation is irrelevant to actual text functioning. Where the writer composes, what might be viewed from the writer's window during the composing process, what music might have provided inspiration—all these aspects of the composer's situation while writing are functionally irrelevant. Pieces of writing do not function communicatively at the time of their creation; they only bear a potential for communication. Learning to write is precisely learning to create such a potential. This potential is realized, moreover, only when writer and reader finally come together by way of the text. It is this situation of the reader reading which defines context of use in written communication, for it is this moment precisely when the writer finally speaks to the reader and the text must do its communicative thing.

As we have seen, this point has been a source of considerable confusion in many comparisons of spoken and written language. The doctrine of autonomous texts defines context narrowly in terms of immediate context of production—mainly such paralinguistic features as gestures and quizzical looks. Yet the actual context of situation for any communication is far more rich and complex than the physical gestures of the conversants. Relevant factors include the nature of the audience, the medium, and the purpose of the communication. This is no less true for writing than speech. Business executives, for example, know all too well that the complete meaning of an interoffice memorandum frequently involves not just the typed text but myriad contextual details, including (a) why the communication is in writing; (b) who is copied (and has received carbon copies or *cc:*); (c) who is *not* copied; and especially (d) who, though not copied, is nonetheless a recipient (of the "blind" carbon copy or *bcc:*) and perhaps even the main reason for the memo.

It is true, of course, that written texts must function without benefit of hand gesture or eye contact. But it is a serious mistake to view the paralinguistics of speech as a categorical prerequisite to all communication. If **paralinguistics** refers to those phenomena that "occur alongside spoken language, interact with it, and produce together with it a total system of communication [Abercrombie, 1968, p. 55]," then written language may be said to have its own special resources in this regard. These resources, moreover, serve the essential paralinguistic purposes of **modulation** (superimposing upon a text a particular attiduninal coloring) and **punctu-ation** (marking boundaries at the beginning and end of a text and at various points within to emphasize particular expressions, and to segment the utterance into manageable information units) (Lyons, 1977, p. 65). Quotation marks, for example, commonly indicate irony, skepticism, or critical detachment; and exclamation marks and underlining typically show emphasis. Sentence fragments can often be used to show emphasis, particularly at the end of paragraphs. A semicolon can juxtapose two sentence-length assertions, which readers then contrast without any explicit reference made by the author to "contrast" or "comparison." A more complex type of modulation is achieved when writers exploit reader expectations for particular genres of written discourse. The classic example here is irony in Swift's "A Modest Proposal." Because it is in essay form, readers often assume the proposal is serious and the contents are meant to be taken literally.

The increasing availability and sophistication of electronic word-processors substantially increase the range of such paralinguistic modulation available to professional, business, and academic writers. With capabilities previously available only in printers' shops, these machines now sit on many individual writers' desks. Included among these capabilities are the usual marks of punctuation, plus boldface, italics, hanging indents, offsets, and fonts of all sorts. The rhetorical impact of these typographic capabilities in this new setting is not yet clear, especially on writing tasks not usually published. For example, what sorts of correspondence and typescripts should and should not be formatted with justified right margins? Nonetheless, the possibilities of these systems for subtle modulations of text have not been lost on the office systems people, who routinely promote their products not only in terms of increased efficiency but also, and especially, enhanced corporate image. With only a few formatting commands, businesses can present themselves as Baskerville, Palatino, or Bold Roman. No doubt the day of the designer letter is upon us.

In addition to such possibilities for paralinguistic modulation, writers have access to a wide range of punctuation for marking syntactic, prosodic, and semantic boundaries. Consider the range of devices writers have for setting off particular expressions. A particular phrase that may be subordinated as a non-restrictive clause with commas in:

(4.2)   *Hostilities between countries in the Middle East, which are increasingly armed with weapons made in the USA, threaten to start a world war.*

may be further subordinated with parentheses in:

(4.3)   *Hostilities between countries in the Middle East (which are increasingly armed with weapons made in the USA) threaten to start a world war.*

and may be subordinated further still by asterisking its referent (*countries in the Middle East*) and treating the phrase in a footnote. By contrast, setting the phrase off in dashes marks it with emphasis:

(4.4)   *Hostilities between countries in the Middle East—which are increasingly armed with weapons made in the USA—threaten to start a world war.*

The most significant mark of punctuation for use beyond the sentence, of course, is indentation and paragraphing. The paragraph (from Greek: *para*, beside + *graphos*, mark) was originally a symbol (¶) placed in the margin to indicate conceptual, narrative, and other shifts in the flow of discourse. The original notion persists not only in copy editors' notations but also in the transitive verb *to paragraph* (Rodgers, 1966). This treatment of paragraphing has recently been elaborated by Halliday and Hasan (1976), who see the paragraph as a "device introduced into the written language to suggest . . . periodicity":

> In principle, we shall expect to find a greater degree of cohesion within a paragraph than between paragraphs; and in a great deal of written English this is exactly what we do find. In other writing, however, and perhaps as a characteristic of certain authors, the rhythm is contrapuntal: the writer extends a dense cluster of cohesive ties across the paragraph boundary and leaves the texture within the paragraph relatively loose. And this itself is an instance of a process that is very characteristic of language altogether, a process in which two associated variables come to be dissociated from each other with a very definite semantic and rhetorical effect. Here the two variables in question are the paragraph structure and the cohesive structure [pp. 296–297].

Table 4.5 summarizes the range of punctuation devices available for joining and separating English sentences.

There is another category of devices, which we shall call **metadiscoursal** and which, like punctuation and paragraphing, modulate the meaning of a text, but, unlike punctuation and paragraphing, do so with words and text. Phrases and words like "next," "on the other hand," "in addition," "nevertheless" contribute little or nothing to propositional content but work instead to manage the conduct of discourse. In this sense, they are analogous to "y'know," "well," and "uh" in conversation, which speakers use to "keep the floor" and so manage the conduct of discourse.

Clearly, texts are explicit not just because of what they say but also because of a range of devices, including paralinguistic and metadiscoursal, which accompany the text and cue readers as to its interpretation.

TABLE 4.5
Punctuation Devices for Joining and Separating Sentences

[Sentence₁] <,> [Sentence₂]		Medical researchers now classify 23 sexually transmitted diseases, two new ones in just the last few years. First came Herpes, then came AIDS.
[Sentence₁] <;> [Sentence₂]		Medical researchers now classify 23 sexually transmitted diseases, two new ones in the last few years. First came Herpes; then came AIDS.
[Sentence₁] <, and> [Sentence₂]	INCREASING SEPARATION	Medical researchers now classify 23 sexually transmitted diseases, two new ones in the last few years. First came Herpes, and then came AIDS.
[Sentence₁] <.> [Sentence₂]		Medical researchers now classify 23 sexually transmitted diseases, two new ones in the last few years. First came Herpes. Then came AIDS.
[Sentence₁] <¶> [Sentence₂]		Medical researchers now classify 23 sexually transmitted diseases, two new ones in the last few years. First came Herpes. Then came AIDS.

CONCLUSION

The doctrine of autonomous texts essentially assumes that because writers, unlike speakers, cannot know their audiences, they must take precautions to be explicit so that "the reader" can understand the text. This is a very strange reader, however—one who never reads and one whom no writer ever actually addresses. Instead, this ideal, reified reader is the motivation for countless pedagogical exhortations to beginning writers to be explicit about everything ("so the Reader can understand it"). In fact, almost all writers in actual rhetorical situations address very particular readers about whom they know something. They write letters to friends, memos to employees, notes to themselves. Indeed, it is difficult to think of many actual situations where writers do not know at least something substantial about

their readers' expectations even if they cannot always know them personally. School compositions requiring students to "compose essays" rather
than address audiences are perhaps the only significant exception. Even in
school writing instruction, those essays used as models written for a
universal audience were in their conception addressed to very particular
readers for very particular purposes. Those few writers in our world who
actually compose for a true "general audience" (e.g., newspaper columnists,
professional essayists) do in fact know something about their readers and
particularly about their expectations. Of course, writers addressing general
audiences are hardly typical—no more than Dan Rather as CBS Evening
News anchor is a typical speaker. The typical writer's situation is reasonably
concrete and specific, certainly finite. No one, after all, actually writes for
The Norton Anthology, least of all those authors whose works finally reside
there. "A written text as a whole," Halliday and Hasan note, "still has its
outer context of situation... [1976, p. 50]."

So while it is true that there is not the give and take in writing that there
is in talk, it does not follow from this lack of conspicuous interaction that
writers have any less sense of their audience than speakers do; that the
writer's audience is somehow more anonymous or less specific than the
speaker's is; that writers somehow interact less with readers than speakers
do with listeners; and ergo, that written texts are somehow more autonomous than spoken utterances. Writers, no less than speakers, strive to
maintain a balance of discourse with their readers; and writers, no less than
speakers with their listeners, must carefully fashion texts which will
maintain a balance of discourse with their readers. Reciprocity undergirds
written communication just as much as spoken.

It is clearly a mistake to associate the spontaneity of casual talk with
fragmented expression, and equally wrong to confuse elaborateness of text
with fullness of meaning. The attempt to view writers as somehow
disadvantaged because they are bereft of the paralinguistic resources of
speech, moreover, is a misconception of written communication, and is
consistent with the traditional conception of writing as a defective representation of speech. What is missed by such confusions is how writing and
speech work differently as language systems. If casual conversation with
friends as well as notes to oneself are cryptic whereas formal inquiries to
and from the Internal Revenue Service—either written or spoken—are
comparably elaborate and explicit, this difference mainly means that the
former *can* be more abbreviated while the latter *must* be more elaborated
if coherence is to be maintained, messages are to be adequate, and
communication assured. It does not mean that cryptic texts are necessarily

"semantically inadequate" or unclear to the reader–hearer. And above all, it most definitely does not mean that written texts are "autonomous" whereas spoken utterances are "context-bound." What it mainly means is that speech and writing work differently to maintain reciprocity and the underlying pact of discourse between conversants.

5

Necessary Text Elaborations

INTRODUCTION

Most attempts to predict how hard or easy readers will find texts have been based on the premise that the critical variables are all in the text. The bulk of this readability research has found that difficult texts arc typically characterized by unfamiliar words and complicated sentences. This conclusion is well established, and its predictive validity remains unchallenged after more than half a century of research (Klarc, 1974/75). Nonetheless, it is important to note that virtually all this research has been correlational, which means that, while hard texts are typically characterized by unfamiliar words and complicated sentences, these features no more cause the difficulties than day causes night. Consequently, readability formulas may predict ease or difficulty of reading (especially for large populations such as all American sixth graders), but their critical variables cannot be used by writers as principles of clear writing or effective revision. Hence, *The defendant is a 15-year-old teenager who is accused of shoplifting* is probably easier to understand than *He is the defendant. He is 15 years old. He is in his teens. Someone says he stole from a store*, despite the fact that almost any readability formula would rate the second version easier because of the short sentences (Redish, 1979, p. 8). Indeed, any readability formula that is sensitive only to syntactic and lexical factors cannot tell the difference between a paragraph of scrambled sentences and the original. Readability formulas are crude, atheoretical, predictive measures, having nothing whatever to say about what writers must know and do to communicate clearly.

Among the many puzzles that readability formulas cannot solve are these: Why can a text that is clear for some readers be difficult for others? Why can difficult texts be hard in different ways for different readers, e.g., vague for some but obscure for others? Why, for example, can the same part of the tax code that is ambiguous and consequently troublesome for tax attorneys be abstruse and hard for general taxpayers? Attorneys finding parts of the tax code ambiguous will request more details—elaborations of key points—to understand implications of the tax code whereas taxpayers finding the same text abstruse will request clarification of the main idea to comprehend all the details. The former, less knowledgeable group seeks **further specification**; the latter, more knowledgeable group seeks **category definitions**.

AN ALTERNATIVE APPROACH TO READABILITY: THE KINTSCH-VIPOND READER-TEXT INTERACTION MODEL

Kintsch and Vipond (1979) and Miller and Kintsch (1980) have proposed a major alternative to these primitive measures. Briefly, Kintsch and Vipond contend that readability results from effective interaction between particular readers (with certain information-processing capabilities) and particular texts (with certain text characteristics). Ease of comprehension can be enhanced or assured by facilitating such interactions—specifically by increasing the number of ideas or propositions that readers can derive from the text.

The Kintsch-Vipond model is based on the premise that meaning is a structured quantum of information and a property of the text; and, depending on their information processing capabilities, readers will "extract the meaning [p. 355]" of certain kinds of texts more easily than others: "Reading comprehension is ultimately a process of acquiring information. The nature and structure of that information—that is, the characteristics of the meaning of a text, as well as the processes involved in deriving this meaning from the written text—are, we assume, the real determinants of readability [Kintsch and Vipond, 1979, p. 337]." Not only is meaning a property of the text for Kintsch and Vipond; so is coherence. Texts are coherent in this model if propositions in the textbase share common arguments. According to Kintsch, *Tom waved to Sue. She waved back* is more coherent than *Tom waved to Sue. Mary came indoors* because, though each sentence pair has two propositions, the first set of propositions shares a common argument, namely *Sue*, while the second set of propositions has no arguments in common.

Noting previous studies, they propose the following three text variables in this interaction:

(a) **Propositional density**: Given a set length of text, it is easier to understand few rather than many ideas (Kintsch and Keenan, 1973);

(b) **Number of new concepts per proposition**: It is easier to understand texts that say a lot about a few things than texts that say little about many things (Kintsch, Kozminsky, Steby, McKoon, and Keenan, 1975); and

(c) **Text coherence**, defined as the number of **repeated arguments**: It is easier to understand related ideas than unrelated ideas (Kintsch, 1974).

Kintsch and Vipond emphasize that they are not postulating these three text variables as a new set of "categorical imperatives" for readability—replacing lexical and syntactic complexity, for example, as the fundamental readability factors. Because readability is the result of interaction between readers and texts, they maintain, the full description must take readers as well as texts into account. Some reader variables they suggest (but do not test) are short-term memory capacity (but see Miller and Kintsch, 1980, for data and analysis here), power of inference, purpose, and the use of the reader's knowledge base in acquiring new information. Nonetheless, (a), (b), and (c) are the critical text variables in this interaction, so the Kintsch–Vipond model predicts that readability will generally be enhanced by appropriately revising difficult texts for these three items. When this is done, readability is enhanced because the reader's reinstatements of propositions in working memory are reduced both in number and frequency and also because the reader's reorganizations of the textbase are reduced both in number and complexity. This theory-based approach to readability purports to analyze cause and effect and has potentially major implications for discourse analysis.

In more recent work on comprehension with van Dijk (1983), Kintsch has modified many of these positions. According to van Dijk and Kintsch (1983), comprehension is a dynamic, constructive, strategic process which, in search of a coherent representation of meaning, continuously tests and integrates information from the text with previous text and prior knowledge, as well as the communicative and cultural context. Accordingly, they argue that readers process the text, not periodically in accordance with syntactic boundaries as postulated in Kintsch and van Dijk (1978), but continuously in accordance with their need to maintain a coherent interpretation.

By examining the reader's use of knowledge and strategic interaction with the text, moreover, van Dijk and Kintsch radically shift their focus from *formal* coherence (argument repetition) to *semantic* coherence (relations among concepts constructed by the reader in the course of reading).

Coherence depends on whether readers do in fact make the critical relations between propositions, but this does not always require explicitly increasing referential ties in the text. In this new model, argument repetition is but one "strategy for the establishment of relations between proposition participants [p. 154]." And clearly this is the case. For example, writers and readers may share knowledge independently of the text, in which case the writer need say little: Texts may be cryptic yet fully coherent and meaningful. On the other hand, such congruence of writer-reader knowledge bases may be lacking or weak, in which case writers must be very explicit if readers are to bridge this gap. It is important to note (a) that the resulting semantic coherence is the same in either case and (b) that no propositional analysis of the two texts can reveal this equivalence. Whether the reader does in fact make the critical relations certainly does not depend on whether some predicate calculus shows that all textbase propositions are clearly and neatly related, but only on the extent to which readers do in fact find the communication coherent. As Lyons (1977) notes, "It suffices here to reemphasize the importance of drawing a distinction between correct and successful reference and to insist upon the fact that reference is always, in principle, context-dependent [p. 602]."

This strategic model has several important implications in particular for issues related to readability and difficult text. To begin, the new model suggests a criterion for identifying those parts of a text which might benefit more than others from revision. If readers continuously process text (rather than periodically assimilating semantic units at syntactic boundaries), then difficult texts will best be treated by argument repetition and other local coherence strategies at precisely those points of the text that are likely to impede processing. In addition, where readers are uncertain about the gist of the text, certain text structures will be strategically relevant to the formation of macrostructures. The text structures that van Dijk and Kintsch note (1983, pp. 53-54) include titles, subtitles, initial sentences, summaries, advance organizers, and questions and reminders. By addressing specific troublesources, these devices are effective because they treat the thematic structure of the text. In effect, the local coherence strategies such as argument repetition or co-referential ties involve **comment-level elaborations**, and text structures which bear on macrostructure involve **topic-level elaborations**. These elaborations work to synchronize the writer's production strategies with the readers' comprehension strategies, and as a result, "at least certain kinds of elaborative inferences during comprehension, especially those that produce a tighter integration between the text and the reader's own knowledge structure, result in better learning [pp. 51–52]."

AN EXPERIMENT

By examining this process of synchronization in some detail, we learn not only about processes of comprehension but also about the writer's role in the production of readable texts. To gain some sense of the power of this new model and to examine its implications for issues of readability and difficult text, two revisions were made of a passage of technical prose (on window types: see Text 5.1). In revising the text, the propositional density and the number of different arguments per proposition were both reduced while the number of repeated arguments was increased. This was accomplished by elaborating key lexical items parenthetically according to the research specifications of Dulek (1980). For example, where the original text reads, *These balances are concealed in the jamb by a manually operated ratchet or a friction-type control,* the revised text reads *These balances are concealed (hidden) in the jamb or side by a manually operated ratchet (toothed wheel) or a friction-type control (gear mechanism).* Following Kintsch and Vipond's criteria, these elaborations should increase the readability of the original text by (a) saying less in any set length of text, (b) saying more about the same number of things, and (c) relating ideas more explicitly throughout the text.

Two such revisions were prepared. Since the Kintsch and Vipond (1979) model does not specify which terms require elaboration, they were identified randomly in the first revision. In accordance with the requirements of the van Dijk and Kintsch (1983) model for continuous processing, the second revision specifically targeted difficult lexical items—those trouble spots where the writer's meaning and the readers' comprehension were not adequately matched. In elaborating these particular terms, we followed one of Holland's (1981) "psycholinguistic alternatives to readability formulas": We tested all terms for understanding by the intended

---

TEXT 5.1

Windows are broadly classified as fixed or ventilating. Fixed windows consist of one or more panes of glass that cannot be opened. Ventilating windows consist of one or more sashes within a fixed frame and are classified according to the manner in which the sashes operate.

Double-hung windows and single-hung windows open and close by sliding the movable sash vertically in grooves provided in the stiles of the frame. The sliding sash is held open or closed by various spring balances. These balances are concealed in the jamb by a manually operated ratchet or a friction-type control. Formerly, double-hung sashes were usually counterweighted with sash weights.

From Albert G. H. Dietz. *Dwelling House Construction* (Cambridge, MA: MIT Press, 1946), p. 165. Copyright © 1946, 1954 by Walter C. Voss and Albert G. H. Dietz; Copyright © 1971, 1974 by the Massachusetts Institute of Technology.

TABLE 5.1

Percentages of Readers Missing Each Word
When Deleted from Passage in Clozed Form

Windows are broadly classified as fixed or ventilating. Fixed windows consist of one or
  7   0   100   87   17 49 87   100   63   7   44   0 45 2

more panes of glass that cannot be opened. Ventilating windows consist of one or
  2   78 13 11   22   73   0   82   100   20   9   0 29 5

more sashes within a fixed frame and are classified according to the manner in which
  8   100   76   53 94   70   69 18   95   80   2 13   66   32   0

the sashes operate.
 12   100   78

Double-hung windows and single-hung windows open and close by sliding the movable
     67   8   29   73   31   0   5   2   27   87   12   100

sash vertically in grooves provided in the stiles of the frame. The sliding sash is held
 65   73   69   97   100   69 47 100 17 25   69   20   100   78 11 92

open or closed by various spring balances. These balances are concealed in the jamb
 16   78   4   34   100   56   67   60   45   0   100   40 60 100

by a manually operated ratchet or a friction-type control. Formerly, double-hung
86 40   64   64   100   90 67   100   97   100   98

sashes were usually counterweighted with sash weights.
 100   53   96   97   47 100   71

---

audience. Accordingly, elaboration targets in the second revision were identified after initially screening the original text for difficult terms. In the latter case, hard words were identified empirically by clozing the original passage using an every-fifth-word deletion frequency in five different forms (the cloze procedure involves systematically deleting words and replacing them with blanks for readers to fill in; for details of the cloze procedure the reader is referred to Bormuth, 1969; Taylor, 1953). Each form was com pleted by two randomly selected sections of students in Introductory Freshman Composition (Comp 101) at the University of Illinois at Chicago. Students in two additional sections were randomly assigned each of the five forms to compare all cloze forms within a single test administration. This procedure produced data for every word in the passage (see Table 5.1), which was then revised by elaborating all lexical items missed by 97% or more of the subjects in this preliminary analysis of text. Semantic hedges (e.g., "broadly," "'various") were not elaborated. When a repeated lexical item was identified for elaboration, only its first mention was targeted.

For the purposes of preparing this "hard-word revision," an elaboration was defined as a repeated argument and was typically accomplished with a synonym and sometimes a substitution (an alternative expression). In revising the text, elaborations were introduced as either parenthetical expressions or alternative expressions. These two formats were considered

TEXT 5.2
Random-Word Revision

Windows are broadly classified or categorized as fixed (non-opening) or ventilating. Fixed (non-opening) windows consist of one or more panes, or sheets, of glass that cannot be opened or moved. Ventilating windows consist of one or more sashes within a fixed (stationary) frame and are classified according to the manner in which the sashes (movable panels)operate.

Double-hung windows (two sliding sashes) and single-hung windows open and close by sliding (moving) the movable sash vertically in grooves provided or included in the stiles (sides) of the frame. The sliding sash is held, or kept open, or closed by various spring balances, or devices. These balances are concealed in the jamb by a manually (hand) operated ratchet (a toothed wheel) or a friction-type control. Formerly, double-hung (two sliding) sashes were usually counterweighted with sash weights.

TEXT 5.3
Hard-Word Revision

Windows are broadly classified as fixed or ventilating (opening). Fixed windows consist of one or more panes of glass that cannot be opened. Ventilating windows consist of one or more movable panels called sashes within a fixed frame and are classified according to the manner in which the sashes open or operate.

Double-hung windows (two sliding sashes) and single-hung windows (one fixed sash above and one sliding sash below) open and close by sliding the movable sash vertically in grooves (channels) that are in the stiles of the frame. The sliding or movable sash is held open or closed by various spring balances. These balances are concealed (hidden) in the jamb, or side, by a manually operated ratchet (a toothed wheel) or a friction-type control (gear mechanism). Formerly, double-hung sashes were usually counterweighted (counterbalanced) with heavy weights called sash weights.

equivalent for the purposes of experiment, and a clear style was used as the criterion for choosing one rather than the other in each instance.

The random-word and hard-word revisions are shown in Texts 5.2 and 5.3. Using Turner and Greene's (1978) predicate calculus, propositional textbases were prepared for these revisions as well as the original. Compared to the original, the two revisions are identical or roughly similar in number of words, number of propositions, number of different arguments per propositions, number of words per sentence, number of elaborations, vocabulary level, and Dale–Chall readabilities (see Table 5.2).

Procedures

In the subsequent phase of the study, the original text plus the two revisions were tested with new, randomly selected groups of students from the same course. After reading the assigned passage and performing two distractor

TABLE 5.2

Text Statistics

	Original text	Hard-word revision	Random-word revision
Number of words	106	141	133
Number or propositions	51	73	68
Propositional density (number of propositions per 100 words)	48.11	45.39	42.86
Number of different arguments per proposition	.647	.589	.559
Number of words per sentence	15.14	19.86	19.14
Number of elaborations	0	16	16
Vocabulary level (Dale Score)	28.30	25.53	27.82
Readability (Dale–Chall)	8.86	8.65	8.98
General recall (number wrong out of 10 Wh-Item questions)	5.07	4.12	5.58
Keyed recall (number wrong out of 14 Wh-Item questions tagged to elaborations)	8.11	4.50	7.42
Recognition (number wrong out of 14 multiple-choice Wh-Item ques- questions tagged to elaborations)	5.85	2.80	4.37

tasks (reading an unrelated passage and taking a spelling test), randomly identified students were then tested for either recognition, general recall, or keyed recall. The general recall and recognition tests were created by dividing the text into clauses (and subdividing long clauses) and creating a Wh-item question for each clause. In the case of keyed recall, the Wh-item questions were designed to test recall of the difficult terms identified in the cloze test. In the case of the test of recall, questions were posed in an open-ended format requiring students to fill in a blank (e.g., "What is the moving part of a window called? _____"). In the test of recognition, the same questions were asked in a multiple-choice format (e.g., "What is the moving part of window called? (a) stile, (b) groove, (c) sash, (d) frame"). These multiple-choice recognition items were created according to the specifications of O'Reilly, Schuder, Kidder, and Hayford (1977) for multiple-choice cloze test items.

In addition to these tests of recall and recognition, each student also ranked the text read on a 7-point Likert scale estimating "how easy they found this passage to understand."

Results

The original text and two revisions do not differ significantly in terms of readers' subjective estimates of their readabilities. Yet in spite of all their similarities, the two revisions differ entirely in readabilities as measured by general recall, keyed recall, and recognition. The hard-word revision is markedly easier to read and understand than either the original or the random-word revision as measured by all tests. This is particularly striking in light of the fact that the elaborations enormously complicate the syntax of the original passage.

Readers of the hard-word revision recalled 6% more than readers of the original text whereas readers of the random-word revision recalled 8% less. Readers generally recalled the hard-word revision significantly better than the random-word revision [one-way ANOVA, post hoc: $F(1, 109) = 1.59$; $p = .02$] though neither the hard-word nor the random-word revision was significantly different from the original in this respect. In terms of keyed recall, readers of the hard-word revision remembered 60% more than readers of the original text, whereas the readers of the random-word revision remembered only 12% more. Hence, the hard-word revision was significantly easier to understand than either the original [$F(1, 66) = 21.14$; $p < .0001$) or the random-word revision [$F(1, 66) = 13.59$; $p = .0001$], and compared to the random-word revision, the hard-word revision was far superior: Of 14 items queried, readers of the hard-word revision correctly recalled an average of 9.45 compared to only 6.58 for readers of the random-word revision [ANOVA $F(1, 66) = 13.59$; $p < .0001$]. In terms of recognition, readers again did better with the hard-word revision, recognizing 40% more than readers of the original, and 19% more than readers of the random-word revision. Table 5.3 summarizes the differences in readabilities between the two revisions as well as between each revision and the original by rank ordering all three passages in terms of all variables.

Discussion

There are a number of important implications here for the application of propositional analysis to problems of text analysis generally and written discourse production specifically. The first implication has to do with effective communication. Clearly, the extent of shared knowledge facilitated by relevant lexical elaborations makes a significant difference in the intelligibility of the communication. In effect, first testing the original passage with readers and identifying targets for elaboration by this empirical

TABLE 5.3
Rank Orderings of Proposed Readability Factors

	Relative difficulties of texts		
	Easy	Medium	Hard
Propositional density	Random-word	Hard-word	Original
Number of new arguments per proposition	Random-word	Hard-word	Original
Syntactic complexity	Original	Random-word	Hard-word
Vocabulary level	Hard-word	Random-word	Original
Readability level (Dale–Chall)	Original	Hard-word	Random-word
General recall	Hard-word	Original	Random-word
Keyed recall	Hard-word	Random-word	Original
Recognition	Hard-word	Random-word	Original

procedure effectively simulates the rhetorical behavior of writers who skillfully take the needs and expectations of their readers into account.

In short, readability involves more than effective interaction between readers with certain information processing capabilities and texts with certain text characteristics. More fundamentally, readabilty results from effective interaction between the needs of writers for expression and the expectations and needs of readers for comprehension. Where it is weak, this interaction will be enhanced by either (a) increasing the extent to which writer and reader share relevant knowledge independently of the text or (b) "buttressing" the text precisely in those spots where knowledge bases do not coincide, i.e., in accordance with the terms of the Given–New Contract (Clark and Clark, 1977): "The [writer] agrees (a) to use given information to refer to information she thinks the [reader] can uniquely identify from what he already knows and (b) to use new information to refer to information she believes to be true but is not already known to the [reader] [p. 92]."

Clearly, then, text elaborations may not be random. Instead, they must be carefully keyed to just those terms and concepts which are critical to readers' strategies of comprehension, to those terms that are more new than given. The purpose of these elaborations is to **buttress** precisely those parts of the text which threaten common categorizations and reciprocity between writer and reader. In effect, these elaborations provide explicit bridges between just those propositions whose relations readers might otherwise miss.

The second implication has to do with discourse analysis. The extent to which writers' perspectives and readers' needs coincide or match up cannot be derived from even the closest analysis of text. Rather, it must be based on a detailed assessment of the context of use—namely the needs, expectations, and purposes of readers as they interface with what writers want to say. As Horowitz (1985) notes, "Rhetorical structures create particular configurations of meaning, based on the purpose of the text and writer-reader relationships. Writers and readers who are sensitive to rhetorical structures may have insights about text that go beyond the propositions of a text." As we noted at the start of Chapter 4, the writer's problem is not just being explicit; the writer's problem is knowing what to be explicit about. Readability may well be enhanced by explaining fewer ideas, saying more about fewer things, relating certain ideas more explicitly than others. But which ideas need elaborating? Which ideas might benefit from relating? Which ideas are hard for which readers? What principles of language production and discourse are relevant to these issues?

Dealing with these issues will always require an empirical determination made in accordance with the reciprocity principle for both writer and discourse analyst: The writer must be sensitive to what readers do and do not know just as the discourse analyst must carefully gather data regarding the extent of shared knowledge.

Moreover, the extent to which writers and their readers share knowledge is not just another item which writers must take into account in expressing their ideas. Even in Kintsch's terms, it is not just the expression or interpretation of meaning that is affected by the context of use: It is the textbase or meaning itself. That is, writers do not just express what they have to say a little differently depending on the audience; they actually say different things. Given readers who know a lot about windows, for example, a writer can say *These balances are concealed in the jamb by a manually operated ratchet or a friction-type control*, which, according to Turner and Greene's (1978) predicate calculus, means:

1. (QUAL, RATCHET, MANUALLY OPERATED)
2. (QUAL, CONTROL, FRICTION-TYPE)
3. (DISJ: EITHER/OR, 1, 2)
4. (CONCEAL, A:$, O:BALANCE)
5. (LOC: IN, 4, JAMB)
6. (MANNER: BY, 4, 5)

Given other readers, who have no specialized knowledge or window construction, however, a writer is well advised to write something like *These balances are concealed, or hidden, in the jamb, or side of the window, by a manually operated ratchet (i.e., a toothed wheel) or a friction-type control (e.g., a gear mechanism)*, which, according to Turner and Greene's (1978) predicate calculus, means:

1. (QUAL, RATCHET, MANUALLY OPERATED)
2. (QUAL, WHEEL, TOOTHED)
3. (QUAL, CONTROL, FRICTION-TYPE)
4. (REF, RATCHET, 1)
5. (QUAL, MECHANISM, GEAR)
6. (REF, CONTROL, 3)
7. (DISJ: EITHER/OR,)
8. (CONCEAL, A:$, O: BALANCE)
9. (REF, JAMB, SIDE)
10. (LOC: IN, 7, JAMB)
11. (MANNER: BY, 7, 8)

The critical point here is that text meaning is not autonomous: As van Dijk and Kintsch (1983) affirm, meaning simply cannot be conceptualized profitably for experimental, theoretical, or any other purpose independently of use. Writing is not a matter of first finding something to say and then finding a way to say it. Indeed, these investigations suggest just the opposite: The writer's meaning, or what the writer has to say, actually depends on the context or situation of use. Hence, skilled writers do not modify what they have to say in light of their readers' knowledge or lack thereof; what they actually write—indeed, *what they have to say*—is largely a result of this situation.

THE WRITER-READER INTERACTION HYPOTHESIS

In terms of readability and difficulty of text, we see that "the salient features of clear written communication lie . . . not in the interaction of reader and text, but rather in the *interaction between writer and reader by way of the text* [Nystrand, 1982b, p.70]." In terms of this interaction, we see clearly how meaning cannot be not a property of the text to be extracted by readers but *comes about phenomenally when readers activate the semantic potential of the text* (Nystrand, 1982c). From this point of view, texts function when they establish and maintain shared perspectives and common categorizations between writers and readers; and meaning results when writers create texts which are properly attuned to their contexts of their use. In these terms, texts are readable when writers elaborate or "buttress" them precisely in those places where reciprocity is threatened, i.e., where readers need the help.

According to Kintsch in his (1980) monograph on discourse production, the speaker or writer takes into account the context of use—audience, setting, listener/reader knowledge, and so on—when translating the textbase into actual text. The actual linguistic form given thought is consequently treated as a pragmatic problem of use; it is a secondary variable. In other words, the choice of one text form over another does not, according to Kintsch, alter the meaning of the utterance. Hence (BAKE, MARY, CAKE) may be expressed as *Mary bakes a cake, Mary is baking a cake, A cake is being baked by Mary, The baking of a cake by Mary*, or *Mary's baking of a cake*; they all mean the same thing, namely (BAKE, MARY, CAKE) [Kintsch, 1974, p. 14]. From the point of view of the writer–reader hypothesis, however, the context of use is no mere ancillary pragmatic factor; it is as fundamentally semantic as it is pragmatic. As Lyons (1977) notes:

> Given that the truth-conditional definition of presupposition is, to say the least, of very restricted coverage and cannot be applied to actual or potential utterances unless certain assumptions are made about the thematic structure of the utterances and about the contexts in which they occur, there would seem to be little point in drawing a theoretical distinction between two kinds of presupposition in terms of the distinction between semantics and pragmatics—a distinction which is, in general, of doubtful value as far as the analysis of the structure of natural language is concerned [pp. 602-603].

A text is never simply or even primarily a matter of translating thoughts into well-chosen words; and language production is never entirely ancillary to cognition, coming as it were "after the ideational fact." Writing is not just a matter of finding words for thoughts. More than anything, language is an activity motivated by the user's need to make things known in particular ways for particular purposes and to establish and maintain common understandings with others; and the form that a particular text takes is always determined as much by the users' need to function in these situations as it is by whatever it is they wish to express.

A COMPARISON OF DEMANDS ON WRITERS ADDRESSING KNOWLEDGEABLE AND UNKNOWLEDGEABLE READERS

That a given text can be ambiguous for some readers and abstruse for others can be demonstrated by showing that knowledgeable and unknowledgeable readers require qualitatively different revisions of troublesome texts for comparable clarity. Specifically, we should expect that knowledgeable and unknowledgeable readers will differ significantly in their use of text elaborations: Unknowledgeable readers should benefit more than their counterparts from the introduction of topical elaborations.

ANOTHER EXPERIMENT

Preliminary Case Studies

In order to examine differences in the comprehension processes between knowledgeable and unknowledgeable readers, 13 subjects were selected randomly from the University of Wisconsin-Madison undergraduate student population. These subjects took a Test of Computer Terminology (see Table 5.4), and each completed 6 clozed passages of computer documentation. In all, 10 passages were tested and of these 2 were selected for use in the subsequent phase of the study. The remaining texts were discarded as either too hard for the less knowledgeable readers or too easy for the knowledgeable readers. The 4 subjects who read each text succeeded in completing 23-48% of the clozed texts with exact words.

In order to get an initial sense of the kinds of questions that knowledgeable and unknowledgeable readers might have with these passages, four subjects were called back to read several texts aloud to the principal investigator. Two of the readers scored highest on the computer literacy test; two scored lowest. Two passages were used: (a) "IBM's Magnificent Keyboard" and (b) "Error Message #5" (See Texts 5.4 and 5.5). The readers had not read these texts originally in clozed form. They were instructed to "comment freely" on the texts and especially to state any questions that came to mind as they read the texts. In collecting these reading protocols, we following the procedures outlined by Swaney, Janik, Bond, and Hayes (1981).

The most interesting session was the fourth. Kirk, who scored highest on the Test of Computer Terminology (getting 89.5% of the questions right), was the only one of the four to think that "IBM" was the more difficult of the two passages. He made a most interesting distinction. He said that "IBM" read better than "#5" but that "#5" was easier to understand. In explaining, he noted that with "IBM" it was very easy to get the main idea but quite difficult to understand the details (understanding the details, he said, would require a complete course in computer architecture), but since the purpose of the piece didn't really hang on the details, one could easily skip over them and get the main idea. Hence, "IBM" was easier to read.

By contrast, he noted that the details in "#5" were critical to the purpose of the piece. He wasn't even sure whether "#5" had a main idea in the same sense that "IBM" did. The whole purpose of "#5" was to instruct users in a particular procedure; hence, each detail was critical. Since he was familiar with the sorts of procedures outlined in "#5" (even though he didn't know this particular procedure), he knew exactly how to read it and how to consider the details. Also, because he was familiar not only with the general

TABLE 5.4

Test of Computer Terminology

Check the best answer(s) to each question. In some cases, more than one answer is correct.

1. When working at a computer, it's best to keep your eyes on the:

___ a. ASCII
___ b. CRT
___ c. CPU
___ d. RAM
___ e. ROM

2. Communication between computers via telephone lines requires a:

___ a. cursor
___ b. disk
___ c. matrix
___ d. modem
___ e. modem and disk

3. Check each of the following if it is a peripheral:

___ a. cursor
___ b. modem
___ c. monitor
___ d. printer
___ e. terminal

4. Which term does NOT belong in this list?

___ a. GOSUB
___ b. GOTO
___ c. PEEK
___ d. POKE
___ e. RAM

5. One byte = (how many?) bits

___ a. 2
___ b. 4
___ c. 6
___ d. 8
___ e. none of the above

6. One bit = (how many?) bytes

___ a. 2
___ b. 4
___ c. 6
___ d. 8
___ e. none of the above

7. Which of the following is part of a monitor?

___ a. baud
___ b. disk
___ c. duplex
___ d. modem
___ e. pixel

8. An RS232C port is typically:

___ a. backed up
___ b. expanded
___ c. monitored
___ d. serial
___ e. thermal

9. Which of the following has/have true descenders?

___ a. cursor
___ b. handshake
___ c. matrix
___ d. monitor
___ e. peripheral

10. Which is likely to be the most expensive new printer?

___ a. dot matrix
___ b. fully formed
___ c. parallel
___ d. serial
___ e. thermal

11. CP/M, MS DOS, and TRSDOS are all:

___ a. daisy wheels
___ b. integrated circuits
___ c. motherboards
___ d. resident RAMs
___ e. operating systems

12. BASIC, FORTRAN, and COBOL are all:

___ a. I/O ports
___ b. interfaces
___ c. languages
___ d. operating systems
___ e. peripherals

Define each of the following terms:

13. CPU:

14. I/O:

15. default value:

16. operand:

TEXT 5.4

IBM's Marvelous Keyboard

One super feature of the IBM keyboard is that you can cause any key combination to create any code you want. To understand how this is done, let's examine the key-encoding scheme. The keyboard contains an Intel 8048 single-chip microcomputer that constantly scans all the keys. It sends out a serial pattern of bits (called the *make code*) when a key makes contact, and a similar pattern (the same pattern but with high-order bit set, called the *break code*) when the contact is broken. If the contact is present for more than 1/2 second, the keyboard sends out the make code repetitively 10 times a second.

Each key is treated identically by the keyboard; any key could represent a shift key, a number, or a special function. And, because the duration of the depression of a key is reported precisely, you can use the keyboard for playing music and simulating simple joysticks, in addition to the usual typewriter applications. Meanwhile, the main computer doesn't have to waste time monitoring and "debouncing" the keyboard—that's all done by the dedicated 8048 microcomputer. The penalty one pays for this completely general flexibility is that the main computer does have to translate the make and break codes into standard ASCII, but that seems a minor price to pay.

From D. Glaco and M. Sargent III, "Using IBM's Marvelous Keyboard," *BYTE*, May, 1983, pp. 402–403f. Reprinted wih permission from *BYTE* magazine, May 1983, © McGraw-Hill, Inc. All rights reserved.

TEXT 5.5

Error Message 5: DISK IS FULL

This could just mean that it's write-protected, and by removing the tab, the problem will go away. Or, it could mean what it says. Beginners often get this message because they don't write-protect drive 0, and didn't specify a drive number for their files. In that case, all new files are written to drive 0, which eventually fills up. Solution: make sure everything is sent to drive 1. Method: copy your text files from zero to one (there is a DOS command called "COPY"), then "KILL" the old copies on drive 0, then put a write-protect tab on drive 0. Of course, if it's a drive-1 disk that has filled up, the solution is even easier: just insert a formatted data disk in drive 1 and try again. If you don't have any preformatted disks lying around for the purpose, you may have a problem. Solution: remove the write-protect tab from drive 0, try to save your text onto drive 0, then press <RESET>, hold down <ENTER> to suppress "AUTO", and format a couple of disks. Then copy the file over from drive 0 to 1, kill it on drive 0, and type the command "NS" to get NEWSCRIPT going again.

From *NEWSCRIPT Release 7* ® *PROSOFT, Inc. 1984, p. 202.*

subject of "IBM" but also with the sort of article it was, he knew it was possible to read it without necessarily understanding all the details.

Kirk showed his knowledge in several ways. Most important, Kirk knew what sorts of articles he was reading (general informative versus procedural). Knowing this, he had some sense of the relevance of the details and their purpose in the article. He knew whether the details were important to know. With "IBM" all you really need, he said, is the main idea; with "#5" all you need (and all you get) are details. In order to totally succeed with "IBM," the reader would need a course in computer architecture. By contrast, the reader of "#5" would need only a primer of terms, maybe a glossary. "IBM" touches on the enormously complicated subject of computer architecture. There is nothing remotely complicated in the same sense about the subject matter of "#5."

These distinctions are consistent with Chiesi, Spilich, and Voss's findings that "hi-and-lo knowledge readers yield performance differences in their ability to use context. . . . This hypothesis is based upon the idea that the HK individuals process the information at input as a unified sequence of related information to a greater extent than LK individuals |1979, p. 268|."

Compare these impressions to those of the two other readers, Mark, another highly knowledgeable reader, and Ross, a less knowledgeable reader (whose scores on the Test of Computer Terminology were 84.2% and 47.4%, respectively). Ross was aware of text, not meaning; Mark was aware of meaning, not text. But Mark was not as aware of meaning as Kirk. Whereas Mark and Kirk were both highly knowledgeable about computers, Kirk knew more than Mark. Kirk knew not only about computers, he knew also how to read computer articles; hence he could make judgments about the relevance of details to the purpose of the genre. By contrast, Mark made more superficial copy-editing suggestions; he went deeper that either Ross or Lois, the other unknowledgeable reader, but his comments did not capture the relevance of the details to the type of article in the same way that Kirk's did. Mark knew a lot about computers, but he didn't know as much as Kirk about *reading about computers*.

From these interviews, it seems clear that, when knowledgeable readers have questions, they will request further specification more than category definitions. Neither Kirk nor Mark expressed any doubt about what the articles were about. Rather, the thrust of their comments was directed entirely at the meaning and use of details. By contrast, Ross and Lois worked at a very different level, and their questions were more directed at getting some sense of the gist of the text in each case.

These differences are consistent with the findings of Spilich, Vesonder, Chiesi, and Voss (1979), who, in studies of "hi- and lo-knowledge" readers' recalls of passages about baseball, showed that "the HK subjects recalled more information that was goal related than the LK subjects, they tended to integrate sequences of goal-related actions more than LK individuals, and they recalled information in the appropriate order more than LK individuals [p. 284]."

These distinctions are also consistent with research conducted by Harris, Begg, and Upfold (1980). Working from the premise that "communication is an interactive process in which there is an implicit contract between the communicants," they tested the hypothesis that misinformation is defined not in terms of inherent truth value but rather extent of congruence between the discourse produced and interpretive frame of the receiver. To do this, they conducted an experiment in which some subjects served as senders and were asked to produce clues for receivers, whose task was to determine the target words for which the clues had been produced. The senders were led to expect either that the receivers would know the general category of which the target was an exemplar (e.g., furniture) or they would not. Whether or not the receivers did in fact know the general category was manipulated randomly by the experimenters. The results showed that "senders who expect that receivers will know the target's category give clues that are beneficial if the receiver does know the category, but are harmful if the receiver is not so informed. Conversely, if senders expect that the target's category is unknown, their clues are helpful to receivers who do not know the category, but harmful to receivers who do. That is, expecting too much or too little categorical information hurts performance, in line with the contractual view [of communication] [p. 603]."

Main Study: Subjects, Materials, and Procedures

Following these initial probes, groups of knowledgeable and unknowledgeable subjects were identified randomly from the University of Wisconsin-Madison population for the purpose of establishing baseline data on new texts that would be revised and used in subsequent tests of the main hypotheses. The group of knowledgeable readers consisted of 9 students who had experience programming microcomputers and scored more than 50% on the Test of Computer Terminology. The group of unknowledgeable subjects consisted of 11 students who had no experience with computers and scored less than 50% on the Test of Computer Terminology. Out of 18 test items on the Test of Computer Terminology, the mean scores of the two groups were 5.27 and 15.44, respectively [t (df 18) $=$ 11.78; p $<$ .0001 (2-tailed test)]. Subjects in both groups also completed the first part of the Davis I(A) Reading Test, which showed that there were no significant differences in the general reading abilities of the two groups [t (18) $=$ .65; p $=$ .53 (2-tailed test)].

These two groups then screened several passages of computer documentation of about 100 words each, to make sure that the passages were not unreasonably hard for the unknowledgeable group and not altogether obvious for the knowledgeable group, and also to precisely identify and characterize troublesources by type. To do this, each subject was asked to execute the instructions outlined in the documentation by actually performing the backup, format, and other miscellaneous tasks outlined by the documentation. The principal investigator promised to answer any and all questions each subject asked and encouraged subjects to ask questions since the questions they asked would become primary data in the experiment. All subjects were paid $10 an hour for their participation. Subjects in each group then executed the instructions in the documentation, indicating as they read where they had questions and what they needed to know to proceed. Errors in executing the instructions were noted, and each subject's performance was timed.

The unknowledgeable subjects asked more questions than the knowledgeable group. As in the preliminary study, they also asked different kinds of questions. The unknowledgeable subjects tended to ask more for **category definitions** (e.g., "What's a disk drive?") compared to their knowledgeable counterparts who tended to ask more for **further specification** (e.g., "Which disk drive?"). Figures 5.1 and 5.2 show the clear relationship between Knowledge of Computer Terminology and Requests for Further Specification and Category Definition. Two raters analyzed all subjects' questions into these two categories, and interrater reliability, computed as a Pearson product–moment correlation was $r = .575$; $F = 83.1$; $p < .00001$. Discrepancies were resolved in discussion, and Table 5.5 shows the criteria used for operationalizing the distinctions between the two sorts of questions. In all, the requests of the unknowledgeable subjects were 41.6% for category definitions and 58.4% for further specification. By contrast, the requests of the knowledgeable subjects were 26.8% for category definitions and 73.2% for further specification. A chi-square test indicated that this difference was significant (chi-square $= 5.35$; $p = .02$).

The requests for category definition were interpreted as need for topic-level elaborations, and the requests for further specification were interpreted as need for additional commentary. Accordingly, two sets of revisions were prepared, each treating the troublesources identified by unknowledgeable and knowledgeable readers respectively. Compared to the original texts, the revisions for unknowledgeable readers included 11 additional topical elaborations and 27 additional comment-level elaborations, whereas the revisions for knowledgeable readers included only 4 additional topic-level elaborations and 25 additional comment-level elaborations.

To test the main hypothesis, 48 new subjects were selected according to the procedures noted previously. Twenty-two were identified as knowledgeable subjects, and 26 were identified as unknowledgeable subjects. The

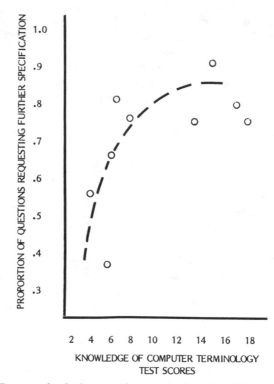

Figure 5.1. Requests for further specification as a function of knowledge of computer terminology.

mean scores of the unknowledgeable and knowledgeable groups on the Test of Computer Terminology were 4.92 and 14.89, respectively [t (df 46) = 13.87; p < .00001 (2-tailed test)]. Subjects in both groups also completed the first part of the Davis I(A) Reading Test, which showed that there were no significant differences in the general reading abilities of the two groups [t (46) = .88; p = .39 (2-tailed test)]. Among each group, subgroups of 7 or 8 were identified randomly, and one of these subgroups read the original passage, another read the revision for knowledgeable readers, and the third read the revision for unknowledgeable readers.

Results: Knowledgeable Subjects

There were no significant differences in the numbers of requests for category definition made in response to Revision #1 or #2 compared to the original. There was, however, a significant decrease in the number of

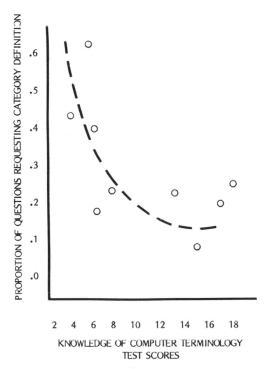

Figure 5.2. Requests for category definition as a function of knowledge of computer terminology.

requests for further specification made in response to Revision #1 compared to the original (ANOVA $F = 5.79$; $p < .0001$).

Results: Unknowledgeable Subjects

The unknowledgeable subjects responded just the opposite from the knowledgeable subjects. There were no significant differences in the numbers of requests for further specifications made in response to Revision #1 or #2, compared to the original. There was, however, a significant decrease in the number of requests for category definition made in response to both Revisions #1 and #2 compared to the original (#1: ANOVA $F = 4.31$; $p < .0001$; #2: $F = 3.06$; $p = .0006$).

Both groups benefited more from Revision #1, but, as predicted, the two groups differed in how they benefited. The knowledgeable group requested significantly fewer specifications, but the unknowledgeable group requested significantly fewer category definitions. We see the benefits of the revision in their performance too: Whereas the unknowledgeable group made nearly

TABLE 5.5

Criteria Defining Requests for Further Specification and
Requests for Category Definition

Further specification	Examples
1) Qualification of an NP with an adjective identifying a plausible attribute	"Are there 40 tracks per inch?"
2) Request for confirmation [possible options: either/or]	"Am I identifying or naming a file?"
3) IS + NP_1 + NP_2? [possible]	"Which button is backspace?"
4) Requests involving collocation	"Is a cylinder a track?"
5) DO + I + VERB + ADV? [possible option]	"Do I press <ENTER> now?"
6) Queries of given information	"Which drive is drive A?"
Category definition	
1) NP + MEAN/BE/REFER TO + $NP_\emptyset$?	"What does 'backup' mean?"
2) Request for information/ confirmation [no apparent options]	"What do I do now?"
3) NP_1 + BE + same/different from NP_2? [queries relationship]	"Is 'backup' the same as 'format'?"
4) Queries of new information	"What's a drive?"
5) "[TEXT]" + MEAN + $NP_\emptyset$?	"What does 'DOS PLUS prompt' mean?"

three times as many errors as the knowledgeable group in working from the original text [.92 versus .35 respectively; t (41) = 2.08; p = .04 (2-tailed test)], there was no significant difference in the number of errors made by the two groups in response to the second revision [.57 versus .46, respectively; t (52) = .47; p = .63 (2-tailed test)]. This equivalence of performance was taken to indicate the semantic adequacy of the revision for each group.

Comparing the two revisions in terms of errors made by the two groups, we find that the significant increase in topical elaborations in Revision #1 over both Revision #2 and the original text significantly reduced the errors made by the unknowledgeable group by 47% [$F(1, 80)$ = 2.92; p = .0002] but made no significant reduction in the errors made by the knowledgeable group. This result is taken to support the main hypothesis that clarification of main idea (i.e., topical elaboration) will improve unknowledgeable readers' comprehension but will not affect the comprehension of knowledgeable readers, who already know the main idea.

Discussion

Regardless of whether a text is clarified for experts or non-experts, the results should be the same: A clear text that allows readers to understand the writer. There will be an easy exchange of ideas in each case since the text is properly attuned to its context. Hence, texts will be clear when they enable writers and readers to share relevant knowledge adequately. Shared knowledge is the salient condition of any clear communication or good document design. Conversely, discrepancies between what the writer has to say and what the reader needs to know is the salient condition of all hard texts and poor document design.

The criterion of shared knowledge as a condition for clear communication constrains skilled writers in their tasks. Writing for experts is very different from writing for nonexperts for just this reason. The problem for the writer, however, is not just that the expert knows more than the nonexpert; the expert's knowledge is also much more highly integrated than the nonexpert's (cf. Spilich, Vesonder, Chiesi, and Voss, 1979). As Faigley (1986) notes, "The readers' knowledge not only influences how they *abstract* the topic, but also how they *reconstruct* the topic [p.22]." Hence, the expert is far more likely than is the nonexpert to come to the text with clearly defined expectations, particularly about the gist or main idea, as well as a ready appreciation for fine points and relationships among concepts and details. Compared to nonexperts, experts who are uncertain about the meaning of a difficult text will seek further elaboration and more detail to be sure of certain implications of the author's meaning, which is likely to seem ambiguous to these readers; additional commentary, which provides further specification, will help. By contrast, nonexperts who are confused by difficult texts will be simply overwhelmed by too many details, and the text will seem abstruse. These readers need the main idea to cope with and organize all the details; topical elaborations, which provide category definition, will help.

These differences between knowledgeable and unknowledgeable readers may well explain the negative results that Reder (1982) reports with students' uses of text elaborations. In several experiments, she compared student recall of text material versus summaries of the same material. In study after study, she found that recall was better for the summaries than for the actual, more elaborated text materials. As Reder concludes, these results should not be interpreted as arguments against using textbooks (and Cliff's *Notes* instead). Her results are probably explained by the fact that her subjects, as students using textbooks, were all unknowledgeable readers and so benefited more from the topic-level elaborations of the summaries than from the comment-level elaborations of the textbooks.

Elsewhere (Nystrand, 1979, 1982b) I have analyzed this problem of abstruseness and ambiguity of text as a problem of mismatch between what the writer has to say and what the reader needs to know. Readers who find texts abstruse seek category definitions when they are unable to assimilate the information the writer provides, e.g., Kintsch's (1974) high propositional-density texts for the average reader. Readers who find texts ambiguous seek further information to understand a writer's meaning, e.g., Kintsch's texts that say too little about too many things, compared to texts that say much about a few things.

As an approach to readability and text design, these distinctions have several important implications and advantages. First, clarity of text obviously depends on the world knowledge that the reader brings to the text. Also, writers compose clearly for their readers when they effectively take into account their readers' knowledge and expectations. To do this, writers must include information and compose texts that will result in common categorizations. Indeed, assuring reciprocity between writer and reader may be said to be a fundamental motive for discourse production. Most important, the incorporation of "situation of use" (knowledgeable and unknowledgeable readers in this case) into the analysis of readability clears up some puzzles we reviewed in the first part of this chapter regarding Kintsch's distinctions between texts that say too much about too little (i.e., high propositional-density texts) and texts that say too little about too much. The extent and organization of the reader's knowledge is a critical factor in each of these situations, and whether a particular text is ambiguous, abstruse, or lucid depends on neither the writer, the reader, nor the text alone but rather on the balance of all three—that is, on how well the writer matches what he or she has to say with what the reader expects and needs to know.

Part II

Learning to Write

The first part of this study principally concerns the communicative options and strategies of the fluent writer, who must establish (a) what sort of text is under way, (b) what sort of topic is under discussion, and (c) exactly what he or she wishes to say about it. In other words, writers proceed by elaborating messages at the levels of genre, topic, and comment, each level progressively constraining the interpretive possibilities of the next.

But what of the learner? How does a child, for example, get to the point where the genre, topic, and comment of written text define meaningful communicative options and considerations? How do these principles operate in adult learning?

In the case study presented in Chapter 6, Margaret Himley reports the growth of a young writer, Samantha, whose early texts, like those of many children, mix drawing and writing in idiosyncratic ways. In effect, Samantha explores the possibilities of the new medium (writing) in terms of capabilities she already possesses (drawing), and at least one early "book" contains nothing but smiling faces and their variations. In the course of her explorations, however, the graphic gives way to the orthographic, the lexical to the syntactic, and eventually the formal to the functional.

There are several key points worth noting about the growth of this writer. First, the medium she chooses to explore is a new option for her expression—namely a text option—and as such it presents to her certain choice points rather than others. But for a beginning writer, there is nothing fixed about these choice points and text options. Indeed, they are continuously fluid, and much of the play of children's writing is given over to experimenting with novel interpretations of both the new options and the choice points that they define. Hence, making a book presents the option of sequential pages, but sequential pages in turn present the writer with

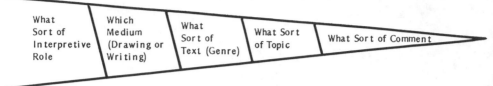

Figure II.1. Hierarchic constraints on the growth of writers.

particular boundaries requiring navigation. New options breed new choice points which, in turn, breed new options, and for this reason the path into textual space is typically bumpy and uneven even for the most assiduous.

Before topic and comment—indeed before genre—come some far more fundamental options and choices for the child who ventures into this brave new world. Most fundamentally, learning to write requires adopting a particular interpretive role in a particular kind of speech community, the world of writers and readers. As such, much early writing is role playing, significant not for what the child tries to *say* but rather for what she *does*. As one of Luria's (1977–78/1929) 3-year-old subjects responded when the psychologist asked the child about the meaning of one of her scribbles, "That's how you write!"

In addition to considerations of genre, topic, and comment, we must add more fundamental levels to the hierarchy of communicative concerns outlined in Chapter 2. The constraints on development we shall explore in this section are depicted in Figure II.1.

When Samantha finally gets going, all these features work in concert. The earliest texts highlight issues of social role (playing author) and medium (both drawing and writing) but little else. As Samantha explores and works through the possibilities of her new role and medium, she increasingly confronts the more intricate concerns of this textual space, and we see a progressive though inconsistent movement through the entire range of developmental issues.

In another case study in Chapter 7, "Where Do the Spaces Go?," we look closely at another child, Paul (cf. Bissex, 1980), and his struggles with one particular kind of choice point—the orthographic puzzle of word segmentation. Here we find a progressive differentiation of *spaces between words* from *spaces within words*. Also, much like the invented spellings of young writers that have been studied by Read (1971), Henderson (1980), and others, the spacing in the early texts is not really haphazard and unpatterned. Rather, the writer's initial segmentation of text is merely at odds with readers' expectations. The development of orthography here is largely a matter of his learning to synchronize choice points and text options with readers' expectations for a particular kind of orthographic coherence.

In both case studies we see that the writer's growth is governed by the principle of reciprocity between writers and readers: Ultimately it is the balance between their own needs for expression and their readers' needs for comprehension that adjudicates each writer's experiments with the possibilities of text; and to the extent that their texts achieve this balance they are functional.

In Chapter 8, we examine learning to write from the point of view of college freshmen. These writers no longer conflate drawing and writing, and the issues that confront them as writers are more strictly those of genre, topic, and comment. Nonetheless, we see that reciprocity is as central and critical to adult learning as it is to children learning.

In this chapter we focus on the uses of peer conferencing in writing instruction. When peer groups work well and writers confront their readers regularly to review their papers, the groups tend to "gravitate" to those parts of the texts that are unclear or troublesome in some way. As long as groups do not engage in excessive "copy editing" but dwell instead on understanding the writer's purpose and its articulation, the discussions focus mainly on these troublesources and uncertainties of text. More to the point, these groups have a keen sense of what problems need solving. They identify key troublesources and deal concretely with how particular text structures and options address them. These troublesources, which range from ambiguities of genre (What sort of text is this?), purpose (What's the purpose of this?), topic (What's this about anyway?), and comment (What's the point?) constitute the subject matter of these sessions. In effect, the discussion examines a continuous set of rhetorical problems, which the group collaborates in solving. Hence, by intensively identifying and resolving rhetorical problems, they shore up, flesh out, and sustain just those parts of their papers that otherwise would be weak and unclear.

It is precisely this process of intensive rhetorical problem-solving that defines the effectiveness of intensive peer review. Peer review is not just a method of teaching writing. Used intensively, it creates an environment, somewhat like the social context of initial language acquisition, where the learner can continuously test hypotheses about the possibilities of written text.

6

Genre as Generative: One Perspective on One Child's Early Writing Growth

MARGARET HIMLEY

INTRODUCTION

Many investigations into how and why a child learns to write have focused primarily on the cognitive aspects of the child's development as a writer. For example, researchers have studied the apparent stages whereby children come to differentiate drawing from writing and to establish phoneme-grapheme correspondences (Ferreiro, 1982), the principles that guide children's mastery of orthographic features of written language such as letter formation (Clay, 1975), hypotheses about spelling (Read, 1975; Henderson and Beers,1980), and possible sequences in the development of children's composing processes (Graves, 1973; 1975). In the case study of one third grader, Calkins (1983) documents Susie's development in "the craft of writing," as part of a larger NIE-funded study seeking "to build a tentative map of children's growth in writing [p. 7]." Calkins looks "through" the texts, in a sense, to expose the "metafeatures" of the child's composing processes and his knowledge of good writing. In particular, she looks for more deliberate and conscious crafting, greater audience aware-ness, and increased ability to plan and select options. A child's text, from this perspective, ideally becomes a window onto the mind, an illumination of the child's cognitive development in terms of the underlying composing process.

Important as it may be, this perspective presents a number of potential limitations. One, an unfortunate split results between content and process, with researchers interested not in what a writer has to say but rather in what a child reveals about her understanding of writing and the writing process (C. Onore, personal communication). Two, this emphasis on the cognitive aspects of writing may lead researchers to conclude that growth in writing is governed primarily by broad developmental processes (e.g., Dyson, 1983). The problem here is that language itself may become trivialized. Such a general cognitive level of analysis is too general to capture the salient features of writing as a *particular mode of discourse*, as a *language act* (cf. Chapter 1, this volume).

In this essay I would like to propose another perspective from which to make sense of *how* and particularly *why* a child grows as a writer. As B. H. Smith (1978) notes, "the verbal behavior of every child we observe arises within a functioning linguistic community and is [therefore] shaped by its practices from the very beginning [p. 131]." Halliday (1978), too, empha-sizes the social context of language learning: "A child creates, first his child tongue, then his mother tongue, in interaction with that little coterie of people who constitute his meaning group [p. 1]." In learning to write (or speak), the learner does not simply exercise expressive and intentional capabilities in written (or spoken) forms. More particularly she learns the ways of making meaning of a particular language community by appropri-ating and reworking those ways to which she has access. The language then "becomes 'one's own'. . . when the speaker populates it with his own intention, his own accent, when he appropriates the word, adapting it to his own semantic and expressive intention [Bakhtin, 1981, p. 293]." Indeed as children are socialized into the language community and as they appropri-ate its practices, they come to learn *new* ways to mean (Halliday, 1978), *new* meanings to have.

This social interactive perspective on language development raises sev-eral key questions:

1. How do particular communities make meaning with written language? What are their unique ways of speaking?
2. How are those ways made available to its new members?
3. How do a community's linguistic "practices" affect a particular child's path of development as a writer?
4. How do children become members of the community?

In search of a full documentary account of this complex transaction between child and community, I have observed and analyzed three young writers for a year and half (Himley, 1983). In this paper, however, I would like to highlight only one dimension of one child's early writing growth: I will examine the effect of that particularly key linguistic practice called "genre" in shaping the early path of development of a 6-year-old writer named Samantha. I intend to show that her evolving interpretations of genre offer insights into the evolving nature of the form, substance, and function of her early texts.

A WORKING DEFINITION OF GENRE

A general dictionary will define *genre* as "a distinctive type or category" of language composition. We may also typically think of "genre" in terms of classes of literary works with similar form or content, such as poetry or drama. I would like to use the term, however, both more theoretically and more broadly and to define genre as "social action [Miller, 1984]." Miller argues convincingly that "a rhetorically sound definition of genre must be centered not on the substance or the form of discourse but on the action it is used to accomplish [p. 151]" and must include a larger range of discourse than we typically associate with the term. Indeed, Halliday (1978) contends, generic structure "is not simply a feature of literary genres: there is generic structure in all discourse, including the most informal spontaneous conversation [p. 134]." Genres emerge, then, in a culture as conventional responses to particular and recurrent situations—situations where discourse can mediate or accomplish some social action. Inaugural speeches, eulogies, letters of recommendation, ransom notes, users' manuals, and sermons, for example, have taken on conventional forms *because* they arise in recurrent situations with similar structures and elements. Genres, in sum, are defined here as "typified rhetorical actions based on recurrent situations [Miller, 1984, p. 159]."

As a child comes to appropriate and rework a genre (to "own" it, in Bakhtin's [1981] sense), she comes to learn not only the typical substance or formal features associated with the discourse, but also—and surely more fundamentally—the situations that typically give rise to the genre, the social action she may accomplish with it, and the social and interpretive roles she may adopt with it. Indeed, what a child learns is a *new* way of acting and making meaning. As Miller concludes, "what we learn when we learn a genre is not just a pattern of forms or even a method of achieving our own ends. We learn, more importantly, what ends we have [p. 165]." We discover new ways to mean and thus how to participate more fully in the actions of the community. To learn how to write most fundamentally requires learning a social role in an interpretive community, or in Nystrand's (1982c) terms, negotiating textual space.

Genre, therefore, represents a significant aspect of children's learning to write. To engage in written discourse—"that is, to produce language that is functional in some context of use—they must skillfully negotiate key text points with appropriate text options [Nystrand and Himley, 1984, p. 199]." These "choice points" focus the writer's attention and resources on particular issues during composing including (a) graphic, orthographic, and formal features of text related to matters of length, spacing (see Chapter 7, this volume), (b) substantive features of text related to beginnings, endings, and various text elaborations (see Chapter 5, this volume), and (c) functional features of text related to the acts and purposes of the particular genre such as reference, persuasion, description, etc. It is the formal features of genre that initially engage Samantha's interest and provide a point of entry for her into the written language community. This path of development may result from her product orientation in learning, from her pleasure in role playing, and from her school's particular presentation of literacy learning. She is drawn more to the social than to the imaginative possibilities for writing: In the beginning at least, she attends more to creating a finished product and acting like a writer than to telling a tale and being a narrator. With time and experience, new choices and options emerge for her. Yet one might speculate about other points of entry for other children, with the functional features of genre, for example, being more salient to a child drawn first to the imaginative possibilities of this new medium.

SAMANTHA: A DOCUMENTARY ACCOUNT

I observed Samantha from March 1982, when she was in senior kindergarten, through March 1983, when she had nearly completed first grade. She lives and attends school in an affluent, family-oriented suburb of Chicago, a suburb that places a high priority on their children's learning to read and, to a lesser degree, on their learning to write. For example, parents complained when their children's CAT spelling scores failed to reach the expected criterion of two grade levels above the national norm. As a result the school promptly instituted (from first grade on up) that venerable educational tradition, the weekly spelling test. This achievement orientation toward literacy was also evidenced in the open, ceaseless class competition among the students—"*I'm* in Book Five!" or "*That* ditto sheet looks simps!"

Briefly portrayed, Samantha is a happy, somewhat emotionally restrained, and well-liked student who efficiently and crisply goes about the business of learning. Engaged in the social world, she attends closely to the interactions of that world, as evidenced by her sensitivity to register and to social rules, her internalization of the teacher's entire Rugtime Routine, her preference for role-playing games during free time, and her ability to produce "communicatively efficient" spoken language discourse when talking with adults and at Show and Tell times.

Samantha's approach to learning may be succinctly characterized as product-oriented: She wants to complete an assignment efficiently and correctly. She conflates task and text: Completing an assigned sequence of pages in her reader is more salient and significant to her than actually understanding the story on those pages. Samantha carefully balances her resources with her intention in order to complete the product. For example, she may simplify a task by focusing on one key part and investing that part with the essence of the whole. Ergo, a book becomes a "book" because it has a title page and a sequence of paginated sheets.

Samantha has adapted well to the reading curriculum, with its sequenced attention first to phonics, next to an evolving sight vocabulary, then to simple sentences, and finally to short stories. She has readily accepted the notion of reading as rule-governed decoding behavior, and has attended more to the local concerns of decoding words than to global matters of comprehension and story organization.

SAMANTHA QUA WRITER

Learning to write, for Samantha, is primarily a (w)rite of passage, a process that engages her interest at the level of producing texts that can be shared with others and therefore marks her as a participating member of the written language community. Typically she writes most prolifically on those occasions when written texts are part of a cultural event (e.g., sending cards for holidays) and when writing is embedded in play with peers—and of course when writing is assigned at school. In Samantha's early development, writing is more a matter of creating and sharing token written language products than inventing worlds or expressing feelings and thoughts or communicating information.

Genre, I contend, has a generative effect on Samantha's early growth as a writer and facilitates moments of microgenesis. As Samantha experiments with the new medium of written language and produces texts, she works within a particular understanding of a particular genre, and this interpretation defines certain text points and options rather than others. Hence, early books have covers and pages and staples, but later books have stories beginning "Once upon a time," characters, plots, and "The End." It is her interpretation of "book" at any moment in her development as a writer that first defines those text points that are salient and then, in turn, appropriate text options. Her notion of the genre—of the social and interpretive roles entailed in that genre—establishes a kind of overall meaning potential (cf. Halliday, 1978). Once she has decided to write a "book," her notion of that genre—including what a book looks like, what content it typically contains, what functions or acts it fulfills in a community of readers, and what an author does—defines a series of choice points for Samantha to identify and respond to. In a sense, then, the genre itself—or more precisely her interpretation of it—generates a kind of momentum that draws Samantha forward as she composes, and that may encourage, perhaps even enable her to discover and invent new text-creating options for negotiating those formal, substantive, and functional textual choice points.

And as Vygotsky (1978) observes, development in writing "does not follow a single direct line in which something like a clear continuity of forms is maintained" but rather is "full of discontinuities [p. 106]," introducing new means of cognitive organization for the writer. As Samantha chooses to act, to be an author, she works with certain choice points and experiments with those text-creating options that are available to her. In the beginning these options are largely graphic, but as she explores this new medium, these options in turn define new choice points which in their own turn define new options (including orthographic, lexical, and syntactic). As she "spirals" her way into this new domain, her growth as a writer is bumpy and uneven.

Let me propose a schematic representation of this thesis as a means of describing how genre may structure the ways new writers create text and thus may facilitate their growth as writers (see Figure 6.1)

In a writer's early development, the impetus to write comes from the situation (e.g., a school assigned task, a part in a play with peers). This situation suggests a genre, a conventional way to realize a particular kind of meaning potential. It also defines particular text points which she negotiates with the options available to her. Her interpretation of that genre, in conjunction with her expressive intentionality, results in her conceptualizing and negotiating various semiotic choice points with available text-creating options at various textual levels. These choice points concern formal, substantive, and functional features and determine in part the character of the text so produced. To illustrate this thesis and to suggest the possible productiveness of this perspective, I now analyze several texts

SITUATION ⟶ GENRE + Samantha's intentionality and knowledge ⟶
CHOICE POINTS ⟶ TEXT OPTIONS ⟶ TEXT

Figure 6.1. Genre as a factor in Samantha's text production.

Samantha wrote during the last months of senior kindergarten (from February 1982 to June 1982). I have divided the texts into three groups based on Samantha's evolving notions of genre and the analysis proceeds chronologically within each group.

SAMANTHA MAKING THINGS

The "book" has been Samantha's favorite genre in the sense that she has produced a large number of such books and often initiated this project in play with her sister and friends. An early example is shown in Figure 6.2.

Here Samantha appropriates certain mostly formal features of the genre "book": A title page, a written title with capital letters, stapled sheets of pages with alternating pagination, and the left-to-right, top-to-bottom directionality required of book "content." The content of this book, however, consists of a smile-face schema, repeated with minor modifications and embellishments, such as with or without glasses, happy or sad facial configurations, varying sizes, etc. Samantha's centering the title in large letters on the title page and her careful placement of smile faces on the following pages reflect her concern with visual orientation and balance. This book may well constitute what Gundlach (1982a) calls a "mixed medium" and illustrates his claim that children first use writing as a "bridge" to extend functions already served by other, more established semiotic activities.

The composing pattern here does closely resemble the way Samantha draws. Typically she divides the available space up mentally into smaller chunks, usually horizontal or vertical thirds, and proceeds to fill that space with items, often repeated and unrelated to each other, from her graphic repertoire. Once when I asked her whether she knew ahead of time what she would draw, she said, "No, I just draw." This comment suggests little planning or intention beyond creating a visually appealing and balanced product, beyond acting as an artist. It is easy to see Samantha's "bridge" from drawing to writing here.

For Samantha, then, the genre "book," as she understands it, creates for her a particular kind of textual space or meaning potential to be realized. She participates in this "space" and proceeds to realize its potential initially with available options, in this case items from her graphic repertoire. Planning takes place at the global level, and the salient choice points define graphic options. The "right" amount of content is determined spatially and visually—so the product looks like a book.

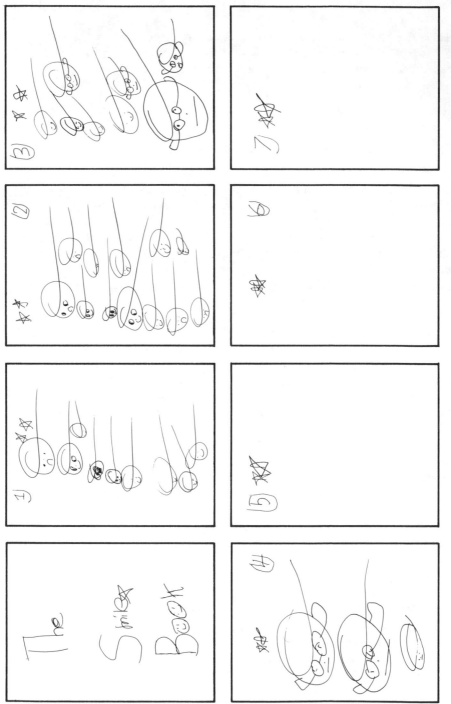

Figure 6.2. The Smile Book.

I observed this attention to visual orientation and balance in other ways, too. Samantha more frequently erases a word in order to correct the spacing than the spelling. When checking books out of the library, she copies and recopies the title until it "fits" between the lines. The sizes of houses or persons or flowers in her drawings are influenced more by their relation to the space on the paper than by their relation proportionately to each other. Things have to look "right" overall, with the parts relating more to the overall page boundaries and space than to each other.

In the spring of Samantha's kindergarten year, her teacher introduced a new, school-sponsored genre—the Draw and Write. The teacher provided special paper, with the top half empty and thus available for drawing, the bottom half lined and thus available for writing. Students initially were encouraged to draw first and then to write words, simple sentences, and little stories. At times a specific assignment was made, but more frequently students were instructed to write "anything" and were allowed 15–20 minutes to do so. The teacher's main function was to provide spelling assistance (apparently her primary pedagogical purpose) and generally to praise all efforts. The texts then went home in the Friday Folder with no other response, either oral or written.

Samantha structures these vague Draw and Write tasks in several ways. The most salient requirement of this genre, as Samantha herself informed me directly, is length. She said that if students didn't write "enough," the teacher told them to do more. For Samantha "enough" comes to mean three lines, each filled from left to right. These lines are unrelated to the requirements of any discernable communicative situation. They do not address true functional text points. Rather they are canonical text parts, invoked regardless of purpose, context, and circumstance. At this point in Samantha's growth as a writer, a text is a text for her only if it has three parts, and as we shall shortly see, she writes a great number of these **canonical tripartite texts** (cf. Nystrand and Himley, 1984).

In this first Draw and Write (see Figure 6.3), the orthographic items are derived in part from a story in one of Samantha's readers in which a rat and a kitten become friends. In both texts Samantha begins at the top, left-hand margin and lays out a sequence of lexical items. Here the start of each line inevitably defines a choice point defining syntactic options for Samantha; she begins a new sentence at the start of each line even if she has not completed the sentence in the previous line. The text is elaborated for the first two lines via orthographic repetition—reminiscent of the elaboration via repeated graphic schema in the book. The first two lines filled, Samantha begins to cast items into syntactic form, but when she hits the end of the requisite third line, she stops. Perhaps laying out the items orthographically generates a kind of semantic field, and perhaps from an overlap of such fields

Figure 6.3. The rat and baby texts.

an image or narrative begins to burgeon. Or perhaps the line begins to elaborate the narrative or imagistic potential suggested in the drawing. At any rate, it appears to have emerged while writing; it was not planned.

In both texts, too, it appears that Samantha's purpose primarily is to act like a student and to fulfill a class assignment—and to do so within her understanding of the Draw and Write genre. In effect, the textual choice points that seem salient to her are defined by the start of each line, and her options include building up graphically, if not semantically or syntactically, a written language text by laying out orthographic items. The shift in the third line toward syntactic relationships among the items and toward semantic content suggests growth (i.e., the discovery of a new option) and her concomitant attention to a higher level of text functioning—a transition that may have been facilitated by the three-line length requirement of the genre, as it pulls the text forward. The genre allows Samantha to stabilize her knowledge (lexical items, spelling) as well as to stretch a little (beginning syntax, evolving purpose). That is, in exploring new options she redefines text points, which in turn define new options.

In sum, the genre of these early formal texts defines for Samantha a sequence of semiotic choice points for her to negotiate:

1. Pseudogenres defined by arbitrary length requirements, e.g., an appropriate number of pages for a book, three lines for a Draw and Write;
2. The start of each line regardless of syntax.

In negotiating with these choice points, her text options include elaborations within these graphic and formal parameters, i.e., repeated graphic or orthographic items are laid out visually more than syntactically or semantically.

SAMANTHA SAYING SOMETHING

Samantha did the Draw and Write shown in Figure 6.4 at home with her mother's help, and it represents a beginning shift from merely formal concerns (that a text look like a particular written product) toward communicative ones (that a text say something). As the teacher had not specified a subject matter, Samantha's mother suggested that she write about the circus the family had seen over the weekend. When they had left the circus, her mother had asked the children what part they had liked best, and Samantha had preferred the scene depicted in the drawing—a man on a bike balancing on a tightrope with a lady in a cage attached below. Together they wrote the text, which succinctly summarizes who did what when. The second t-unit—"and we had popcorn"—adds an elaborative detail that fills out the text to the requisite three lines and also replays the syntactic/semantic pattern of the first t-unit. Unlike the previous text, her sentences span more than one line; choice points are more fully syntactic here.

Figure 6.4. "We went to the circus."

This text shows her experimentation with a new text option—the written language sentence—and illustrates a new act for the writer—saying something to someone. The form and function (a short, declarative sentence that sums up or asserts something for a public yet immediate audience) resembles strongly Samantha's spoken language discourse style in Show and Tell and in conversation with certain adults, and thus suggests yet another "bridge" into writing. This choice point requires planning at a higher textual level.

The drawing illustrates the written language text—two versions of the same idea. The relationship of the drawing to the written text in the earlier two Drawing and Write examples was much more ambiguous, with a developed drawing and a sketchy, unfinished text. Here both drawing and text could stand separately, with the drawing depicting a particular scene and the written text summing up the whole event. With her mother's help, Samantha has come to understand a new way to realize the meaning potential of the Draw and Write, and her negotiation of textual space is orthographic as well as graphic, syntactic as well as lexical, communicative as well as citational.

Three days later at school Samantha wrote the text shown in Figure 6.5 all on her own—a writing episode I observed. She drew the three parts of the drawing first: The stick figure and notes on the left, the nested and three-tiered building on the right, the smaller stick figure in the middle with the final notes. The first two t-units of the written text, apparently planned one t-unit at a time, comment on the drawing—that is, they say something

Figure 6.5. "I can make music."

about the drawings, by asserting *who* is singing and that *the* building is shaking. They provide comments on the topics depicted in the drawing. It may well be the length requirement of the genre that pulls Samantha on; as she apparently had nothing further to say about the drawing after completing line 3, she reverts to an old strategy—laying out lexical items—but this time in syntactic form. She took the third t-unit from the words and figures on the calendar board in the front of the classroom and then concatenated them to make a rather anomalous sentence. The proposition that emerges from these words does not really make sense though it is grammatical.

Leaning back in her chair, Samantha reread the text aloud, and Eileen, sitting next to her, commented, "That doesn't make sense." Samantha did not respond and appeared indifferent to that implicit textual criterion. While the text does cohere in relation to the drawing, the three sentences taken together, as fluent reader would expect, do not. [The reader may note similarities here between Samantha's idiosyncratic relation of text and graphic, on the one hand, and Paul Bissex's idiosyncratic word segmentation as discussed in Chapter 8, on the other hand. In each case, there is a mismatch between what the writer does and what readers expect.] As she had done earlier with words, Samantha now lays out sentences in visual, but not semantic sequence.

The composing strategy in the Draw and Write shown in Figure 6.6 resembles the earlier ones: Samantha fills her requisite three lines by asserting the role of the rabbit at Easter. The first part of the text sums up a major feature of the Easter holiday in a rather formal register, as Samantha

Figure 6.6. "The rabbit can bring eggs."

might explain it in a Show-and-Tell context, and the heavily drawn period suggests that that was all Samantha had planned to say and that it constitutes the "text." But it is too short, not meeting the genre requirement of three lines—a requirement that draws the writer forward. Driven by the syntactic–semantic momentum of the first part, Samantha "invents" a new object [flowers] for the rabbit to bring on a new holiday [Violet Day]. Neither her teacher nor her mother can explain the reference to Violet Day. When I asked Samantha herself, she grinned sheepishly and merely shrugged. In a sense, it is the genre, not Samantha, speaking. To complete the assignment—to fulfill the genre requirements as she interprets them— Samantha introduces new content consistent with the syntactic–semantic pattern already established.

The Draw and Write shown in Figure 6.7 was done in a period when the kindergarten teacher had been discussing butterflies with the students, and the class together had generated a chart-board story:

> The Butterfly
>
> Butterflies are pretty.
> Butterflies have four wings.
> First they lay eggs ... *etc.*

For the Draw-and-Write period, the teacher requested that students either write an original story about butterflies or take a part of the class-written story.

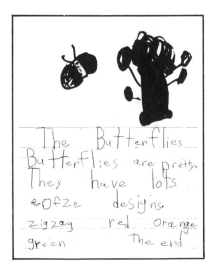

Figure 6.7. The butterflies."

I joined Samantha and a few of her classmates at the table as they began
the assignment. Samantha wrote the title and then the first line quickly,
apparently copying it from the chart board. She paused, looked around the
room and commented to me, "Mrs. C. tells you to write more if it's not long
enough."

Although I typically observed more than participated when Samantha
wrote, this time I prompted her by asking, "What makes butterflies pretty?"
She immediately replied, "They have lots of designs." She then began
writing, without further prompting from me, realizing immediately that I
had helped her with material for the next line. She asked me for spelling
assistance on "they," "lots," and "designs." She wrote word by word, pausing
frequently to chat, commenting that her favorite part of writing was putting
"The End" at the bottom of the page. The anomalous "oefze" construction
seems to have resulted from her somehow adding the plural marker from
"designs" to the "of"—evidence of her producing words and inflectional
markers separately (a salience of parts even within words). After a brief
discussion about periods, led by this overly persistent researcher, Samantha
independently added the words at the bottom of the page, requesting
spelling assistance on all but "red." These words apparently elaborate
further on the "pretty" and "design" topic. When she finished, she drew a
multicolored butterfly and a tree at the top of the paper.

Three text elaboration strategies are at work here: (1) copying text, (2)
making a new assertion, and (3) laying out key lexical items to fill up the
lines. The text exceeds her three line requirement—the page itself is filled.
My simple prompt question indicates that the hesitation for Samantha was
not a problem with knowledge of butterflies or with generating language,
but rather with writing, with how to make meaning within the con-
straints/potentials of this *particular* medium. She can lay out/spell words,
she can assert things, but she is still unsure of how and why to create
particular written texts/genres.

In sum, the genre of Draw and Write takes on a new dimension for
Samantha when she "bridges" from her spoken language discourse patterns,
and these texts represent a kind of three-way "mixed medium" of drawing,
speaking, and writing. The choice points are further differentiated, and her
range of text-creating options has grown:

1. Arbitrary requirements for length continue to define key choice points
   and draw the text forward in these three cases;
2. Text elaboration is now planned at the t-unit level and exhibits the
   form and function of Samantha's spoken discourse summational pattern;
3. If an assertion fills less than the requisite three lines, further text

elaboration picks up on and extends the syntactic and semantic
possibilities of the major t-unit and often includes the invention of
new but similar information;

4. Samantha's text options extend beyond formal text features to functional text structures which "say something."

I find the invented material ["March day is shamrock day"; "flowers and for
Violet Day"] particularly striking. Consider alternatives: Samantha might
have discussed what she does on Easter or how she likes eggs or when she
decorates them—any number of events that might relate to Easter and its
rituals. In the other text Samantha might have said more about the singing
person or the shaking building—or made many other sorts of claims. Instead
she strove to complete the text with imaginative, invented "days." Conceiv-
ably this results from her still evolving understanding of written language
genres and from her still vague sense that written language texts are about
certain kinds of things and make certain kinds of claims, claims that belong
to the universe of "fictive discourse" (cf. B.H. Smith, 1978) and are
impersonal and invented. I wonder, that is, if her choices here reflect her
nascent notions of the *particular* medium of written language and its genres
and their *particular* ways of making meaning.

SAMANTHA CREATING TEXTS

In the Draw and Write shown in Figure 6.8, Samantha not only fulfills an
assignment and fills the lines but also tells a tale. This intention is focused
and shifts her attention from merely formal features to the features of
mature narrative. Experience with the Draw and Write may have encouraged, even enabled, Samantha to stretch a bit beyond her visual and formal
approach to making texts. The text here portrays a typical event from
Samantha's everyday social life, but it begins to exhibit features more
characteristic of fictive than natural discourse. This is not just Samantha
recounting in conversational style a time she asked Tracy to play with her:
She is becoming more deeply aware of text possibilities. The story switches
perspective back and forth between the characters, there is reported
dialogue, and the "Samantha/I" double subject form suggests a waffling
between a third- and a first-person narrator. These features suggest a shift
from the social act of telling an anecdote (natural discourse) to the act of
telling a tale (fictive discourse). The momentum of the tale draws the text
beyond the three-line length of earlier texts. Planning must have occurred
at the genre level of deciding to tell a specific tale so that the parts here
mediate the whole—they combine integratively, not incrementally. It is also

Figure 6.8. "I met Tracy."

interesting to note that the "content" consists of combined and recombined words—a pattern strikingly reminiscent of the combined and recombined smile faces of The Smile Book. This pattern is now directed, however, in terms of narrative requirements, not spatial ones. The text is shaped by Samantha's growing understanding of how to compose in the genre of written narrative.

The text of the Easter Bunny Letter (see Figure 6.9) arose out of a situation at home. Each Easter Samantha and her older sister left a note for the Easter Bunny in an empty basket. In the morning they always awoke to a filled basket with the note having been "delivered." This particular Easter, Samantha had been bothered by her sister's taunting accusation that the Easter Bunny wasn't real. Troubled by this possibility, she discussed it with

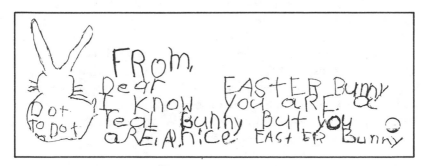

Figure 6.9. "Dear Easter Bunny."

Figure 6.10. "The bunnies went out to play with other friends."

her mother, who assured her that her sister was wrong and that the Easter Bunny was indeed real. In the genre of a letter—and a very formal one at that, written to an important public figure—Samantha acts like a letter writer and asserts her belief in the Easter Bunny's existence and her confidence in his good character. This letter exhibits essential features of the mature genre: it has a salutation [Dear Easter Bunny] and a closing [From, Samantha Freeland]. She also follows, though in reverse order, the formal structure of a letter. The tone is formal and polite, and all the extra periods and attempts at cursive further suggest how Samantha seeks to use all appropriate written language conventions. After all, she has an important audience, the Easter Bunny—who she truly believes is real—and an important statement to make. Unlike the above narrative, this text clearly belongs more within the realm of natural discourse—someone ("I") saying something in a particular situation to a specific audience ("you").

This final text, written four months after The Smile Book, reveals Samantha's growth as a writer, her shift from texts informed primarily by the formal features and choice points of the genre, toward texts informed by the formal, substantive, and functional features of the genre (see Figure 6.10).

Samantha and two of her friends had been experimenting with writing books in the kindergarten class (copying directly, adapting a specific book) so her teacher provided them with a blank "book" that consisted of a construction paper cover with a sheet of typing paper stapled inside. The title for this text on the cover reads "Bunnes in the trees." Apparently on her own, Samantha had written the following first line in the book:

The Funnes wet out to Play with some other people Then

The next day the teacher returned the books for the children to complete. Because one of her friends had just returned to class, Samantha immediately asked her to join in the project and volunteered to recopy the text so far into her friend's book. The friend agreed. Once the recopying was completed, Samantha traced and retraced the word "Then"—apparently a key text point. Samantha traced and traced. I asked her if she had any idea what to do next, and she said no and eagerly accepted another friend's invitation to work together on the hardest puzzle in the world. Then it was clean-up time, and as Samantha put the book away, I again asked if she knew what she'd write next: She shrugged and said no. Samantha never finished the book at school, and it ended up at home in a stack of papers that her mother saved for me in the kitchen. On her own, Samantha decided to finish the text: She first changed "people" to "friends," added the second t-unit, and drew the schematic pictures of bunny heads and park play equipment. She happily brought the finished product to school and read it aloud at Show and Tell.

Bunnies, Samantha had once told me, were her favorite things to write about though this is the only text I have in which she actually did, except for the Letter to the Easter Bunny. So I am not surprised that they were the first characters to pop into Samantha's head when she was given the book. Her text and her text elaborations here suggest Samantha's evolving interpretation of the genre "book." Clearly this genre belongs to the universe of fictive discourse—the suspension of the particularity and contextuality of natural discourse. Samantha begins with invented and imaginative characters and places them in two rather generic locales [the trees, the park]. This is the anytime–anywhere world of the imagination: The events are decontextualized (in the sense that this is not a particular park), dehistoricized (in the sense that this could occur anytime, not just last Tuesday), and depersonalized. These are features, according to B. H. Smith (1978), of fictive discourse, and, of course, appropriate to the genre she is working in.

Samantha plays in the park often with friends, and surely she could recount anecdotes about what she and her friends do there. The problem is not content or knowledge of playing in parks. Her difficulty in elaborating text seems to result more from Samantha's vague sense of relevant choice points and appropriate text options related to fictive characters acting in a fictive world and telling a tale. This is not to disparage her efforts; indeed it is evidence of a child's learning to work, to make meaning within a new medium/genre.

Samantha finally elaborates the written version of the text by recombining the agents/actions from the first t-unit into a slightly modified version in the second t-unit. "Bunnes" collapses into the referential pronoun "they," and "play" expands into "in the park." The rest of the meaning potential is realized graphically as Samantha has divided the remaining space into thirds and filled the middle third with three items of play equipment, the bottom third with three highly stylized and balanced bunny heads. That strategy is familiar by now. Here, however, the drawings supplement the written text. Indeed, the drawings mark both topic [bunnies] and comment [play in the park]. The text—both written and graphic—is highly summative and communicatively efficient. Even though Samantha has yet to learn how to unpack that image into narrative, it nonetheless highlights agent and action. Here we see the beginnings of her experiments with a fully mature genre, and we see how these initiatives probe certain new choice points involving new text options.

In sum, in these last three texts (last logically, not chronologically), Samantha experiments with the functional options and constraints of a mature genre and negotiates more abstract textual choice points:

1. Length continues to be salient as Samantha fulfills the writing task by filling the available space;
2. Unlike those of early, formal texts, the salient choice points for Samantha transcend superficial play with a particular social and interpretive role (e.g., pretending to be a writer, making "books") and begin to encompass the integral concerns of functional texts—writing a story about something, writing a letter to someone. That is to say, Samantha exercises text options not only at the level of interpretive role and genre but also of topic and comment; she is learning how to write.
3. The initial choice of genre shapes more particular choices along the way;
4. One sees the beginnings of Samantha's growing understanding of the forms and functions of various genres;
5. Text elaboration occurs within the resources of written language

CONCLUSION

How and *why* does a child learn to write? For Samantha, the effect of genre is clearly generative. Her notion of how a particular genre works—the social role the writer adopts, the interpretive act she performs, the situations that give rise to the genre, the discourse features—defines for her a series of textual choice points which she negotiates as she creates text. First, understanding primarily formal textual features, Samantha attends to decisions about overall design and about filling the appropriate length with "content," usually from her repertoire of graphic and orthographic items. Samantha then tests the possibilities of topic and comment for "saying something," and writes texts that resemble her spoken language pattern in public discourse situations. In the last three texts, we see the beginnings of more functional genres as Samantha begins to use the resources of written language for new ways to mean—to tell a tale, to write a letter to an important public figure, and to produce a children's story book. She moves from texts that "look like" certain genres to texts that "say something" and then to texts that mean solely within the resources of written language.

This growth is facilitated by her evolving notions of genre. To experiment with a genre is a way to create new situations, to learn new ways to make meaning and to interpret events and to *be*. In a sense, genre is like the hub of a wheel, related to and bringing together the several aspects of writing. Once Samantha comes to understand the genre of children's books, for example, she also comes to understand how to create fictive discourse, how to interpret and present the world in that way, how to negotiate the choice points with appropriate text-creating options—in other words, how to *be* an author. That is a beginning for Samantha in understanding what the genre offers.

7

Where Do the Spaces Go? The Development of Word Segmentation in the Bissex Texts

INTRODUCTION

Glenda Bissex's *Gnys at Wrk: A Child Learns to Write and Read* (1980) is the story and case study of how the author's son Paul learned to write and read, processes that Bissex observed over a span of 6 years. The study is a benchmark largely because it was among the first case studies about children who learned to write before going to school (Read, 1982), and also because it corroborated much extant literature on early written language development, for example early work of Luria (1929/1978) on the semiotic character of children's scribbles, and Read's (1975) work on invented spelling.

One aspect of Paul's writing, which Bissex describes in great detail in her case study but which has never been systematically researched, is the development of word segmentation in children's writing. At first, Paul put no spaces at all between words: EFUKANOPNKAZIWILGEVUAKANOPENR, for example, is the nonstop text which he writes at age 5;2 to say, "If you can open cans, I will give you a can opener." This period of no spaces—or equal spaces, if you will—is actually preceded by a period of irregular spacing (age 5;1 to 5;5) and then followed by another period (age 5;5 to 6;5) of segmentation by dots, e.g., PAULZ.HOZ.PLANF.ELD.VRMAT [Paul's house, Plainfield, Vermont]. At the end of this latter period, the dots drop away like training wheels from a bike, and there emerges a reasonably mature orthography, replete with punctuation and upper- and lowercase distinctions.

The purpose of the study reported in this chapter is to examine the development of word segmentation in the early Bissex texts and to describe certain patterns which seem evident. I have chosen to use the Bissex texts, with the author's permission, largely because the author has meticulously collected, described, and chronicled everything. Studying these texts has the additional advantage that, because Paul learned to write before starting school and especially because he was given no instruction in handwriting, his texts provide an excellent opportunity to examine the kinds of spontaneous intuitions a writer makes about how and where to space written text.

INITIAL IMPRESSIONS

I first examined the original Bissex texts in the summer of 1981, when I visited the Bissexes at their home in Plainfield, Vermont, for that purpose. The very first texts (age 5;1) were typed, not handwritten, and they were as unspaced as the first handwritten texts. But some intuitions about word segmentation do seem evident as early as the third text (see Figure 7.1: Text 1) written at age 5;1, where the morpheme -*S* seems to be separated from the name PAUL. Nonetheless, in first examining the texts from the first 2 months—six in all—I was struck not only by unconventional word segmentation but also by unconventional treatment of words at the ends of lines, e.g., Text 4 where TALAFON and BOOTH are both split as the edge of the page dictates.

At age 5;2 the mother commented to Paul that writers normally put spaces between words, and the texts after age 5;2 reflect this observation. Indeed, at age 5;5 Paul formalizes this advice by marking word boundaries not just with spaces (i.e., by leaving something out) but with dots (i.e., by actually putting something in as noted above). During this period, which lasts a year, the spacing within words becomes increasingly irregular—even more so than during the pre-dot period. Paul masters the spaces between words more easily than the spaces within. But then when the dots do drop away—12 months after they appear and 6 months after he begins first grade—the spacing both between and within words has become quite regular, and the orthography shows other developments as well, including punctuation, genre conventions such as letter form, and upper- and lower-

Figure 7.1: Text 1

Figure 7.1: Text 2

Figure 7.1: Text 3

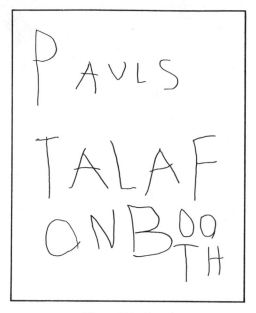

Figure 7.1: Text 4

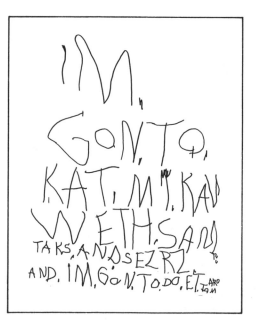

Figure 7.1: Text 5

Figure 7.1: Text 6

Figure 7.1: Text 7

Figure 7.1: Text 8 (From Bissex, 1980. Reprinted by permission.)

Figure 7.1: Text 9

Figure 7.1: Text 10

Figure 7.1: Text 11

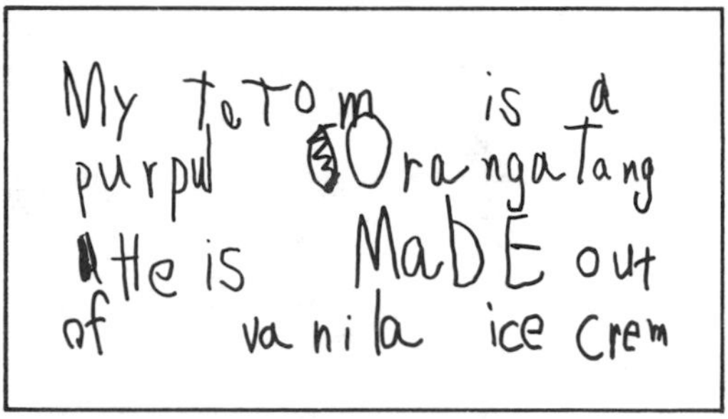
My TeTOm is a
purpul Orangatang
He is MaDE out
of vanila ice Crem

Figure 7.1: Text 12

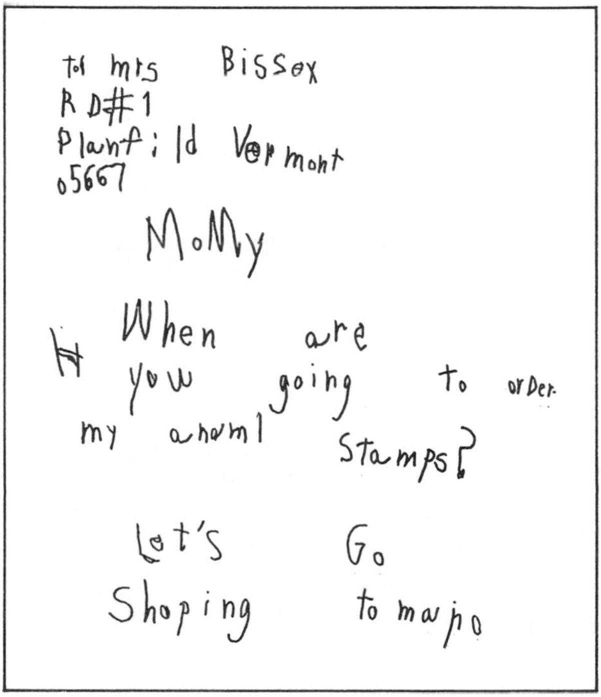
To mrs Bissex
RD#1
Planfild Vermont
05667
MoMy
When are
you going to orDer
my anaml Stamps?
Let's Go
Shoping to mapo

Figure 7.1: Text 13

Figure 7.1: Text 14

Figure 7.1: Text 15 (From Bissex, 1980. Reprinted by permission.)

case distinctions (see Texts 13, 14, and 15). When I first saw the texts, I suspected that the dots were Paul's way to control boundaries, as a kind of place holder, so that he might more easily address the more complicated problems of orthography within words. I decided to examine the texts more closely. I was especially interested in uncovering patterns of development in spacing between and within words. I would test my intuition that spacing between words occurs before mastery of spacing between characters and that the spacing within words actually becomes more irregular before it normalizes.

TEXT SAMPLE

To proceed with my study, Bissex sent me, per my request, a random sample of one text a month written between ages 5;1 and 6;8. As things turned out there were many months missing, since Paul didn't write every month. Also, the pre-dot period lasted only a couple months, and the texts written during this period were never more than a couple words each, so I deliberately skewed my corpus of texts by using four texts from the first month in order to create approximately equal numbers of pre-dot, dot, and post-dot texts. I also added a text, published in the book, from Paul's work at age 8;3. Hence, the corpus of 15 texts is not entirely random but probably representative nonetheless.

Procedures

How to measure spaces between words in children's writing is not intuitively obvious. Reliable physical measurement with a ruler is impossible. Even if one might know where to place the ruler—at the bottom of the line where "A" and "H" are close, for example, or at the top of the line where the letters are not so close, or in the middle as a kind of compromise—one must first confront the reality that children don't always write in or on lines and certainly not on straight ones. They squiggle a lot. Some texts are small, others big. Most are highly irregular, e.g., becoming cramped as the writer squeezes letters into the edge of the page. As J. Martin (1967, 1971) concludes in experimental investigation of hesitation phenomena in speech, "one may as well use scorer judgments as physical measures to locate them, particularly since all the other usual types of hesitation . . . must be identified by listener judgment [Martin, 1971, p. 64]."

To estimate spaces in these texts, then, I asked two readers independently to examine each space in each text—including spaces both between and within words—and to score it blind for size on a scale of 1 (for very small) to 7 (for very big). I organized these texts randomly into booklets so that no two subjects read the texts in the same order. I instructed them to let their intuitions be their guide, and to try to be consistent for any given text. All readers in this preliminary investigation were college juniors at the University of Wisconsin-Madison and knew nothing of the purpose of study. They wrote their estimates in the spaces themselves as they read each text. My first trials with this procedure presented two problems. First, there was great variation from subject to subject; some people have bigger ideas of "big" than others. To solve the first problem, I normalized each subject's ratings by calculating the mean rating of spaces by each subject for each text and then adjusted each original estimate with exactly that increment which would force the text mean to 3.5, the midpoint on my Likert scale. In addition, subjects responded to the dots between words differently. Whereas some ignored the dots and rated each space with a single estimate, others actually rated the spaces on both sides of the dots, yielding two judgments between words instead of the desired one. When this happened, I eliminated such responses altogether from my data summary. I recorded the scores only of those readers who categorically regarded each space as a single space. Figures 7.3 to 7.5 present these data as histograms.

Results: Trials

Figure 7.2 actually depicts the mature orthography of one of the readers from the trials and provides an instructive contrast to Paul's developing orthography. To gain some sense of how adults print, I asked the readers to write (print) notes to each other, which they then exchanged and rated for spaces (further analysis of these samples is not presented in this chapter). The maturity of the orthography is evident here in both (a) prominent, regular word boundaries (i.e., the spaces between words are about twice as big as the spaces between characters), and (b) very little variability in within-word spacing. Paul's early texts stand in sharp contrast to this. Figure 7.3 charts Text 1 [a pre-dot period text written at age 5;1]. Figure 7.4 shows Text 6 [a dot-period text written at age age 5;9], and in this transitional text, we can see word boundaries emerging as the spaces between words clearly begin to exceed the spaces between characters. (At the end of the text, the spaces all become smaller: This results from Paul's cramming the last several words into the corner of the paper, a border he has not yet learned to navigate.)

Figure 7.5 shows Text 15 [a post-dot period text written at age 8;4]. Here we see the maturity of Paul's written text segmentation, which, as in the adult sample, shows regular spacing between characters, plus spacing

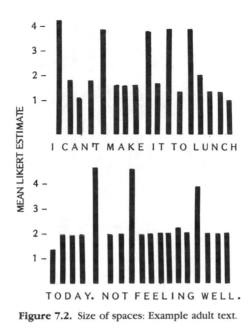

Figure 7.2. Size of spaces: Example adult text.

between words that is regularly about twice that of spacing between characters.

The direction of development is clear in these texts. Apparently undifferentiated at first in its spacing, Paul's orthography changes progressively in two fundamental ways. On the one hand, the spacing between characters becomes increasingly regular. On the other hand, the spacing between words becomes about twice as great as the spacing between characters. These parallel developments in word segmentation are analogous to other aspects of language development which progressively articulate **significant differences** and **minimal contrasts** (e.g., phonetic contrasts: Jakobson, 1968; semantic categorization and overgeneralization: E. Clark, 1975; or invented spelling: Read, 1971).

MAIN STUDY

To sum up, these histograms clearly depict development in word segmentation characterized by (a) an increasing contrast between *spaces between words* and *spaces between characters* and (b) an increasing regularity in the spacing within words.

These two orthographic developments are amenable to two sorts of statistical examination. The first deals with a simple ratio of *spaces between words* to *spaces between characters*. In this study we will call this con-

Text 1

Figure 7.3. Size of spaces: Pre-dot period text.

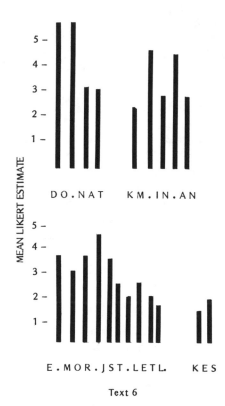

Text 6

Figure 7.4. Size of spaces: Dot period
text.

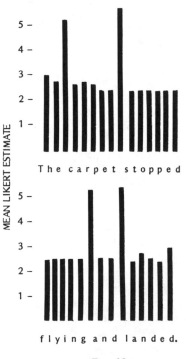

Text 15

Figure 7.5. Size of spaces: Post-dot
period text.

trast **the ratio of the means**, and in fully mature texts we will expect this ratio to be about 2:1. The other statistic is more complicated. In order to gauge the development of spacing between characters, it is necessary to measure the extent to which they are regular and consistent. Hence, instead of examining the extent to which there are differences in treatment means (as with analysis of variance), the issue of interest here is just the opposite: We need to measure the extent to which there is consistency or homogeneity among within-group variances (in this case spaces within words). In this study this variance is termed **grapholexical variance**, i.e., the variability among spaces within words. This use of variance as a descriptive statistic has occasionally been used to examine developmental issues (e.g., Birch and Lefford, 1967) and has great potential for the study of individual development over time.

To investigate the development of spacing in the Bissex texts, all 15 were randomly ordered into new booklets and presented to new readers, no two of whom read the texts in the same order. Two main hypotheses were tested. The first related to the ratio of the means and predicted that spaces between words would increasingly distinguish themselves from spaces within words. The second hypothesis had to do with spaces within words and predicted diminishing estimates of grapholexical variance. In this latter case, the null hypothesis was that there would be no consistency in within-word variance among all 15 texts; the experimental hypothesis was that this variance would decrease progressively from Text 1 to Text 15 and that only the later texts would exhibit no significant variability among spaces within words (i.e., the spaces would be homogeneous). The Box Test for Homogeneity of Variance (Box, 1953) was used for this latter analysis because of its robustness with nonnormal populations (Martin and Games, 1977), precisely the situation of a beginning writer's texts.[1]

Subjects

Subjects for the main study were 27 students in a summer course taught by Professor John Kean and sponsored jointly by the University of Wisconsin-Madison Department of English and Wisconsin Writing Project. The students were all experienced teachers, most of them English teachers, and about a third of them teachers of elementary language arts. I did not pay them, nor did they receive course credit for their participation. Nonetheless, they appeared to take the tasks quite seriously, and many asked for copies of the final report. I explained my project to them only by soliciting their "help in an experiment about how children learn to write." I did not tell them that all texts were written by the same child.

Procedures

I asked the readers to do three tasks:

1. Write down on a prepared form "what you think the child is trying to say."

2. Mark on a 9-point Likert scale "Are you sure?"

```
+------+------+------+------+------+------+------+------+
```

| I don't   I'm   I'm |
| know   pretty   certain |
| sure |

3. Evaluate each space—both between and within words—by writing a number from 1 (for very small) to 7 (for very big) in the space itself.

Much research has shown that reader comprehension is a major factor in reducing irregularity in any text (cf. Miller, 1956). In fact, one major definition of comprehension is the reduction of uncertainty (cf. Smith, 1971). For example, readers will often penetrate an otherwise illegible scrawl once they perceive the overall gist of the text. Hence, in order to investigate how reader comprehension might affect readers' estimates of the spaces, I counterbalanced the deciphering and space-estimating tasks so that half the subjects rated the spaces before they were given the form asking them to record what they thought the child was trying to say, as well as how sure they were of its meaning. The other half first tried to make sense of each text, and when they were done, they went on to rating spaces. It is impossible to know, of course, the extent to which the spaces-first subjects did not actually read the texts for meaning before they rated the spaces, but the group that completed the comprehension task first no doubt ignored the spaces altogether until they received instructions to rate them. The data analysis shows clear differences in the responses of the two groups.

Results

There was substantial subject loss. I eliminated the forms of subjects who, for one reason or another, did not rate all the spaces. I eliminated one subject's responses altogether because she had just started reading Bissex's book. In all, there were from 14 to 21 sets of responses to each text with the exception of Texts 10 ($N = 11$) and 11 ($N = 6$), where because of experimenter inadvertence only spaces-first subjects responded to Text 10 and only comprehension-first subjects responded to Text 11.

I first tested the possibility that the elementary school teachers might have a special advantage in reading children's writing by comparing the K-3 teachers' comprehension of the texts from that of other teachers. All comprehension scores were computed as the proportion of correctly deciphered words in each text. Synonyms were not accepted (and in fact none was suggested by any subject in interpreting any text). In Texts 1 and 4 the morpheme -s was counted as a word because an initial screening of the responses indicated that subjects' comprehension differed in these texts on this item. This initial comparison of elementary (K–3) and other teachers showed that the two groups did not differ significantly in terms of their comprehension of the texts. Hence, the elementary teachers' responses were not excluded from the remaining analyses.

Both experimental hypotheses were supported. On the one hand, the ratio of *spaces within words* to *spaces between words*, which is less than 1.0 in Text 1, progressively increases to almost 2.0 in Text 15 (see Figure 7.6). By contrast, the spacing within words becomes increasingly regular as we see in Figure 7.7, which shows progressively diminishing estimates of grapholexical variance.

These developments in orthography are reflected in reader comprehension and confidence about the meanings of the texts. Both comprehension and confidence increase as the spaces between words distinguish themselves from spaces within words and also as the spaces within words normalize. Obviously at the same time that Paul's orthography matures, other things normalize (notably spelling). Nonetheless, in terms of reader comprehension and confidence, spacing—both between and within words—accounts for 34.3% and 37.5%, respectively, of the variance. There are positive correlations between the ratio of the means and both comprehension and reader confidence[2] and negative correlations between grapholexical variance and both comprehension and reader confidence.[3] Curiously, in terms of comprehension the ratio of the means is nearly twice as important as grapholexical variance[4] whereas just the opposite is true of reader confidence: In terms of reader confidence, grapholexical variance is nearly twice as important as the ratio of the means.[5] In other words, comprehension relates more to the spaces between words whereas confidence about the texts' meanings relates more to the regularity of spacing within words.

Discussion

Obviously this study does not really measure the spaces in Paul's texts per se. *Rather, it assesses reader's attribution of qualities of text in terms of these spaces.* Hence, the ratio of the means is really a measure of readers' attribution of word boundaries, and grapholexical variance is really a statistical construct dealing with reader's attribution of orthographic coherence. And clearly these measures are appropriate since the spaces themselves have no linguistic or communicative value as mere physical, graphic vacancies.

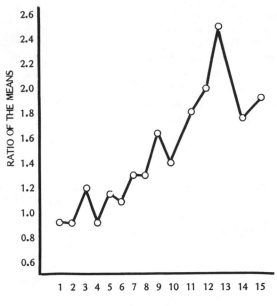

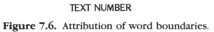

Figure 7.6. Attribution of word boundaries.

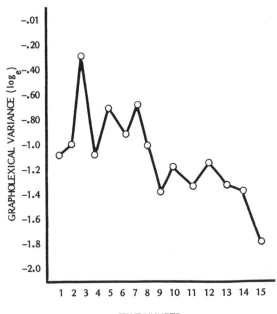

Figure 7.7. Variability among spaces within words.

Learning where the spaces go is a puzzle for Paul. But the dimensions of this puzzle are defined by the requirement that the texts must function in some context of use, i.e., they must be meaningful to fluent readers. For this reason the proper measures of this exchange are readers' attribution of word boundaries and orthographic coherence, which are valid signs of functioning texts. The spaces are as phenomenological as much as they are physical, and their valid measure is the reader's comprehension because it is this moment precisely when the writer finally speaks to the reader and the text must serve its communicative function.

When do readers attribute spaces to Paul's texts? We gain some insight into this question as we examine the responses of the spaces-first readers versus those of the comprehension-first readers. The spaces-first readers were far more aware of the spaces than the comprehension-first readers. Unlike the spaces-first readers, whose initial task was deliberately to focus on spaces, the comprehension-first readers made a deliberate first attempt at comprehension, and these readers tended more to overlook and hence underestimate what, to their counterparts, were more obvious graphic irregularities. Specifically, the variability of spacing within words figures into the responses of the spaces-first readers more prominently than those of the comprehension-first readers; this is true of reader comprehension[6] and especially reader confidence.[7] It is as if those readers who first read for meaning, compared to those readers who first estimated spaces, were largely unaware of the spaces within words. In and of itself, the variability of spacing within words is not a significant element in either the comprehension or confidence of these readers who first read for meaning though it clearly is for the spaces-first subjects.[8]

Yet reader comprehension is only half the story. The progressive clarity of Paul's texts results not just from reader comprehension but also from the development of Paul's orthography, and especially from the increasing synchronization of the former with the latter. The importance of this synchronization is evident in the pattern of word segmentation in the early texts. For example, there is evidence to suggest that Paul's working hypothesis about word segmentation in Text 1 [PAULSELEFIT] is syllabic (much like a later, dot-period text, PAULZ.HOZ.PLANF.ELD.VRMAT). When analyzed in this way, overall estimates of the ratio of the means for this text are 1.20,[9] and estimates of grapholexical variance are -1.42.[10] These revised values for the ratio of the means are comparable to those for the more advanced texts 5 and 6, and for grapholexical variance texts 9 and 12. Reanalysis of Text 2 supports the syllabic hypothesis in this text too. These results highlight the sort of linguistic intelligence involved in these apparently aberrant texts at the same time that they explain fluent readers' difficulties with them. Much like invented spellings, the problem is not that the spacing is unpatterned, only that Paul's initial segmentation of text is at odds with readers' expectations. The development of Paul's orthography is largely a matter of his learning to synchronize resources of text with readers' expectations for orthographic coherence.

For Rommetveit (1979), words "emerge" in the process of reading. A word is "a very complex and hierarchically organized *process* [emphasis in the original]" whereby the meaning potential of the text is activated by what the reader knows and expects. Rommetveit draws this conclusion from his own research on the stereoscopic presentation of words, as well as from Kolers' (1965) research on bilinguals' recall of mixed French and English words. Following this line of reasoning, we see that readers attribute specifically orthographic spaces to Paul's texts when, in comprehending his texts, they are able to transform what might otherwise be empty perceptual forms or visual arrays of letters into meaningful semiotic forms, or words— that is, when the dominance of perceptual form over meaning is inverted, and meaning dominates perceptual form. The reader is aware of the word not as a visual array but rather as a meaningful semiotic form, a sign.

In "The Structure of Textual Space [1982c]," I make a similar distinction:

> If I board a train in Lisbon and overhear a conversation, I will not understand it. For me this talk is impenetrable. If I board a train in Chicago or London, however, I may well find myself absorbed in the conversation of others—even if I do not mean to listen. If the conversation intrigues me, only such radical action as a change of seat or departure from the train can prevent my silent participation in this talk. I cannot understand talk in Lisbon even if I need to, whereas in Chicago I am an unwitting participant even if I mean not to be.
>
> In Lisbon, speakers share a certain space from which I am effectively excluded. Though not material or physical, this space is quite real, as my exclusion from the conversation clearly shows. The space is textual; and to move around and get on in it, one clearly needs to know its rules and distinctive features.
>
> Participation in textual space is characterized for the participants by a "trans-parency" of language. . . . In Chicago I am aware of meaning, not text; in Lisbon I am aware of text, not meaning: Words of a truly foreign tongue are either ambiguous or opaque—depending on how urgently I need to understand them [p. 75].

In this essay I go on to show how the International Harvester logo can be interpreted either verbally or visually. Interpreted verbally (the usual way), readers read the initials "I.H."; interpreted visually, viewers see a tractor. In the first instance, a message emerges; in the second instance, an image emerges. In both cases a figure of meaning emerges in contrast to the ground of its interpretation. In the final analysis the figure that stands out (image or message) does so largely as a result of the context (visual or verbal) in which it is set. Plainly put, "what you see" depends on "how you look."

We may now understand where the spaces go. Writers elaborate words orthographically literally by clustering letters and appropriately segmenting words. It is the purpose of the spaces between the words—the blanks—to work as ground against which these clusters—the verbal figures of words— may emerge. The spaces between words, regularly twice as large as the spaces within words, provide readers with a uniquely orthographic context, cuing them to interpret the forms verbally as words, not visually as images. The purpose of the spacing is nothing less than to index an entire semiotic system.

In his classic study of the acquisition of diagonality, David Olson (1970) contrasts performatory and perceptual acts in terms of the development of just such concept systems. He notes that "it is the performatory acts in various media that confront the individual with the alternatives for which he then select[s] further information. It is this performatory activity, therefore, that provides the occasions for the radical elaboration of the perceptual world [p. 201]." Following this line of reasoning it is very tempting to speculate that the steady rise in the ratio of the means accompanied by the decline in grapholexical variance actually traces the development of Paul's concept of word in his explorations of the written medium. This line of reasoning makes sense, of course, if one thinks of *word* not as a lower-level sentence constituent nor as a bundle of semantic features but rather, in Halliday's (1978) terms, as one aspect of the textual function of language. That is, the effective management of word boundaries and grapholexical variance are part of how the writer learns to manage the written text-forming component of the linguistic system. In this respect words are learned as a way of spacing written text—not as embodiments of meaning but rather as enablers of meaning. They are the orthographic resources available to writers for accomplishing the interpersonal and ideational functions of language.

If we view writing as a process of elaborating possibilities, associative paths, and interpretive contexts, we see that this process of text elaboration has two general parts for the writer: (a) recognizing when and where elaboration is possible, i.e., understanding the choice points of written discourse; and (b) understanding the options for elaboration which are available at each choice point. In negotiating choice points with appropriate text options, the writer effectively elaborates certain associative paths rather than others and in so doing prompts certain reader expectations rather than others. In this way, the writer creates and builds up a uniquely textual space.

To sum up: Paul's texts become increasingly clear to the extent that the readers endeavor to understand them. Compared to their counterparts who first assessed the spaces, those readers who first read the texts for meaning tended to "see through them" and as a result underestimated the variability of spacing within words. To the extent that readers were aware of meaning and not text, the texts were "transparent." This transparency depended not only on how the readers approached the texts, however, but also on the extent to which their expectations were matched by Paul's orthography. Significantly, this phenomenal dependency of writer and reader speaks to the reciprocity of their respective roles, i.e., to their joint participation in a common textual space.

NOTES

[1]The Box Test was used as follows. First, it was used to test only spaces within words since the object of the analysis was to assess homogeneity of variance within this particular category. After between-word data were deleted from the original data set, each remaining group was randomly divided into groups of three observations. This was accomplished by "shuffling" each group into a new, randomly ordered group and then dividing this new group into subsamples of three observations each. Variance estimates were then calculated for each of the three subsamples, and each estimate was converted into $\log_e$. This conversion permitted comparisons of variances, which otherwise cannot be compared. The Box test is then conducted as a straightforward ANOVA using the $\log_e$ values as observations.

I am indebted to Dr. Dale Liebert of the Wisconsin Center for Education Research for his assistance in writing the computer subroutine that accomplished the shuffle.

[2]COMPREHENSION: $r = .596$; $F(1, 13) = 7.12$; $p = .018$; CONFIDENCE: $r = .57$; $F(1, 13) = 9.75$; $p = .026$

[3]COMPREHENSION: $r = -.56$; $F(1, 13) = 5.83$; $p = .030$; CONFIDENCE: $r = -.62$; $F(1, 13) = 7.92$; $p = .014$

[4]In terms of comprehension, the ratio of the means and grapholexical variance account for 13.005% versus 8.49% of the variance respectively.

[5]In terms of reader confidence, the ratio of the means and grapholexical variance account for 14.09% versus 8.78% of the variance respectively.

[6]SPACES-FIRST READERS: $r = -.53$; $F(1, 12) = 4.69$; $p = .049$; COMPREHENSION-FIRST READERS: $r = -.50$; $F(1, 12) = 4.01$; $p = .066$

[7]SPACES-FIRST READERS: $r = -.61$; $F(1, 12) = 9.62$; $p = .019$; COMPREHENSION-FIRST READERS: $r = -.45$; $F(1, 12) = 3.07$; $p = .102$.

[8]Multiple regressions estimating the contribution of grapholexical variance and the ratio of the means to reader comprehension and confidence are each significant for spaces-first readers [COMPREHENSION: $r^2 = .421$; $F(2, 11) = 3.996$; $p = .0488$; CONFIDENCE: $r^2 = .473$; $F(2, 11) = 4.927$; $p = .0293$] but not in either case for comprehension-first readers [COMPREHENSION: $r^2 = .343$; $F(2, 11) = 2.877$; $p = .098$; CONFIDENCE: $r^2 = .375$; $F(2, 11) = 3.304$; $p = .074$].

[9]For all subjects, 1.20; for spaces-first subjects, 1.21; and for comprehension-first subjects 1.196.

[10]For all subjects, -1.42; for spaces-first subjects, -1.21; and for comprehension-first subjects, -1.87.

8

Learning to Write by Talking about Writing: A Summary of Research on Intensive Peer Review in Expository Writing Instruction at the University of Wisconsin-Madison

INTRODUCTION

In this chapter we move from the problems of young writers to those of adults. We gain special access to the writing development of college freshmen as we examine their writing for each other and their discussions with each other about this writing. In this situation, known as peer conferencing or intensive peer review, we see that adult learners confront many of the same problems as their younger peers. Though the intricacies of the written medium, especially orthography, do not present major hurdles for adult writers, they must nonetheless experiment with text options that are essentially defined by the need for reciprocity at the levels of topic, comment, and genre.

WHAT IS INTENSIVE PEER REVIEW?

Intensive peer review is a method of teaching expository writing developed by Professor A. N. Doane and now used extensively in Freshman Expository Writing at the University of Wisconsin-Madison. Students in these so-called writing studios meet regularly in groups of four or five, and the same groups meet three times a week over the course of the term for the purpose of sharing and critiquing each other's writing. The instructor assigns few if any topics and gives students no checklists to use in monitoring their discussion. Rather, students keep journals and prepare pieces of exposition from these notebooks for presentation to classmates at every class meeting. Students are required to prepare a new paper or a substantial revision for each class. They are instructed to consider the extent to which the author achieves his or her purpose; they are to avoid checking spelling, punctuation, and usage; and they are required to provide each member of their group with a photocopy of their work. Periodically the instructor collects the best papers from each student for evaluation, but she does relatively little direct instruction, and intervention in these groups is minimal.

The use of peer review is not new to writing instruction. The idea dates back at least to James Moffett's *Teaching the Universe of Discourse* (1968a); other references include Beaven, 1977; Benson, 1979; Britton, 1971; Bruffee, 1973, 1984; Buxton, 1975; Elbow, 1973; Fox, 1980; Gebhardt, 1980; Gere and Stevens, 1985; Gere and Abbott, 1985; Hawkins, 1976; Murray, 1969; Nystrand, 1983b; Nystrand and Doane, in preparation; Zoellner, 1969. This research finds that peer work contributes to gains in critical thinking, organization, and appropriateness (Lagana, 1973); revision (Benson, 1979); attention to prewriting and increased awareness of one's own writing processes (Nystrand, 1983b); and writer confidence (Fox, 1980).

What accounts for the effectiveness of peer review? Generally, its practice is consistent with what is known about effective response to student writing. For example, Moffett originally justified the method in pragmatic terms as "the only way, short of tutorial, to provide individual students enough experience and feedback [1968b, p. 12]." Even more important, students receive feedback on drafts in process, not just after they have completed their final (or only) draft (cf. Beach, 1979), and in this respect the interactive processes of peer review are very much like those of a writing conference (Freedman, 1981). Peer review also broadens the kind of feedback that students receive, and substantial research shows that writers benefit from more than just teacher comments (Freedman and Sperling, 1985; Gere and Stevens, 1985; Hillocks, 1982). Furthermore, because teachers respond to student writing in several different roles (e.g., judge, evaluator, interested reader, copy editor; cf. Britton et al., 1975), they are not always as consistent as students' peers, who, when they say "I don't understand that," always mean exactly that (Freedman and Sperling, 1984).

Immediate feedback, of course, is a sound pedagogical principle. But in light of recent research into discourse production, the composing process, and classroom context, what can we now say about the nature of this feedback in terms of the composing process itself? Exactly how does peer editing impact upon the composing process? And what sorts of classroom activities foster its development?

WHAT SPECIFIC EVIDENCE SHOWS THAT INTENSIVE PEER REVIEW IS EFFECTIVE?

The studies reported here were undertaken in order to examine the effectiveness of intensive peer review in college freshman writing instruction at the University of Wisconsin-Madison. In order to see how writing develops in studio and nonstudio classes, many writing samples were collected. These writing samples included argumentative and personal essays, as well as each writer's characterization of her or his writing process. These writing samples were examined not only for writing quality but also for insight into the ideas about writing which students develop in their work with peers. In order to consider the effects of group work, several groups of writers in studio settings were videotaped. Altogether, this study examined 250 essays, videotaped five groups twice each (10 hours total), and compiled 411 composing process profiles—data representing the work of 250 students in 13 classes over a period of 3 years. None of the students in this study was required to take the course involved in these studies, and while no one was therefore a remedial student, very few if any were truly outstanding writers. The average College Qualifying Test (Verbal) score was 42.14; these were average college freshmen.

Results: Writing Sample

One of the writing tasks that students in all classes completed as part of this research was a personal essay, both at the beginning and end of the term. All students wrote about some important personal experience and explained its significance. These writing samples were evaluated using the Britton et al. (1975) scale of "transactional-informative" (i.e., expository) prose. For Britton, writing is largely an interpretive activity, and the development of writing ability is the increasing power to conceptualize experience and render the results in clear, explicit prose. The lower levels of development,

Britton contends, consist of **recording** and **reporting**; the middle levels involve **drawing inferences** and **generalizing**; and the highest level involves **theorizing**, speculating explicitly about one's inferences and generalizations. Britton derives his categories from a theoretical conception of writing ability inspired generally by Piaget's ideas on cognitive develop-ment and expressed in slightly different terms by James Moffett in his work at Harvard in the late 1960s.

Based on this conception of writing ability, there were no significant differences among the personal essays written by studio and nonstudio students assessed at the start of the term [one-way ANOVA, post hoc: $F(1, 119) = .079; p > .05$]. By the end of the term, however, the studio students were significantly ahead of their nonstudio counterparts [one-way ANOVA, post hoc $F(1, 119) = 3.018; p = .0023$]. The mean writing ability scores for the two groups at the end of the term were 2.2 for nonstudio and 2.7 for studio writers; 2 on this scale indicates **report**, and 3 indicates **generali-zation**.

These results were also examined as "gain" against placement and ability test scores. This was done by performing two analyses of covariance (ANCOVA) involving UW English Placement Test (EPT) and College Qualify-ing Test/Verbal (CQT) scores, respectively, as the two covariates after a separate analysis of variance (ANOVA) showed that there were no significant differences among classes on either variable [on the EPT, $F(6, 167) = 1.02; p = .42$; on the CQT, $F(6, 165) = .72; p = 1.00$]. Both the analyses of covariance and the analysis of variance showed positive results. In terms of both the EPT and CQT, studio students made significantly more progress in the development of their writing abilities [on the EPT, $F(1, 107) = 8.62; p < .0001$; on the CQT, $F = 2.26; p = .0044$].

Results: Premises about Writing

Part of the reason studio students made significantly more progress than their counterparts in learning the art and skill of exposition is related to key differences in how the two groups of students learned to revise. Each student was asked to write for 20 minutes about how he or she generally writes, and then these writing samples (which averaged more than 200 words each) were analyzed by two independent readers for what students said about revision and several other things (see "Composing Process Profile" form, Table 8.1). Overall interrater reliability, computed as a Pearson product-moment correlation, was $r = .829$ [$F(1, 226) = 583.5; p < .0001$]. This analysis showed that, over the course of the semester, *nonstudio students came increasingly to see revision as a matter of*

TABLE 8.1

Composing Process Profile

Read each of the enclosed writing samples on "How I generally write," and rate the writer according to the following categories.

1. To what extent is the writer's characterization of his or her composing process *stylized and undetailed* or *personalized and richly detailed*? (Circle one)

1	2	3	4	5	6
stylized ◄———————————			average ——————————►		personalized

2. To what extent is the composing process desribed as a *recipe-like linear process* ("First I think, then I write, and then—sometimes—I change a few things before I hand it in") or an *unpredictable process of improvisation and experimentation*?

1	2	3	4	5	6
linear ◄———————————			average ——————————►		improvised

3. How much emphasis is there on *prewriting* (gathering thoughts even if this involves writing, e.g., brainstorming, jotting down notes, outlining, etc)?

1	2	3	4	5	6
NONE			SOME		A LOT

4. How much emphasis is there on *revising as editing*?

1	2	3	4	5	6
NONE			SOME		A LOT

5. How much emphasis is there on *revising as reconceptualization*?

1	2	3	4	5	6
NONE			SOME		A LOT

6. To what extent is the reader viewed as a judge?

1	2	3	4	5	6
NONE			SOME		A LOT

7. To what extent is the reader viewed as a collaborator?

1	2	3	4	5	6
NONE			SOME		A LOT

8. How much does the writer say that *topic* affects his/her writing process?

1	2	3	4	5	6
NONE			SOME		A LOT

9. At what level of generality is this description of the writing process organized?

1	2	3	4	5	6
simple report			generalized narrative		lo-level analogic

10. To what extent are the writer's attitudes toward writing positive?

1	2	3	4	5	6
very negative			positive		very positive

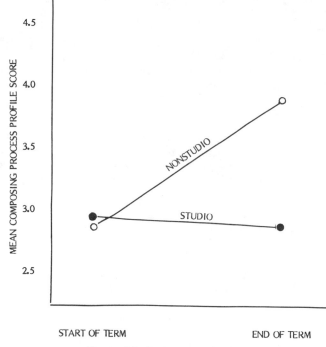

Figure 8.1. Revision as editing.

editing whereas *studio students increasingly treated it as a matter of "reconceptualization."* Both these changes were statistically significant.

Data from these composing process profiles were then analyzed in two one-way multivariate analyses of variance, one at the start of the term and another at the end. These analyses showed striking contrasts between the studio and nonstudio classes at these two points in time. Specifically, we see that how these students learned to write was significantly related to how they viewed their readers. We gain some insight into this especially as we examine students' ideas of revision. To the extent that these writers viewed their readers as judges, for example, they saw revision increasingly as a matter of editing and tidying up texts $[r = .23; F (1, 113) = 6.586; p = .01]$, and their focus was mainly on lexical and syntactical concerns. The studio sections stand in sharp contrast to the nonstudio sections in this respect. Whereas nonstudio students increasingly treated revision as a matter of editing [start of term: no significant difference; end of term: $F (1, 105) = 15.986; p < .001$; see Figure 8.1], studio students increasingly viewed their readers less as judges of their writing and more as collaborators in a process of communication [start of the term: no significant

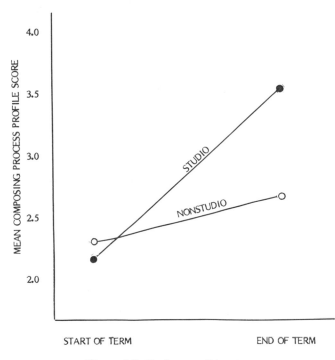

Figure 8.2. Reader as collaborator.

difference; end of term: $F(1, 105) = 7.55; p < .007$; see Figure 8.2] and increasingly treated revision as a matter of reconceptualization [start of term: no significant difference; end of term $F(1, 105) = 4.931; p = .029$; see Figure 8.3]. Over the course of the term, studio students increasingly saw their texts not as something to be judged (along with them) but rather as the functional means and their best chance for balancing their own purposes as writers with the expectations of their readers. Finally, we see that studio students' attitudes about writing became increasingly more positive [start of term: no significant difference; end of term: $F(1, 105) = 3.465; p = .065$; see Figure 8.4].

One college student explains the effects of peer review as follows:

> Personally, peer editing has been a success because it suspends any judgement regarding the essay. For example, there is no authority figure in the group who is assigning grades. This relieves a tremendous amount of pressure on me when I write an essay . . . because I know that the piece doesn't have to be perfect. I know that I can submit a very rough draft for my group to review and that they'll take it from there. Futhermore, there is no pressure to succeed in my group but rather a genuine desire to do so. In other words, the group is there for my benefit, not my benevolence. This results in a more relaxed attitude towards my writing because

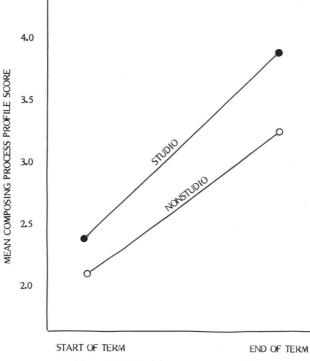

Figure 8.3. Revision as reconceptualization.

I'm not wondering what grade I received on the paper. Rather I am able to concentrate on the piece itself.

In addition, the group has no expectations of a student's writing. The paper does not have to be five pages long, typed and double-spaced in perfect grammatical form. In other words, arbitrary requirements are disregarded. Still, the outstanding advantage of suspending judgment . . . is that the group helps the student see his paper more objectively. They aren't giving out grades and so their suggestions relate to the very core of the essay itself (Alling, personal communication).

Gere and Stevens (1985) come to a similar conclusion. They cogently argue that group response is aimed at "an actual text, one which communicates the meaning students find inherent in the text presented" whereas teacher response is more concerned with "an ideal text, one which possesses certain abstract features of writing quite independently of any meaning. . . . [W]riting groups unconsciously assume that the purpose of writing is rhetorical, that it is meant to have some influence or effect on a reader," whereas "the teacher assumes that the purpose of the writing is pedagogical, that it is an exercise meant to train the student in the use of certain

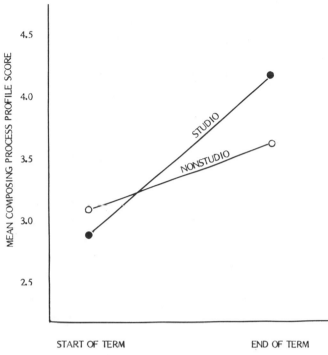

Figure 8.4. Positive attitudes toward writing.

rhetorical forms [p. 103]." Largely as a consequence of this difference in textual orientation, groups tend to deal with errors more functionally than instructors: Groups more consistently than teachers work with errors as evidence of what the writer is trying to say (Nystrand, 1982b; Shaughnessy, 1977).

Composing process research has focused almost exclusively and perhaps necessarily on the writer writing—the solitary situation of the individual confronting (and confronted by) his or her thoughts and a sheet of paper. It is a very lonely situation, no doubt a fundamental fact of the writer's situation. Good writers do indeed, as Flower and Hayes (1981) point out, work more fundamentally and substantially than novice writers at the level of purpose; specifically they plan more. To understand why this should be so, however, requires that looking beyond the individual writer to the context in which he or she learns to write. Then we understand that good writers are good not simply *because* they plan more; rather good writers plan more *because they have grappled more extensively with the demands that are made on writers when they write for authentic purposes with actual readers*. Our study of intensive peer review demonstrates that classroom context—when its inherent diversity is exploited by intensive peer review—can be an important factor in the process of learning to write. This context offers, indeed it defines an invaluable rhetorical situation in which writers can both heighten their awareness of the possibilities of written text and test their capabilities in addressing readers.

Results: Talk about Writing

To gain some understanding of the kind of talk that goes on when students write for each other and discuss this writing intensively, five groups were videotaped over the course of a semester, each group once near the start of the term and once toward the end.

Generally we find that some writing studio students are initially anxious about the prospect of learning anything from other studio students. (Indeed, some instructors have similar anxieties and wonder how their students will learn if they don't conspicuously "teach.") Many students are initially awkward about their roles in the groups. Some are too polite and superficial in their readings of each other's papers. Others are just the opposite and assume a rather schoolmarmish posture, referring to hand-books and dictionaries as a kind of martial law. In their responses to other students' papers, these students seldom go beyond considerations of spelling, punctuation, and usage. And they don't really interact much either. Instead they recite their suggestions for copy editing and go on to the next paper.

By contrast, the groups that work have extended discussions of substantial issues. They may note spelling and punctuation problems, but they mainly note them in passing on to larger considerations of the writer's purpose, organization, rhetorical effect, and adequate development. They are rigorous and direct in their comments, and the other members of these groups regard such comments as constructive criticism and seriously consider them when revising. When observed at work, these groups have the appearance and character of a busy newsroom.

Effective groups work by collectively examining written texts rather than by merely listening to oral readings by authors. That is to say, some groups proceed by listening to authors read their papers aloud whereas other groups proceed by collectively reading photocopies of the texts which the authors bring to class. This difference between groups listening and groups reading is fundamental to how groups respond to the texts so read. There is an apparent relationship between visually examining (i.e., reading) written texts on the one hand and considering higher order writing problems (such as structure of argument, presentation of arguments, paragraph development, etc.) on the other hand. By contrast, there seems to be another relationship between listening to oral readings of written texts on the one hand and considering lower order writing problems (e.g., word choice, usage, and phrasing) on the other hand. In short, groups that proceed by listening rather than by reading rarely go beyond sentence-level concerns.

This distinction between oral and written language processes is similar to one made in some developmental research between monitoring production by sight versus sound (e.g., checking spellings by examining the way words *look* rather than listening to how they *sound*). In particular, the use of visual comprehension strategies seems to correlate generally with insights into the possibilities and workings of written text—especially those idiosyncratic feaures of written language that have no direct equivalents or analogs in the spoken language (including homonym distinctions; most punctuation; quotation marks; upper- and lowercase distinctions; conventions of paragraphing; spelling patterns and other morphophonemic regularities; and certain genres of discourse that do not exist in speech, e.g., essays). It is not surprising, then, that studio groups consider different kinds of issues about writing depending on whether they proceed by listening or by reading.

Groups differ significantly in how they deal with writing problems. Some groups seek to identify a single, general problem ("You need to be more specific"; "Your focus isn't clear") and consider their tasks complete when they have identified one such problem in summary fashion. The problem is only labeled; it is not discussed in terms of particular parts of text. A curious variation of this same procedure is considering an author's points out of context (as from an outline); the validity of the points is weighed, but their presentation is treated superficially if at all. Other groups are more specific about problems (e.g., "You need to give more examples") but still do not actually examine the troublesources in any detail. Yet other groups are not only specific about key problems but also actually work through revisions in some detail.

ANALYSIS OF TALK IN WRITING GROUPS

We now consider this process in more detail by analyzing two discussions of college freshmen about papers they have written. The first is instructive because of the range of text issues—including genre, topic, and comment— that are implicated by the talk. The second is useful because it clarifies the role of such talk in the revision process. By examining these discussions closely, we get a clear sense of how students can learn to write by talking about their writing.

In the first discussion, students discuss the draft of a paper arguing that the newsmedia too often put profits ahead of information. The author develops her thesis partly by relating a conversation she overheard on the bus one day. The group spends considerable time debating whether such personal narrative is appropriate to the intended character of the piece as a critical essay. Consequently the discussion deals not only with the writer's purpose and thesis but also with the group's ideas of a critical essay.

Here is the original draft of the paper discussed:

[NO TITLE]

"The NBC Nightly News", "The Capital Times", "WIBA-AM" and other TV, newspaper and radio stations are constantly competing to get the highest ratings on the largest circulation: Making the news eyecatching can be difficult. Not many people will be alarmed by the invasion of a tiny island, but if the media slants the story or introduces theories that the attack could be a threat to our nation more people will be concerned. The station and papers that are able to catch the audiences attention the best will attract advertisers and advertisers bring money into the market. The media is a very competitive business, and because it is so competitive we need to be very careful about what we will believe as 100% truth.

It is very difficult for us to distinguish between what is true and what isnt. For example the average American is not an economist who can detect when a table or graph has been drawn to accent or hide the current rate of inflation. If the graph just shows how much the price of a candy bar has gone up in the last 20 years of course it will look awful. A rise from 5¢ to 40¢ is a 35¢ could make a graph look terribly depressing. In order to come up with the real increase in cost the graph would need to allow for the increase in wages over the last 20 years. Not everyone would catch the fact that this very important component was left out and they would be astonished at the 800% increase.

One day on the way to school I overheard a conversation that gave a perfect example of a medium slanting a story. A man on the bus was telling another about an interview which lead to a story written by a Madison newspaper reporter. The man is a foreign student who is here to earn a degree and then return to his country with his education. His country is supporting him while he is here. The reporter was interviewing the student to find out how he felt about the support that he was receiving from the government in his country. The man explained that he had enough money, but that he didn't receive as much as some of the other students from his country, who where also being supported by the government. The money was given to the students according to need. The paper left out this very important part and made the man's government sound unfair. By carefully choosing which questions and answers to print the paper changed the meaning of the entire story. More people were probably attracted by the idea of another country treating its people poorly, than would have been attracted if the country was fair to its people. Interesting stories attract and retain readers, readers attract advertisers, and advertisers bring money and profit to the paper.

Most people trust the media and rely on it for information. Our opinions about issues are formed largely by the information we receive from the media. We can not all be experts in every area, so we need to turn to some other sources for information. We all need to be aware of the fact that these others forms of information may be trying to excite us in order to hold our attention. We should not believe everything that the media gives us. We need to use our own instincts to realize when a story sounds a little too dramatic in order to keep a realistic picture of the world.

Part I: Genre

The discussion begins by focusing on the third paragraph. The issue is whether or not the author's reference to a conversation she overheard "one day on the way to school" is too personal a subject for a critical essay about the media slanting of the news. Jean and Tom advise the author to "detach it more," "make it general"—not too "close." There is considerable discussion about what "you can and can't do in 'this sort of paper.'" For example, you can't write about "something that I overheard." The group evaluates examples and presentations that are appropriate to this sort of a text, and in so doing they sort out genre-level concerns. Whereas it was okay for Jean to use personal experience in her personal narrative on high school band, it is not okay for the author to include such examples in her critical essay on media slanting of news; this is not that sort of paper.

Tom. That was really—I—I enjoyed the first paragraph really good. I thought it—um—"slant"—"slant" was a good word—"slant their stories"—um—stuff like that—um—

Jean. Um—this one right here on the second page it says "one day on the way to school"—I think that's too related to you—It's—you gotta detach it more.

Tom. Yeah—Make it—make it general.

Jean. Should I do that on my paper too?

Rick. You can't do that on your paper.

Jean. Maybe my whole paper just stinks.

Rick. No, just 'cause you have personal experience in it doesn't mean it stinks. I don'—*your* paper was about band. When you document—you know—you can't use documented proof on something like that.

Jean. So I have to use my own—right.

Rick. Well, unless you know of something—

Jean. 'Cause when she was reading that through I noticed it on hers and then I thought it's the same on—as mi——mine—like—

Rick. But hers—hers is a paper where she could get—you know?—examples and stories that didn't *have* to deal with her.

Tom. Yeah. I think that would end up—you have to—

These issues about genre lead directly to issues about text. For example, the group discusses whether or not it's okay to use "I" in this sort of text.

Then Jean recommends that the author delete reference to the author's bus ride because "it doesn't have anything to do with the story." And the group debates whether or not reference to Madison is appropriate i.e., whether or not reference to a local setting is consistent with a more universal theme; they conclude it's okay.

Rick . That's why I think that you—it—it—

Jean. You just have to change the phrasing a little bit.

[Author]. How about if I just started out "I heard a conversation that gave a perfect example of the media slanting a story"?

Jean. That's still—I think it's still too close.

Tom. Yeah.

Rick. But if she doesn't do that she's gonna have to like say where—where she got this information from—That's what I—I kinda want to know about this.

Jean. What is the bus? What does the bus have to do with it maybe? Take the bus out too—

Rick. That's where—where she heard it

[Author]. Yeah

Jean. Right. But that doesn't have anything to do with the story.

Tom. No. It doesn't.

[Author]. Okay

Jean. And that's kind of—

[Author]. How could I—how could I introduce the story into the paper so that it didn't sound like something—that—something that I'm just making up?

Jean. Okay.

Tom. Does anybody have that one paper on—um—

Jean. How 'bout for—for instance—um—

Rick. Mention the conversation a little bit.

Jean. "I overheard a man explaining to a man—about something—" okay?—I don't even know if you have to use "I"—in this paper, do you?

The author quickly sees the dilemma created by this suggestion: If she omits reference to herself and recasts her experience on the bus in more general terms, it may not be clear that she is in fact relating a true story. On the one hand, her "I" potentially marks a too personal and perhaps insufficiently "critical" text; on the other hand, the omission of "I" possibly marks a fiction. As the group works through this problem, we see clearly how some solutions to rhetorical problems do themselves create new problems by taking the text in new and unexpected directions. Through a process of trial and error, then, the group benefits not merely by finding acceptable revisions for problem passages but also and especially by evaluating possible revisions, even if many possibilities do in the end prove inadequate.

In this discussion, the author learns that she needs to establish clearly that this is not just a story she has made up—that it is in fact true. The group acknowledges this problem but wants her to do more than acknowledge its truth; they want her to depersonalize and generalize it.

Rick. No. But if she doesn't do that [mention "I"] then—like the reader's gonna question where this information came from. You know. It doesn't say at all where the information came from.

[Author]. If it was a paper I wouldn't—if I read it in a newspaper or something, I wouldn't—if I read it in a newspaper or something, I wouldn't have to say, "I read it in a newspaper." I would just say, "The newspaper said—"

Rick. Oh, yeah—like—like the *Daily Cardinal* said or the—

Jean. Yeah.

Rick. Otherwise she's not stating her source of information. I—I—think—

Tom and Jean then propose that the author start with a fictitious headline ("Immigrant gets half of what everyone else . . ."), depersonalizing and generalizing everything in a single stroke. But is it fair to make things up in exposition, i.e., in writing that is supposed to tell the truth? The author says she feels uncomfortable "slanting" her piece too much. The author says it's okay to "make things up as long as they're real" and suggests that she factually report a newspaper article that she has learned about only indirectly. After much discussion, the author and her group agree that "you don't have to mention the two people [whom the author overheard on the bus] and yourself. You can just mention this man and his problem," which the author will use as a good example of her more general thesis that the news media sometimes seriously distort the news in order to sell the news and stay on top of the ratings.

Jean. Why don't you start it backwards? Why don't you say—you can make up things as long as they're real, right?

Tom. You can make stuff up.

Jean. Start like—um—start like reading the headline, you saw in the paper—and then—

[Author]. But I didn't read the paper. But I didn't see the article.

Jean. But that's not—you don't have to say that.

Tom. No. You can say you read this article and then—

Jean. And then—

[Author]. And then, what?

Tom. Later—later—the person

Jean. Later—er—later heard—er—an editorial reacted to this——by interview or you—you heard it on interview on television—that would be
   changing a—

Tom. Isn't it *Absence of Malice* that did this?

Jean. Wouldn't that work though? I mean, wouldn't that get your attention
   if you started with the headline—um—"Immigrant Gets Half of What
   Everyone Else"—or something—er—

Rick. No, but that—you're talking about—you're—

Jean. You're not slanting the story too much

[Author]. I know—but then—I'm slanting it

Rick. What?

[Author]. Yeah. Right. But then I'm really slanting it.

Rick. She's—she's using this as a source of evidence—I think when you
   start screwing around with evidence—

[Author]. I want to keep it clean.

Rick. —on our personal papers it was okay to lie 'cause how would
   anybody tell us otherwise?

Tom. Yeah.

Jean. Well, you didn't get to see the article, right? Was it a news interview,
   or was it an article?

[Author]. It was an article, but—you know—you have to interview a person
   before you write an article. The person interviewed—

Jean. You just have to tell it—

Tom. She's just telling it in a certain way.

Jean. You just have to tell it—backwards—and then go back somehow—
   you know—tell what the news article said and then go back and show
   how it was wrong

Tom. Like did you see *Absence of Malice*?

[Author]. I saw part of it and then we walked out.

Tom. Well, there was—it's part of—just—the lady wrote up a story—
   and then you can just—there was an editorial that—you know—she
   had to reclaim everything—that—'cause there was just lies—you
   know—and that's the same thing, you know—you can say it was like—
   "I read in the paper one day—they reclaimed it and said it was wrong.
   And that's what you can—I dunno—bring—

[Author]. I just don't know if I want to lie that much because this
   is true—

Rick. Yeah.

[Author]. You know, and I'm trying to—to use it to back up what I'm
   saying so that—

Jean. Well, it is true. Just switch—just say the article—you don't have to say very much about the article, you just have to say what you told us already—and then at the—after you're done describing the article

Rick. Or maybe not even say that—mention an incident—"there was a man, you know"—

[Author]. There was a man who said this? Okay, okay. Yeah. I don't have to—I see what you mean.

Jean. What are—what are you saying?

Rick. Just like when you start. Just say—just say for example, one incident when a man—you know—an incident occur—you know—

Tom. Yeah, you don't—

Jean. You don't have to mention the two people and yourself. You can just mention this man

Tom. Yeah. And you don't have to—Yeah. You—mention the problem. I think it'll be a lot shorter, but leave out "like Madison" or something maybe? No, that's not—

Tom. "Madison"'s okay.

Rick proceeds to suggest a thesis—that "these sources of media are more like businesses rather than—and actually less like news sources." But what is interesting here is not just Rick's clarification of the thesis. The group immediately picks up on this suggestion in terms of its potential for clarifying the genre: "I could say 'business' up at the top too—maybe to get the idea rolling a little bit." By stating this idea explicitly at the start of the paper, the author will clearly establish that this paper is not about her ride on the bus but rather about the character of the news media as businesses.

Jean. I like this—this—I like the part about "a perfect example of a medium slanting a story." I don't—maybe that—

Tom. No. That's good

[Author]. Where? Oh—"gave a perfect example of a medium slanting a story"?—

Jean. Well, you can use that. You just have to rephr—put in a different sentence. — —okay

Tom. Um—Maybe you can say "the story goes as such . . ." and you can tell them where they slanted it—even though you didn't read the story, you know—you know what went on in it because—you heard—you heard the guy talking about it.

Rick. You might want to bring into the paper—maybe you could persuade us—that us—that's just a general idea. Maybe you can just try and persuade us that—uh—these—these sources of media are—you know—like—that paper that we saw in that videotape? It said like the football teams that were just like businesses.

[Author]. Yeah.

Rick. Well, maybe you could state—stress more that like these sources of
media are more like businesses rather than—and actually less like
sources of information

[Author]. Yeah. Okay. I tried to do that down at the bottom but I could say
it maybe—

Jean. What's the medium?

[Author]. I said the medium [is] a very competitive business but I could say
"business" up at the top too—maybe to get the idea rolling a little bit.

Tom. Yeah. Foreshadow and stuff.

Part II. Topic and Comment: Thesis

The group moves now directly to the author's thesis having to do with the
business nature of the news media. Jean begins by noting ambiguity in the
author's treatment of the topic ("the 'business' word didn't catch my eye"),
and the group then proposes and discusses several possible revisions
designed to resolve this misconstraint—potential elaborations explicitly
stating the author's idea that the newsmedia put business before information.

They also move to strike the author's reference to the U.S. invasion of
Grenada in the second sentence of the first paragraph. This inappropriate
elaboration not only contributes nothing to the thesis but is actually
misleading by suggesting a direction to the paper which the author never
follows up. As such, it violates the *elaboration construction corollary*,
which prohibits constructions that complicate rather than clarify and
thereby threatens rather than maintains reciprocity. Clearly, the first paragraph will be tightened by (a) eliminating potentially spurious interpretations prompted by reference to the Grenadian invasion and (b) buttressing
the text at the level of comment by stressing the profit motive of the
newsmedia. As we noted in Chapter 3, the writer gets the reader off and
running by setting the text in one particular direction rather than another,
loading the communication in favor of certain possibilities and interpretive
contexts rather than others.

Jean. Um—what is—what is—what are you trying to show us?

[Author]. What do you think I'm trying to show you?

Jean. I didn't see—I didn't—the "business" word didn't catch my mind
[*identifies troublesource*]

Rick. See, I think you could make that a lot stronger and strengthen the
paper at the same time

Jean. And—all I got was for you to tell people to look closer [*notes
insufficient elaboration*].

[Author]. That's—what I was trying to persuade you

Rick. But maybe that would be more obvious if you said like—if you said "Media are ... businesses and not necessarily—" [*potential elaboration*].

Tom. —"trying to sell a product" [*potential elaboration*].

Rick. "when they're going to sensationalize the story maybe in order to catch the reader's eye or the viewer's eye in order to retain more viewers for the advertising."

Tom. Is that a government public service?

Rick. You touched on—you touched on it—you didn't—I don't think you went into it deep enough that—it was a major point in your paper [*potential elaboration*].

Tom. It sounded like a government public service where they just give you blah-blah-blah the facts.

Rick. Yeah.

Tom. They were boring.

Rick. You were going—I think that you were going sometimes—

[Author]. Okay. I think maybe how 'bout if I—if I cross out this whole thing about the tiny island and stick something else in there. That's kinda—[*identifies inappropriate elaboration: violates elaboration construction corollary*].

Tom. That could help too—that could happen—you know—

[Author]. That didn't really support very much there—that example right away—

Jean. —but that—is that—that's giving personal opinion, you know—you might be alarmed, but a lot of people, you know—

[Author]. Okay—right.

Jean. But to tell you the truth, I don't think a lot of people would be alarmed—if they heard today that some small island was attacked— there's so much other stuff going on that they wouldn't really care.

Rick. No. Madison would—would take offense to any—

Tom. They jump on anyone. They jump on anything. But no I was—

Jean. But what I'm saying is I think she's right. I think this can be edited back into the paper somewhere else.

Tom. But all right, you're offering a different opinion that doesn't fit in the rest of the paper. Right? You don't really give a lot of—

Jean. In your intro you shouldn't really give examples more than you should just state facts.

[Author]. Maybe if I just cross it out, the whole thing would be better—you know—[*reads proposed revision*]: "Making the news eyecatching can be difficult. The station and the papers that are able to catch the audience's attention best will attract advertisers, and advertisers bring

money into the market. The media's a very competitive business and because it is—"

Eliminating reference to Grenada will tighten the paper but possibly create another problem: Will the paper be too short to satisfy the instructor's requirement? This problem, of course, is wholly pedagogical and entirely unrhetorical in nature. Fortunately the group quickly returns to more essential problems of text and spends little time discussing it.

Jean. You know what you're doing? You're gonna shorten your paper a lot— not only taking this out but taking out what we said before. So you're gonna have to lengthen it.

[Author]. Well, I don't care. Maybe I could add—well . . .

Jean. Persuade it.

Rick. I think you can add a lot—when you—

[Author]. I'm not real worried about the length too much because—I dunno—one of those ones that he have us he gave the person an "A" and it only had three pages.

Tom. Yeah, I—uh—yeah—you could add a lot to it too.

Rick. You've got a great paper, and if it's only two and a half pages and—and it would be—it would be senseless to—to lengthen the paper and have it suffer in the end and I think—I—I—I always—if I didn't have enough to write about I would stop way—way short of the deadline if I thought that going on with it would ruin the paper.

Tom. I wouldn't. I'd keep writing so I'd have enough.

Rick. But right here—

Tom. Quantity not quality.

Rick. When you say—you know—maybe you could say it more obviously. In order to keep more viewers they're gonna slant—you know—slant the story or sensationalize it or in—in another situation—like—let's say—well, you could bring in politics—you know—I mean—like—like when you're bringing up this economic thing—I give up—like maybe if you were in a state that was—you know, the majority was Democratic— you're not gonna—you're gonna slant the story—before—to make like the President look bad.

[Author]. You mean so like if it—like if it's kind of a Democratic newspaper or something then they're gonna slant the story to make it seem—

Rick. Well, you know, some states are more—more Democratic or strongly like that they wouldn't probably—like you could find an example of them using a table like this against making—or some public—

[Author]. The thing is that I couldn't find any examples.

Jean. You couldn't find any examples? Hah, hah, hah.

Rick. You know what you might wanna do? Ask—

[Author]. So I didn't really want to say anything about them—

Rick. Ask Prof. Xxx. Say you're writing a paper—

Jean. Well, are you real up on Democratic views—are you real up on Democratic and Republican views 'cause you can read a paper and tell—

[Author]. Yeah.

Rick. You know that it—

Tom. Yeah. That thing on economics in there—

[Author]. If you were in like—maybe a—a state that was mostly Democratic, you're not gonna—I think most newspapers aren't gonna write— something that's gonna make the Republican Party look better. Like they're gonna try and take facts and distort them and make the Republican Party look worse—er—the President look worse—er—the President look worse or whatever—

Tom. Yeah. Maybe you can say something to the elections coming up how they really distort—you know, the elections 'cause they can change a lot of people's opinions—when they go and vote.

Rick. Facts and figures can kind of be twisted around.

Tom. Yeah. And then like—during the election they have all those things like—they—they have what's-his-name out in front—Mondale out in front of Hart out in front or, you know—that's gonna change a lot of people's opinions like especially like during the stupid primaries.

Rick. Yeah. That's a good point, though, 'cause like most of those medias, ours are, you know, they're supported by advertisements. For that you need viewers and so you gotta kinda—

Jean. Did you see that arti—did you see that commercial about—um—this just comes to mind—about that girl who's riding the bike and says all those Democratic ideas aren't so new?

[Author]. Yeah, yeah.

Tom. Yeah, yeah. They go "Of course"

Jean. "Vote Republican."

Tom. Yeah—that's a nasty commercial paper.

Jean. Don't you think that's kind of slanting?

[Author]. Well, no. That's advertising—I don't really want to get into advertising. I want to get into news more because everybody kinda knows that advertisers are gonna try to—you know—

Rick. Well, advertising has to have—I think we expect it out of advertisers and I think they should have the right—they're—they're paying their own way in advertising and they—they did pay for that commercial, you know. It's their time to express their view, but—the news is like something that I think that people have always depended on—for—

[Author]. Straightforward facts—

Rick. Straightforward information—and like if it doesn't come that way, I still think people believe it.

[Author]. Yeah. That's—That's kinda what I said, you know. It's hard for us to distinguish between what's true and what isn't. Because, I mean, you really don't know much about important things than—things we read and hear on the radio. Nobody knows Reagan personally to know if—you know—he really feels this way—or—if this is—you know—the paper's just making it sound that way—or—just really what he's got being him.

Tom. I didn't read that in there. You know. Put that in there 'cause—you know—we're getting this—you know—only half the picture here and that's what most people—

Rick. Just brainstorm for awhile 'cause think if you can [get] more ideas about the paper to add on, I think you could make this a lot longer by putting in some of the stuff you just told us.

[Author]. So what did I just say?

Rick. You said like—well—bring up the example—like if you don't know a person personally for example, the President. If he's misquoted—you know—that can slip right by you.

Tom. Or if the story's slanted, you're gonna go "Oh I really like this guy."

Jean. Remember that controversy about—uh—Jackson's saying something bad against Jews and he, of course, denied it right away—a media guy picked it up—but you couldn't use that to your benefit.

Rick. Well, how do you know he was quoted right?

Jean. Because later on he said he was quoted right and he—ah—he apologized. Didn't you hear that?

Tom. Well, I don't listen to Jackson anyway. He's a nerd.

Jean. Well, I don't listen to him either.

Tom. He just pulled a lucky one to get that guy out of whatever it was. Israel?

Jean. Yeah, right.

Tom. He just—

Jean. What? What did he do?

Tom. When he got that guy out.

Rick. Don't talk to me about the news. I haven't read a newspaper in—

Jean. I know. I haven't read a newspaper in so long—I never read the newspapers—frequently—like every other day or everyday or—it's too depressing.

Rick. —the presidential campaign. I'm not going to know about it.

Tom. I am—'cause I don't want to study. But anyway—

Jean. I listen to the news.

Tom. I've written about six letters in the last two days.

Rick. Look here—in your first paragraph where you do all that—I think you could be more clearcut and straightforward.

Tom. About—like maybe not—maybe say like just—a money making business—you know—because everything in a sense is a like a business, you know? Bring in the money, you know? Make 'em look greedy.

Jean suggests that the author might go on to discuss the ethics of editorial policies in the news media ("Do they or don't they have the right?") and then notes that this "could be a whole new paper." Once again, we see how the solution to one rhetorical problem prompts yet another problem as the text develops. This particular candidate for elaboration—the ethics of the news media—is bound by the *elaboration episode corollary*, which requires that substantially new text segments be marked as such.

Tom. Yeah. I liked the last paragraph.

Jean. Do you want to go into—if you don't have enough room—I don't know if this could be a whole paper that the media doesn't have a right—to—when—

Rick. Do they or don't they have the right, though? That could be a whole new paper.

Jean. I haven't even told you yet.

Tom. Well, they—

Jean. —to say—to say such things like they do—say things that they don't really know—you know? They don't have all the facts on?

[Author]. Yeah?

Rick. I know. But do they or don't they have the right?

Jean. Well, see, with freedom of speech they do, supposedly—but then again, somebody in a crowded theatre couldn't yell fire. You know, I mean—there's a fine line.

Tom. No, but—um—

Rick. That's almost—um—you could go into a whole 'nother paper than that.

Jean. Yeah—I suppose—

[Author]. That's awful—

Tom. But that's freedom of—that's freedom of speech.

Rick. No, I just think that maybe you should make the audience aware that it's a money-making business and that—because if she starts getting into that, she's gonna have to support that.

Tom. Oh, you didn't even—

Jean. Ratings—you could go into ratings.

Tom. Oh, you didn't even—

[Author]. Well, I did kinda, but not really, 'cause I said ratings—you know—because—uhm—advertisers were attacked too.

Jean. You mention that—you went—you went on the surface too much.
[Author]. Well, I did about three times.
Tom. You think there—well, wait a minute.
[Author]. I brou—I kinda brought it up about three times but—

Jean now notes an explanation that is too technical and therefore unhelpful to someone like Jean with only a nonexpert's understanding of economics. Other members of the group, namely those with a background in economics, are not troubled by this explanation, however, and for them it is not a troublesource. Here the nature of misconstraints—discrepancies between what the writer has to say and what the reader expects and needs to know—becomes clear. There is nothing categorical about misconstraints; they are defined entirely in terms of reader expectations. For this reason, Jean's problems provide useful feedback for the author and identify an important troublesource. Elaborations that threaten rather than maintain reciprocity violate the *elaboration construction corollary*.

Jean. Go into more of the money-making things. And I don't understand
    your example [*identifies troublesource*].
[Author]. Which one?
Jean. I'm—maybe I'm just—I mean, inflation—sure, looking at a graph that
    five cents that—that went up forty cents now and there's a thirty-five
    cents difference—also you have to fix that phrase.
[Author]. Yeah, right.
Jean. But I don't understand how that was wrong. I mean, I know it's gotta
    be wrong.
Rick. I think you gotta make that example real—real clearcut 'cause I
    understood it but that's 'cause I'm in the same econ class.
Tom. Yeah. I understood it too but—
Jean. I'm not in econ. It didn't make sense to me.
Rick. See, she's showing that—you're making this price—this price increase
    so dramatic, you know? But they haven't even considered that wages
    have increased as much or more, you know? If wages increase as much
    as—as the price does, there's virtually no effect, right?
Jean. But you gotta—
[Author]. Wages could have increased more than that—and then there
    would be a better deal to buy a candy bar than it would—
Rick. Yeah. Make it real clear cut—like state a couple of examples of wages
    and freeze, you know? As much—you—you know—there wouldn't be
    no change—[*potential elaboration*].
Jean. You know, you could—could bring something like—um—no, you
    couldn't. Forget it.

Then they consider asking their economics professor for examples:

Rick. You know, if you do have time, you might want to ask Prof. Xxx if he knows of any examples off-hand, you know, that would—

Jean. Ask who?

Rick. Our professor—he—he might—he brought this up—this—uh—point about inflation and stuff—how, you know, there's **real** and **nominal** and—if you don't use nominal, you're kind of—

Jean. "Real" and "nominal"—would not—the average person wouldn't know what you're saying [*identifies misconstraint*].

Rick. —doesn't give the whole picture really...

[Author]. That's right—so that's kind of my point too.

Jean. That's kind of my point too because *nominal*—you know—you could say that it's nominal and everybody would say "oh, yeah, ok"—it went up so much, and they'd just think it did and it was terrible, you know? But really, nominal—

Rick. But there are other factors if you consider more than wages.

[Author]. So that's—that's exactly my point. People don't understand everything that—they're—that they're being told, you know, and—

And so another rhetorical problem is identified and solved. It turns out, however, that the point of these examples, which introduces a distinction between real and nominal inflation, does itself potentially violate the *elaboration construction corollary.* That is, the proposed elaboration creates a potential troublesource and hence complicates things more than it clarifies. Finally Jean and Tom propose the solution of marking the point as an explanation:

Jean. State a sentence like that and the right afterwards say, "Do you know what this means?" and then go into it [*potential elaboration*].

Tom. Yeah—you can—tell—tell them that the news is taking advantage of them. You know, certain parts of our—our ignorance [*potential elaboration*].

The group concludes by briefly examining the conclusion and the title:

Jean. I liked your conclusion.

[Author]. Oh, that's good.

Tom. Yeah. I did.

[Author]. That's nice. Good. What?

Jean. Bring up the experts on—these areas.

[Author]. Yeah—how 'bout—uh—

Jean. Like something like this—"do the media assume we know more—

does the me-—oh—here—like this how—does the media assume we know more or does it want purposely to delude us?"

Tom. Ooh—ooh—that's good. I like that one.

[Author]. I like that one too.

Jean. It just occurred to me.

Tom. "Delude" is a great word—oh, wow—

. . . .

Jean. What are you going to name—what are you going to name this?

[Author]. Something—something that makes it sound like a business. I don't know yet, but—

Rick. "Fact or Fiction"—

Jean. Ha, ha, ha, ha—

Rick. Sorry.

Tom. "Service or Profit"?—"Provid—Providing a Service or Making a Profit"?

[Author]. That's kinda good.

Tom. I don't know.

Jean. Why—why can't you think of a title for *my* paper?

Rick. "Business as Usual"

Jean. Ha, ha, ha, ha.

[Author]. "Business as Usual"?

Jean. Should I just drop that paper? I still think I should.

Tom. No—no, that paper—you can make something of it.

Jean. What—what did you say?

Rick. I—think "Business as Usual" is quite good, you know?—

Jean. Or come up with one of your own—as usual.

[Author]. But I don't know—what—what did you say?

Tom. "Service or Profit"

Jean. You guys gotta come up with one for me now.

We clearly see in this discussion the process of negotiation whereby the writer shapes her text by balancing her own needs for expression with the expectations and needs of her readers for comprehension. In focusing primarily on their own problems in understanding the text, the readers provide essential feedback to the writer on just which points need attention and just which revisions might help. Many of these suggestions are in the final analysis inappropriate, but it seems clear that much learning, for both the writer and the readers, results from proposing and evaluating these revisions even if, in the end, they are not quite right. In effect, each such revision is a **text hypothesis**, which the writer tests with the group. It is worth noting, furthermore, that many potential revisions turn out to be inappropriate not because they fail to address the problems that prompted their consideration in the first place but rather because they raise new problems. In other words, elaborations do not just address trouble spots; they can also create them.

At several points in the discussion, we see that members of the group allude to other texts. For example, one person continuously compares her own paper (on marching bands) to the paper under discussion. There are allusions to articles in the *Daily Cardinal* (a student newspaper) and also to the film *Absence of Malice*. At one point, someone mentions previous personal essays written by the whole class, and in another section, someone alludes to the videotaped discussion of a paper written in another class.

There are also several points in the discussion which seem tangential to the actual text in question. For a little while the group talks about President Reagan and then the Rev. Jesse Jackson, and it is not altogether clear that this talk is functional in terms of the rhetorical problems the group ultimately addresses. It seems entirely possible, however, that these allusions help the group think through essential issues mainly by providing foils to the text under consideration. For example, the group decides it's okay to slant advertising (as in the Reagan campaign ads) but not the author's paper, which is not advertising; it's okay to recount "conversations overheard on a bus one day on the way to school" in a personal essay though the same topic can present a problem in a critical essay; and so on and so forth. As with all conversation, there is an ebb and flow to this talk, and while it is not altogether clear whether or not this ebbing is essential or peripheral to the flow, it seems entirely plausible that its function here is to provide the group an opportunity for reflection and free association which is essential for significant problem solving.

We now consider this process by analyzing the talk of another group in which students discuss the draft of a paper arguing that people who frequent bars are "fake." By examining this discussion closely and especially relating the subsequent changes the author makes in his paper, we get a clear sense of how group talk about writing works its way into the author's revision.

Here is the original draft of the paper discussed:

A Particular Spot

I spend a lot of time in campus bars. I like a change of pace so I tend to discover new bars. No matter where or what bar I end up at, one thing is always the same, people are fake.

Friday afternoon I go to a bar called the Black Bear. Everyone at the BBL is fake. Most of the customers are "Harley Davidson" types. Why do these people wear chains, leather, and long hair? They do this because they are fake. They are trying to tell everybody, "I'm tough, stay away." This is just a front, if they were just themselves they would feel better.

Friday night I do the KK Circle. This is when I go to the Kollege Klub and go inside. I try to walk around but then there are so many students trying to impress each other. Football players flexing girls with tight pants, and well dressed preppies. I start my circle by walking through the bar browsing and staring at everyone. Everyone here is fake also; they are just putting up a front. Not the tough guy front: they have a new front the nice guy. They are playing a Richie Cunningham role. The irony is that they drink, smoke, and fight as much as the "Harley Davidsons."

My third and last stop is at Charlie's Place. Most of their customers are older and more grown up. But they are still fake, just a little bit older. They might be drinking JB on the rocks instead of Huber beer.

What's the difference between a leather jacket, a polo shirt, or a Brooks suit? Nothing is different: it is all a front. It is the same as a red or brown building they are all hiding something. But everything and everyone is hiding something. I am hiding something. Everyone is fake; okay I am fake too.

The group immediately focuses on the author's, Steve's, contention that people frequenting campus bars are "fake," challenging him to explain what he means by it. Steve responds by reassuring everyone that there's nothing wrong with being "fake," but the group emphasizes that the problem is not with their feelings but with his paper: He needs to define "fake" and to explain what he means by it. Specifically the problem is in the commentary of the paper.

Ann. Oh, that wasn't very—
[Author]. I don't think so either—
Mary. I don't think everyone is fake—
[Author]. That's just my opinion—I think *every*one's fake—
Ann. I think you go too far though—
Mary. Yea. That bothers me a bit—
Melissa. Do you have any paper?
Ann. Yea. Because—
[Author]. I think everyone is just a little fake.
Mary. Everybody's not just fake.
Mary. They've got something to hide too—
[Author]. Well fine. That's just how I interpret it. But—um—I just person-
   ally think that everyone is trying to hide something—
Melissa. But what would they be if they weren't fake then?
[Author]. No. Well there's nothing wrong with it. There's also at the end
   where I say that I'm fake too. I mean there's nothing wrong with being
   fake.
Melissa. What would be a non-fake person?
[Author]. It would be new—
Melissa. What would be a non-fake personality—

Ann. Come on—

Melissa. What would be a non-fake personality?

Mary. What do you want to do? Do you want everyone to sit there and tell you that's human nature?

[Author]. No. Everyone's fake—

Melissa. You mean that's human nature?

[Author]. No. I'm just saying—I'm saying that's how it is. That's how it's right. There's nothing wrong with it.

Melissa. But what is—I mean if you took away this fakeness, what would you be left? I mean everybody's fake then.

[Author]. Right. But that's all I'm trying to say. Everybody's fake. That's the way it should be. Everyone's fake. I mean—there's nothing wrong with it—

Mary. There are real people.

Melissa. Being fake. How do you define it?

[Author]. I don't think you can define it—

Melissa. It's trying to be something that you're not—

Mary. What's your definition of "fake"? Let's put it that way.

[Author]. Me, I'm fake. You're fake. Everybody's fake.

Ann. No. That's not a definition. That's examples—

[Author]. Maybe. Ok. I think what you just said; trying to be something that you're not. Is that what you were trying to say?

Melissa. Yea—

Mary. I'm not trying to be something I'm not—

[Author]. I'm not saying you are—

Mary. You say I am—

Melissa. But that's what your speech says: Everybody's fake—

Mary. You could use a—

[Author]. I'm just—that's just a word I thought—Well maybe you could use something else—I mean trying to maybe impress someone or something—I don't know if you understand what I'm trying to say. But that's not what I'm trying to say—

Mary. But everybody tries to impress people—Did you watch David Letterman last night?

[Author]. David Letterman tries to impress people just by the way he is—I mean he's funny. He's trying to impress people to make people think he's funny.

Ann. But if people laugh? What about it?

[Author]. Right—

Mary. He's naturally funny—he's not fake.

Melissa. It's entertainment. You can't—

[Author]. Right. Now you're just—you're trying to say—

Mary. What you're saying is that people should keep their mouths shut, stay inside their houses, do not speak to anybody. You really—?
[Author]. No. I'm not saying that. That's what you're interpreting. I'm not saying anything's wrong with being the way you are. I'm saying—
Mary. But you're saying that everybody's fake because of how they are—
[Author]. You're not interpreting it not the same way I'm interpreting it. And I can't explain it. You're, you're—

Melissa finally suggests that Steve "wrote the wrong word," and subsequently, he begins to develop another line of commentary: "They're not really dressed up—just wearing a different type of clothing and talk real different." He proposes to "throw the word 'fake' out the window"—describing this troublesource as "the way I interpret it is—not the same way you're interpreting it"—and proposes a replacement: "Everyone—the people at the pub are a little different from the people at the KK."

Melissa. Maybe you should—in your first paragraph—you should define it.
[Author]. Right, that's what I've been trying to do—
Ann. Define how people's attitudes are influenced by who's around them—
Melissa. Yea. Different—yea—different environments—
Ann. You could say people are changing—every different atmosphere they're in—
[Author]. Yea, I don't think that would bring across the same meaning that I was trying to say. What I'm trying to say is this: There's a different group of people at every bar, and that this group—each bar—each group of people act differently. But they're not—but they're not—but they're not acting the way they really want. But they're just acting—
Melissa. How about if you put down—if you say or turn it around a little bit and say: So many people are trying to change themselves to be what in their own minds—the perfect—something perfect. So they are trying to impress everybody. But everybody's idea of perfect is different. So everybody's trying to impress everybody.
Ann. And if you don't act like yourself, you're not making yourself happy—
Melissa. But how do you write that down?

Steve tries out his new topic and comment: "There's a different group of people at every bar—" It is precisely this idea that Steve uses in his subsequent revision:

Bars at Their Finest

The University of Wisconsin campus has numerous places to have fun. I especially enjoy going to bars. There are all types of bars to choose from, clean or dirty, big or small, and cheap or expensive, all with various types of environments.

The Kollege Klub and Charlie's Place both produce a white collar atmosphere. Charlie's is more of a graduate or "after work" bar. The professional people will stop here for a Bloody Mary after a day at the office. Generally the men are wearing suits and the women are sporting the newest fashions in women's wear. When I order a common beer at Charlie's I seem to provoke the same reaction as when E. F. Hutton talks. Charlie's Place has a very ritzy atmosphere.

Another bar, I call it Charlie Jr., that produces a similar atmosphere is the Kollege Klub (KK). The people here all have their white collars pointed up meant that I was a little better than everyone else. Almost the same as pointing a nose towards the ski. When I overhear conversations at the KK it sounds like someone is always bragging. Once I heard a person saying, "My mother's best friend's sister- in-law has a friend that sold some Mary Kay Cosmetics to someone that knows Brooke Shields." Occasionally what I overhear is so ridiculous that I don't bother to listen, I just watch. At the KK I often see a football player flexing, a blond's tight ass in Guess pants, and a bunch of fraternity apparel. The KK and Charlie's Place both produce a white collar environment.

The Pub and Black Bear Lounge both produce a blue collar atmosphere. The Pub is a place to go to play a game of pool and to relax. There is always a special on beer ranging from one-buck St. Pauli Girls to a good buy on a pitcher of Hamms. The people here seem to have put in a hard day's work and come here to relax, not to brag. There are a lot of pool tables, so there is never a wait to get in a game. I once saw a man in a wheel chair at the Pub. He put the chair in the corner and used the pool table as a crutch. He won the table and had a great time playing pool. During another visit my partner and I decided to let some girls take us on in a game of pool. They beat the pants off us and continued to win against other opponents. Episodes like these are what add interest to visiting a bar like the Pub.

The Black Bear Lounge also has a working man's atmosphere, but the "Bear" has more of a "tough guy" environment. I once was going to the bathroom when I heard some thugs bickering. They were arguing over who is better, Twisted Sister or Black Sabbath. I decided not to get involved. The bar itself has a few pool tables and a juke box, my idea of a nice, pleasant, and smokey atmosphere. The bartenders are always trying to sell the moldiest beer. The Pub and Bear produce a blue collar atmosphere.

This campus has plenty of places to go to do something wild. There is a bar for everyone to spend money in and have fun. I love going to bars because there is a bar for everyone.

To sum up: The draft is a *personal essay* arguing that *people frequenting bars in Madison are fake*. The revision is an *informative paper* showing *how bars on campus offer something to everyone*. The revision is motivated by the groups' assault on the commentary in the original draft. Finding no way to defend this point, the author abandons it and offers an unassailable alternative. Hence, "fake" becomes "something for everyone." In seizing upon the comment "fake," the group focuses on just that element of the text that most threatens reciprocity, a real troublesource. Unable to treat this troublesource with an elaboration (e.g., explaining what he means by "fake"), the author abandons it entirely and invents a new commentary.

The author abandons no more than he has to. (Generally, there seems to be an inertia about discourse: To whatever extent possible the author will seek to preserve what he or she can.) In this case Steve retains the original discourse topic while modifying it slightly (*people frequenting bars* becomes *bars on campus*) and invents a new commentary. Significantly, this shift in discourse topic and commentary implicates a different genre. Whereas the original discourse topic-commentary [PEOPLE FREQUENTING MADISON BARS] [ARE FAKE] entails an **argument**, the revision [BARS ON CAMPUS] [OFFER SOMETHING FOR EVERYONE] entails a **report**. The shift is comparable to a newspaper editor's moving the piece from the editorial page to the travel section. We note concomitant shifts in person, voice, and tone; the revision is noticeably more bland.

This shift reveals a significant contrast between and motivation for argumentative and informational prose. To the extent that TOPIC + COMMENT assert something fundamentally inconsistent with the common expectations and working premises of readers, reciprocity will be threatened, and argumentation will be required to restore writer-reader balance. By contrast, to the extent that TOPIC + COMMENT assert something essentially congruent with the common expectations and working premises of readers, reciprocity will not be threatened at the level of genre but potentially only at the level of commentary where the author is obligated to explain or contextualize the new information that he introduces. In this sense, argumentation is a more radical form of discourse than information.

Two important points follow. First, genre, topic, and comment all implicate or constrain each other, and a shift in one can have implications for the others. Any given text will be a specific configuration of genre, topic, and comment—each level implicating the others. Second, any of the levels can define an "entry" point for revision considerations. (For further discussion of these points, see Nystrand and Brandt (in press).) In this case, the comment most thoroughly upsets the expected balance between writer and readers, but once the old commentary is abandoned and the new commentary is embraced, the genre itself has changed.

RHETORICAL PROBLEM SOLVING

In both these discussions we see how groups engage in extensive collaborative problem solving. This can range from collaborative conversational repairs (where the speaker searches for a word and the group actively enters into the search) to joint revision of a troublesome paragraph. Their discussion ranges from general characterizations of both strengths and weaknesses of particular texts to detailed discussions about reworking problem sections. There is an intricate lacing of high-level concerns (such as purpose and organization) with text-level representations (such as paragraphing and development). When peer groups work well and writers confront their readers regularly to review their papers, the groups tend to "gravitate" to those parts of the texts that are unclear or troublesome in some way. As long as groups do not engage in excessive "copy editing" but dwell instead on understanding the writer's purpose and its articulation, the discussions focus mainly on these troublesources and uncertainties of text. More to the point, these groups have a keen sense of what problems need solving. They identify key troublesources and deal concretely with how particular text structures address them. These troublesources, which range from ambiguities of genre (What sort of text is this?), purpose (What's the purpose of this?), topic (What's this about anyway?), and comment (What's the point?) constitute the subject matter of these sessions. In effect, the discussion examines a continuous set of rhetorical problems, which the group collaborates in solving. Hence, by intensively identifying and resolving rhetorical problems, they shore up, flesh out, and sustain just those parts of their papers that otherwise would be weak and unclear. In addition, after several weeks of such work, students can anticipate potential troublesources *as they write*. Indeed, students involved in peer review often say about halfway through the term that they can anticipate their readers during the composing process. That is, they develop a sensitivity to the possibilities of text, which effectively enables them to monitor their composing processes, no doubt the chief long-term benefit of instruction.

In Vygotskyan terms, we may regard intensive peer review as a formative social arrangement in which writers become consciously aware of the functional significance of composing behaviors, discourse strategies, and elements of text by managing them all in anticipation of continuous reader feedback. This is not to argue that writers in peer groups come to control their rhetorical problem-solving efforts by somehow conducting "in their heads" the same conversations that formerly were carried out in their groups. Rather, it means that the composing processes and discourse strategies that writers take from their groups largely emerge in ways that are often evident first in the social interaction of peer review.

It is precisely this process of intensive rhetorical problem-solving that defines the effectiveness of intensive peer review. Peer review is not just a method of teaching writing. Used intensively, it creates an environment, somewhat like the social context of initial language acquisition, where the learner can continuously test hypotheses about the possibilities of written text.

References

Abercrombie, D. Elements of phonetics. Edinburgh: Edinhburgh University Press, 1967.

Applebee, A. N. The child's concept of story: Ages two to seventeen. Chicago: University of Chicago Press, 1978.

———. Writing and learning in school settings. In M. Nystrand (Ed.), What writers know: The language, process, and structure of written discourse. New York: Academic Press, 1982.

Bach, L, and Harnish, R. M. Linguistic communication and speech acts. Cambridge, MA: MIT Press, 1979.

Bakhtin, M. M. [Vološinov] Marxism and the philosophy of language. Translated by Ladislav Matejka and I. R. Titunik. New York: Seminar Press, 1973.

———. Freudianism, a Marxist critique. Translated by I. R. Titunik. New York: Academic Press, 1976.

———. The dialogic imagination. Austin: University of Texas Press, 1981.

———. Problems of Dostoevsky's poetics. Translated by Caryl Emerson. Minneapolis: University of Minnesota Press, 1983.

Bates, E. Language and context: The acquisition of pragmatics. New York: Academic Press, 1976.

Beach, R. The effects of between-draft teacher evaluation versus student self-evaluation of high school students' revising of rough drafts. Research in the Teaching of English, 1979, 13, 111–119.

Beaugrande, R. de. Psychology and composition: Past, present, and future. In M. Nystrand (Ed.), What writers know: The language, process, and structure of written discourse. New York: Academic Press, 1982.

Beaven, M.H. Individualized goal setting, self-evaluation, and peer evaluation. In C. R. Cooper and L. Odell (Eds.), Evaluating writing: Describing, measuring, judging. Urbana, IL: National Council of Teachers of English, 1977, 135–156.

Benes, E. The beginning of the German sentence from the point of view of functional sentence perspective. Casopis pro moderni fililogii, 1959, 41, 205–217 [cited in Firbas, 1966].

Bennett, J. Linguistic behaviour. London: Cambridge University Press, 1976.

Benson, N. The effects of peer feedback during the writing process on writing performance, revision behavior, and attitude toward writing. Unpublished Ph.D. dissertation: The University of Colorado, 1979.

Bereiter, C. and Scardamalia, M. From conversation to composition: The role of instruction in a developmental process. In R. Glaser (Ed.), Advances in instructional psychology (Vol. 2). Hillsdale, NJ: Lawrence Erlbaum, 1981.

Bickard, M. On models of knowledge and communication. In M. Hickmann (Ed.), Proceedings of a working conference on the social foundations of language and thought. Chicago: Center for Psychosocial Studies and the University of Chicago, 1980.

Birch, H. G. and Lefford, A. Visual differentiation, intersensory integration, and voluntary motor control. Monographs of the Society for Research in Child Development, 1967, 32(2), Serial No. 110.

Bissex, G. Gnys at wrk: A child learns to write and read. Cambridge, MA: Harvard University Press, 1980.

Black J. and Wilkes-Gibbs. Distortions of the writing process by verbal reports of mental processes. Unpublished paper presented at the 1982 Annual Convention of the AERA.

Boggs, S. T. The development of verbal disputing in part-Hawaiian children. Language in Society, 1978, 7, 325–344.

Bormuth, J. Factor validity of cloze tests as measures of reading comprehension ability. Reading Research Quarterly, 1969, 4, 358–365.

Box, G. E. P. Non-normality and tests on variances. Biometrika, 1953, 40, 318–335.

Bransford, J. and Johnson, M. D. Contextual prerequisites for understanding: Some investigations of comprehension and recall. Journal of Verbal Learning and Verbal Behavior, 1972, 11, 717–726.

Brazelton, T. B., Koslowski, B., and Main, M. The origins of reciprocity: The early mother-infant interaction. In M. Lewis and L. Rosenblum (Eds.), The effects of the infant on its caregiver. New York: Wiley, 1974.

Britton, J. Talking to learn. In D. Barnes, Britton, J., and Rosen, H. (Eds.), Language, the learner, and the school. Harmondsworth: Penguin, 1971.

————. Burgess, T., Martin, M., McLeod, A., and Rosen, H. The development of writing abilities: 11–18. London: Macmillan, 1975.

Brown, A. L. Knowing when, where and how to remember: A problem of metacognition. In R. Glaser (Ed.), Advances in instructional psychology. Hillsdale, N.J.: Lawrence Erlbaum, 1978.

————. Metacognitive development and reading. In R. J. Spiro, B. Bruce, and W.F. Brewer (Eds.), Theoretical issues in reading comprehension. Hillsdale, N.J.: Lawrence Erlbaum, 1980.

Bruffee, K. Collaborative learning: Some practical models. College English, 1973, 34, 634–643.

————. Collaborative learning and the "conversation of mankind." College English, 1984, 46, 635–652.

Bruner, J. S. Processes of cognitive growth: Infancy. Worcester, MA: Clark University Press, 1968.

————. From communication to language: A psychological perspective. Cognition, 1975, 3, 255–287. (a).

————. The ontogenesis of speech acts. Journal of Child Language, 1975, 2, 1–19. (b).

————. Acquiring the uses of language. Canadian Journal of Psychology, 1978, 32(4), 204–218.

————. The social context of language acquisition. Language and Communication, 1981, 1(2/3), 155–178.

Buxton, E. W. An experiment to test the effects of writing frequency and guided practice upon students' skill in written expression. Unpublished doctoral dissertation, Stanford University, Stanford, 1958 [cited in Gere and Stevens, 1985].

Calkins, L. Lessons from a child: On the teaching and learning of writing. Exeter, NH: Heinemann Educational Books, 1983.

Cassirer, E. Essay on man. New Haven: Yale University Press, 1944.

Cattell, J. M. The time taken up by cerebral operation. Mind, 1886, 11, 220–242.

Chafe, W. Integration and involvement in speaking, writing, and oral literature. In D. Tannen (Ed.), Spoken and written language: Exploring orality and literacy. Norwood, NJ: ABLEX Publishing Corp., 1982.

Chiesi, H., Spilich, G., and Voss J. Acquisition of domain-related information in relation to high and low domain knowledge. Journal of Verbal Learning and Verbal Behavior, 1979, 18, 257–273.

Chomsky, N. Syntactic structures. The Hague: Mouton, 1957.

————. Aspects of the theory of syntax. Cambridge, MA: MIT Press, 1965.

Cicourel, A. Language and society. Cognitive, cultural, and linguistic aspects of language use. In Sozialwissenschaftliche Annalen, Band 2, Seite B25–B58. Vienna: Physica, 1978.

Clark, E. Knowledge, context, and strategy in the acquisition of meaning. In D. P. Dato (Ed.), Georgetown University round table on languages and linguistics 1975. Washington, DC: Georgetown University Press, 1975, pp. 77–98.

Clark, H. and Clark, E. Psychology and language. New York: Harcourt Brace Jovanovich, 1977.

Clark, H. J. and Carlson, T. B. Speech acts and hearers' beliefs. In N. V. Smith (Ed.), Mutual knowledge. London: Academic Press, 1982.

Clark, H. and Haviland, S. Comprehension and the given-new contract. In R. O. Freedle (Ed.), Discourse production and comprehension. Norwood, NJ: ABLEX Publishing Corp., 1977, pp. 1–40.

Clark, H. and Marshall, C. Definite reference and mutual knowledge. In A. K. Joshi, I. Sag, and B. Webber (Eds.), Elements of discourse understanding. Cambridge: Cambridge University Press, 1981.

Clay, M. M. What did I write? London: Heinemann Educational Books, 1975.

Collins, J. and Williamson, Michael. Spoken language and semantic abbreviation in writing. Research in the Teaching of English, 1981, 14, 23–35.

Condon, W. S. and Sander, L. W. Neonate movement is synchronized with adult speech: Interactional participation and language acquisition. Science, 1974, 183, 99–101.

Cook-Gumperz, J. Situated instructions: Language socialization of school age children. In S. Ervin-Tripp & C. Mitchell-Kernan (Eds.), Child discourse. New York: Academic Press, 1977.

———. The child as practical reasoner. In M. Sanches & B. Blount (Eds.), Sociocultural dimensions of language use. New York: Academic Press, 1977.

Cooper, C., Marquis, A., and Ayers-Lopez, S. Peer learning in the classroom: Tracing developmental patterns and consequences of children's spontaneous interactions. In L.C. Wilkinson (Ed.), Communicating in the classroom. New York: Academic Press, 1982.

Cooper, M. Context as vehicle: Implicatures in writing. In M. Nystrand (Ed.), What writers know: The language, process, and structure of written discourse. New York: Academic Press, 1982.

Corbin, A. L. The interpretation of words and the parole evidence rule. Cornell Law Quarterly, 1965, 50, 161–190.

Corsaro, W. The clarification request as a feature of adult interactive styles with young children. Language in Society, 1977, 6, 183–207.

———. Communicative processes in studies of social organization: Sociological approaches to discourse analysis. Text, 1981, 1(1), 5–63.

Cox, R. R. Schutz's theory of relevance: A phenomenological critique. The Hague: Martinus Nijhoff, 1978.

Cronbach, L. J. Test validation. In R. L. Thorndike (Ed.), Educational measurement (2nd edition). Washington, DC: American Council of Education, 1971.

Daneš, F. A three-level approach to syntax. Travaux Linguistiques de Pragues, 1964, 1, 225–240.

———. Functional sentence perspective and the organization of the text. In F. Daneš (Ed.), Papers on functional sentence perspective. Prague: Academia, 1974.

DeStefano, J., Pepinsky, H., & Sanders, T. Discourse rules for literacy learning in a classroom. In L. C. Wilkinson (Ed.), Communicating in the classroom. New York: Academic Press, 1982.

Diederich, P. G., French, J. W., and Carlton, S. T. Factors in judgments of writing ability. Princeton, NJ: Educational Testing Service, 1961.

Dillon, G. Constructing texts: Elements of a theory of composition and style. Bloomington, IN: Indiana University Press, 1981.

Donaldson, M. Children's minds. London: Fontana, 1978.

Dulek, R. Writing to unknown readers. IEEE Transactions on Professional Communication, 1980, *3*, 125–127.

Dyson, A. H. The role of oral language in early writing processes. Research in the Teaching of English, 1983, *17*, 1–30.

Eder, D. Differences in communicative styles across ability groups. In L. C. Wilkinson (Ed.), Communicating in the classroom. New York: Academic Press, 1982.

Eisenberg, A. and Garvey, C. Children's use of verbal strategies in resolving conflicts. Discourse Processes, 1981, *4*(2), 149–170.

Elbow, P. Writing without teachers. New York: Oxford University press, 1973.

Emig, J. The composing processes of twelfth graders. NCTE Research Report No. 6. Urbana, IL: National Council of Teachers of English, 1971.

Erickson, F. Talking down: Some cultural sources of miscommunication in interracial interviews. In Aaron Wolfgang (Ed.), Nonverbal behavior: Applications and cultural implications. New York: Academic Press, 1979.

Faigley, L. The problem of topic in texts. In D. McQuade (Ed.), The territory of language. Carbondale: Southern Illinois University Press, 1986.

————— , Cherry, R., Jolliffe, D., and Skinner, A. Assessing writers' knowledge and processes of composing. Norwood, NJ: ABLEX Publishing Corporation, 1985.

Faigley, L. and Witte, S. Analyzing revision. College Composition and Communication, 1981, *32*, 400–414.

Ferreiro, E. What is written in a written sentence? A developmental answer. Journal of Education, 1978, *160*, 25–39.

————— and Teberosky, A. Literacy before schooling. Exeter, NH: Heinemann Educational Books, 1982.

Fillmore, C. J. The case for case. In E. Harms & R. T. Harms (Eds.), Universals of linguistic theory. New York: Holt, Rinehart & Winston, 1968.

Firbas, J. On defining the theme in functional sentence perspective. Travaux Linguistiques de Prague, 1964, *1*, 267–280.

————— . Non-thematic subjects in contemporary English. Travaux Linguistiques de Prague, 1966, *2*, 239–256.

Firth, J. R. Papers in linguistics, 1934–1951. New York: Oxford University Press, 1957.

Flavell, J. H. and Wellman, H. M. Meta-memory. In R. V. Kail, Jr. and J. W. Hagen (Eds.), Perspectives on the development of memory and cognition. Hillsdale, NJ.: Lawrence Erlbaum, 1977.

Flower, L. and Hayes, J. R. Problem-solving strategies and the writing process. College English, 1977, *39*, 449–461.

————— . Identifying the organization of writing proesses. In L. Gregg and E. Steinberg (Eds.), Cognitive processes in writing. Hillsdale, NJ: Lawrence Erlbaum, 1980(a).

————— . The dynamics of composing: Making plans and juggling constraints. In L. Gregg and E. Steinberg (Eds.), Cognitive processes in writing. Hillsdale, NJ: Lawrence Erlbaum, 1980(b).

————— . A cognitive process theory of writing. College Composition and Communication, 1981, *32*, 365–387.

Fox, R. Treatment of writing apprehension and its effects on composition. Research in the Teaching of English, 1980, *14*, 39–49.

Freedman, S. W. Evaluation in the writing conference: An interactive process. In M. Hairston and C. Selfe (Eds.), Selected papers from the 1981 Texas Writing Research Conference. Austin: The University of Texas at Austin, 1981.

────── and Sperling, M. Teacher-student interaction in the writing conference: Response and teaching. In S. Freedman (Ed.), The acquisition of written language: Revision and response. Norwood, NJ: ABLEX Publishing Corp., 1985.

────── . Research on response to writing: A review. Unpublished paper presented at the annual convention of the National Council of Teachers of English, Detroit, November, 1984.

Garvey, C. The contingent query: A dependent act in conversation. In M. Lewis and L. Rosenblum (Eds.), Interaction, conversation, and the development of language. New York: Wiley, 1977.

────── . An approach to the study of children's role play. Laboratory of Comparative Human Cognition Newsletter, 1979, 1(4), 69-73.

Gebhardt, R. Teamwork and feedback: Broadening the base of collaborative writing. College Composition and Communication, 1980, 31, 69–74.

Genishi, C. and DiPaolo, M. Learning through argument in a preschool. In L. C. Wilkinson (Ed.), Communicating in the classroom. New York: Academic Press, 1982.

Gere, A. R. and Abbott, R. D. Talking about writing: The language of writing groups. Research in the Teaching of English, 1985, 19, 362–385.

Gere, A. R. and Stevens, R. S. The language of writing groups: How oral response shapes revision. In S. Freedman (Ed.), The acquisition of written language: Revision and response. Norwood, NJ: ABLEX Publishing Corp., 1985.

Gingrich, P. A measure of text cohesion. Paper presented at the 1980 Annual Meeting of the American Educational Research Association.

Goffman, I. Footing. Semiotica, 1979, 25, 1–29.

Goldman-Eisler, F. A comparative study of two hesitation phenomena. Language and Speech, 1961, 4, 18–26.

────── . Pauses, clauses, and sentences. Language and Speech, 1972, 15, 103,113.

Goodman, K. Reading: A psycholinguistic guessing game. Journal of the Reading Specialist, 1967, 4, 126–135.

Goodwin, C. Conversational organization: Interaction between speakers and hearers. New York: Academic Press, 1981.

Goody, J. and Watt, I. The consequences of literacy. In J. Goody (Ed.), Literacy in traditional societies. New York: Cambridge University Press, 1968.

Gould, J. D. Experiments on composing letters: Some fact, some myths, and some observations. In L. W. Gregg & E. R. Steinberg (Eds.), Cognitive processes in writing. Hillsdale, NJ: Lawrence Erlbaum, 1980.

Graves, D. H. Children's writing: Research directions and hypotheses based upon an examination of the writing processes of seven-year-old children. Unpublished Ph.D. dissertation at the State University of New York at Buffalo, 1973.

────── . An examination of the writing processes of seven-year-old children. Research in the Teaching of English, 1975, 9, 227–241.

Greenfield, P. M. Oral and written language: The consequences for cognitive development in Africa, the United States, and England. Language and Speech, 1972, 15, 169–172.

Gregg, L. and Steinberg, E. (Eds.). Cognitive processes in writing. Hillsdale, NJ: Lawrence Erlbaum, 1980.

Gregory, M. and Carroll, S. Language and situation: Language varieties and their social context. London: Routledge & Kegan Paul, 1978.

Grice, H. P. Logic and conversation. In P. Cole and J. L. Morgan (Eds.), Syntax and semantics (Vol.3): Speech acts. New York: Academic Press, 1975, pp. 41–58.

Gundlach, R. A. On the nature and development of children's writing. In C.F. Frederiksen & J.F. Dominic (Eds.), Writing: Process, development, and communication. Hillsdale, NJ: Lawrence Erlbaum Associates, 1981.

————— . Children as writers: The beginnings of learning to write. In M. Nystrand (Ed.), What writers know: The language, process, and structure of written discourse. New York: Academic Press, 1982(a).

————— . Notes for the Erikson study group on children's writing development. Unpublished paper, 1982(b).

Guthrie, J. T. Themes and progressions in research on English. Unpublished paper prepared for the Mid-Decade Seminar on Future Directions of Research, of the National Conference on Research on English, Chicago, March 29–31, 1985.

Haas, W. Phono-graphic translation. Manchester: Manchester University Press, 1970.

Halliday, M. A. K. Notes on transitivity and theme in English, Part 2. Journal of Linguistics, 1967, 213(20), 199–244.

————— . Learning how to mean. London: Arnold, 1974.

————— . Language as social semiotic: The social interpretation of language and meaning. Baltimore: University Park Press, 1978.

————— . Spoken and written modes of meaning. In R. Horowitz and S. Jay Samuels (Eds.), Comprehending oral and written language. Orlando: Academic Press, in press.

————— and Hasan, R. Cohesion in English. London: Longman, 1976.

Harder, P. and Kock, C. The theory of presupposition failure. Copenhagen: Akademisk Forlag, 1976.

Harris, G., Begg, I. and Upfold, D. On the role of the speaker's expectations in interpersonal communication. Journal of Verbal Learning and Verbal Behavior, 1980, 19, 597–607.

Harweg, Rolland. Beginning a text. Discourse Processes, 1980, 3, 313–326.

Haviland, S. E. and Clark, H. H. What's new? Acquiring new information as a process of comprehension. Journal of Verbal Learning and Verbal Behavior, 1974, 13, 512–521.

Havilock, E. A. Preface to Plato. Cambridge, MA: Harvard University Press, 1963.

————— . The origins of Western literacy. Toronto: The Ontario Institute for Studies in Education, 1977.

Hawkins, L. Group inquiry techniques for teaching writing. Urbana, IL: National Council of Teachers of English, 1976.

Heath, S. B. Protean shapes in literacy events: Ever-shifting oral and literate traditions. In D. Tannen (Ed.), Spoken and written language: Exploring orality and literacy. Volume IX in Advances in Discourse Processes. Norwood, NJ: ABLEX Publishing Corporation, 1982.

Henderson, E. H. J. and Beers, J. W. (Eds.). Developmental and cognitive aspects of learning to spell. Newark, DE: International Reading Association, 1980.

Hermann, D. J. and Neisser, U. An inventory of everyday memory experiences. In M.M. Gruneberg, P. E. Morris, and R. M. Sykes (Eds.), Practical aspects of memory. New York: Academic Press, 1978.

Hickmann, M. Introduction: The context-dependence of linguistic and cognitive processes. In M. Hickmann (Ed.), Proceedings of a working conference on the social foundations of language and thought. Chicago: Center for Psychosocial Studies, 1980.

Hildyard, A. and Olson, D. R. On the comprehension and memory of oral vs. written discourse. In D. Tannen (Ed.), Spoken and written language: Exploring orality and literacy. Volume IX in Advances in Discourse Processes. Norwood, NJ: ABLEX Publishing Corporation, 1982.

Hillocks, G. The interaction of instruction, teacher comment, and revision in teaching the composing process. Research in the Teaching of English, 1982, 16, 261–278.

Himley, M. First encounters of a written kind: Points of entry and paths of development for three beginning writers. Unpublished Ph.D. dissertation at the University of Illinois at Chicago, 1983.

Hirsch, E. D. Jr. The philosophy of composition. Chicago: The University of Chicago Press, 1977.

Holland, V. M. Psycholinguistic alternatives to readability formulas. Washington, D.C.: American Institutes for Research, 1981.

Holquist, M. The politics of representation. The Quarterly Newsletter of the Laboratory of Comparative Human Cognition, 1983, 5(1), 2–9.

Horowitz, R. The limitations of contrasted rhetorical predicates on reader recall of expository English prose. Unpublished Ph.D. dissertation, University of Minnesota, 1982.

Householder, F. W. Linguistic speculations. London and New York: Cambridge University Press, 1971.

Huey, E. B. The psychology and pedagogy of reading. New York: Macmillan, 1908.

Humes, A. Research on the composing process. Review of Educational Research, 1983, 153(2), 201–216.

Jakobson, R. Child language, aphasia and phonological universals. The Hague: Mouton, 1968.

Jefferson, G. Error correction as an interactional resource. Language in Society, 1974, 2, 181–199.

Johnson, Walter and Kieras, David. Representation-saving effects of prior knowledge in memory for simple technical prose. Unpublished paper, n.d.

Johnson-Laird, P. N. Mutual ignorance: Comments on Clark and Carlson's paper. In N. V. Smith (Ed.), Mutual knowledge. London: Academic Press, 1982.

Kintsch, W. The representation of meaning in memory. Hillsdale, NJ: Lawrence Erlbaum, 1974.

———. Psychological processes in discourse production. Technical report no. 99. Boulder, Colorado: Institute of Cognitive Science, 1980.

——— and Keenan, J. M. Reading rate and retention as a function of the number of propositions in the base structure of sentences. Cognitive Psychology, 1973, 5, 257–274.

Kintsch, W., Kozminsky, E. Steby, W. J., McKoon, G., and Keenan, J. M. Comprehension and recall of text as a function of content variables. Journal of Verbal Learning and Verbal Behavior, 1975, 14, 196–214.

Kintsch, W. and van Dijk, T. A. Toward a model of text comprehension and production. Psychological Review, 1978, 85, 363–394.

Kintsch, W. and Vipond, D. Reading comprehension and readability in educational practice and psychological theory. In Lars-Göran Nilsson (Ed.), Perspectives on memory research. Hillsdale, NJ: Lawrence Erlbaum Associates, 1979.

Klare, G. R. Assessing readability. Reading Research Quarterly, 1974/75, 10, 62–102.

Kleiven, J and Rommetveit, R. Meaning and frequency in a binocular rivalry situation. Scandanavian Journal of Psychology, 1970, 11, 17–20.

Kolers, P. Bilingual facilitation of short-term memory words remembered with respect to semantic rather than morphemic properties. Unpublished paper presented at the Eastern Psychological Association Meeting in Atlantic City, NJ, 1965.

Kroll, B. Developmental relationships between speaking and writing. In B. Kroll & R. Vann (Eds.), Exploring speaking-writing relationships: Connections and contrasts. Urbana, IL: National Council of Teachers of English, 1981.

Kucer, S. B. The cognitive base of reading and writing. Unpublished paper prepared for the Mid-Decade Seminar on Future Directions of Research, of the National Conference on Research on English, Chicago, March 29–31, 1985.

Lagana, J. The development, implementation, and evaluation of a model for teaching composition which utilizes individualized learning and peer grouping. Unpublished doctoral dissertation, University of Pittsburgh, 1973 [cited in Gere and Stevens, 1985].

Lakoff, R. Some of my favorite writers are literate: The mingling of oral and literate strategies in written communication. In D. Tannen (Ed.), Spoken and written language: Exploring orality and literacy. Norwood, NJ: ABLEX Publishing Corporation, 1982.

Langer, S. Philosophy in a new key. Cambridge, MA: Harvard University Press, 1942.

Leithwood, K. F. Maynes, Baxter, P, and Montgomery, D. The Peterborough project. Toronto: The Ontario Institute for Studies in Education, 1976.

Lewis, D. K. Convention. Cambridge, MA: Harvard University Press, 1969.

Lewis, M. and Freedle, R.O. Mother-infant dyad: The cradle of meaning. In P. Pliner, L. Krames, & T. Alloway (Eds.), Communication and affect. New York: Academic Press, 1973.

Luria, A. The development of writing in the child. Soviet Psychology, 1977-78, *16*(20), 65–14. From [Problems of Marxist education]. Moscow: Academy of Community Education, 1929.

———— . Language and cognition. J. V. Wertsch (Ed.). New York: John Wiley & Sons, 1982.

Lyons, J. Semantics (2 vols.). London: Cambridge University Press, 1977.

Martin, C. G. and Games, P. A. ANOVA tests for homogeneity of variance: Nonnormality and unequal samples. Journal of Educational Statistics, 1977, *2*(3), 187–206.

Martin, J. Hesitations in the speaker's production and listener's reproduction of utterances. Journal of Verbal Learning and Verbal Behavior, 1967, *6*, 903–909.

———— . Some acoustic and grammatical features of spontaneous speech. In D. L. Horton and J. J. Jenkins (Eds.), The perception of language. Columbus, OH: Charles E. Merrill, 1971.

Mathesius, V. On the so-called functional sentence perspective. Slovo a Slovesnost, 1939, *5*, 171–174 [cited in Firbas, 1966].

Matsuhashi, A. Explorations in the real-time production of written discourse. In M. Nystrand (Ed.), What writers know: The language, process, and structure of written discourse. New York: Academic Press, 1982.

Messick, S. The standard problem: Meaning and values in measurement and evaluation. The American Psychologist, 1975, *30*, 955–966.

Meyer, B. A selected review and discussion of basic research on prose comprehension. Tempe: Arizona State University Prose Learning Series Research Report 4, 1979.

Michaels, S. "Sharing time": Children's narrative styles and differential access to literacy. Language in Society, 1981, *10*, 423–442.

Michaels, W. B. Against formalism: Chickens and rocks. In L. Michaels and C. Ricks (Eds.), The state of the language. Berkeley: University of California Press, 1980.

Millar, B. and Nystrand, M. The language trap. English Journal, 1979, *68*(3), 36–41.

Miller, C. R. Genre as social action. Quarterly Journal of Speech, 1984, *70*, 151–167.

Miller, G. A. The magical number seven, plus or minus two: Some limits on our capacity for processing information. Psychological Review, 1956, *63*, 81–92.

Miller, J. and Kintsch, W. Readability and recall of short prose passages: A theoretical analysis. Journal of Experimental Psychology: Human Learning and Memory, 1980, *6*(4), 335–354.

Moffett, J. Teaching the universe of discourse. Boston: Houghton Mifflin, 1968(a).

———— . A student-centered language arts curriculum: K–13. Boston: Houghton Mifflin, 1968(b).

Murray, D. A writer teaches writing. Boston: Houghton Mifflin, 1968.

Nelson, K. How young children represent knowledge of their world. In and out of language: A preliminary report. In R. Siegler (Ed.), Children's thinking: What develops. Hillsdale, NJ: Lawrence Erlbaum, 1978.

Newkirk, T. "Direction and misdirection in peer response." College Composition and Communication, 1984, *34*, 301–311.

Ninio, A. and Bruner, J.S. The achievement and antecedents of labelling. Journal of Child Language, 1978, *5*, 1–15.

Nystrand, M. Using readability research to investigate writing. Research in the Teaching of English, 1979, *113*(3), 231–242.

———. Necessary lexical elaborations. Unpublished paper presented at the 1981 Convention of the Conference on Composition and Communication, Dallas, March 26, 1981.

———. Rhetoric's "audience" and linguistics' "speech community": Implications for understanding writing, reading, and text. In M. Nystrand (Ed.), What writers know: The language, process, and structure of written discourse. New York: Academic Press, 1982(a).

———. An analysis of errors in written communication. In M. Nystrand (Ed.), What writers know: The language, process, and structure of written discourse. New York: Academic press, 1982(b).

———. The structure of textual space. In M. Nystrand (Ed.), What writers know: The language, process, and structure of written discourse. New York: Academic Press, 1982(c).

———. The role of context in written communication. The Nottingham Linguistic Circular, 1983, *12*(1), 55–65.

———. Increasing writers' awareness of their own composing processes. Unpublished proposal for research to the National Institute of Education, 1983.

———. Learning to write by talking about writing: A summary of research on intensive peer review in expository writing instruction at the University of Wisconsin-Madison. Unpublished Final Report to the National Institute of Education (Grant No. NIE-G-84-0008), 1985.

——— and Brandt, D. Response to writing as a context for learning to write. In C. Anson (ed.), Responding to student writing: Models, methods, and curricular change. Urbana, IL: National Council of Teachers of English, in press.

Nystrand, M. and Doane, A. N. The expository writing studio method: Research and practice at the University of Wisconsin-Madison (in preparation).

Nystrand, M. and Himley, M. Written text as social interaction. Access to meaning: Spoken and written language. Theory into Practice, 1984, *23*(3), 198–207.

Ochs, E. Language acquisition and folk epistemology. In M. Hickmann (Ed.), Social and functional approaches to language and thought. New York: Academic Press, in press.

——— and Schiefflin, B. Developmental pragmatics. New York: Academic Press, 1979.

Olson, D. R. Cognitive development: The child's acquisition of diagonality. New York: Academic Press, 1970.

———. From utterance to text: The bias of language in speech and writing. The Harvard Educational Review, 1977, *47*, 257-281.

———. Writing: The divorce of the author from the text. In B. Kroll and R. Vann (Eds.), Exploring speaking-writing relationships: Connections and contrasts. Urbana, IL: National Council of Teachers of English, 1981.

———. Writing and literal meaning. In M. Martlew (Ed.), The psychology of written language. London: John Wiley & Sons, Ltd., 1983.

O'Reilly, R. Personal communication, 1976.

———, Schuder, R., Kidder, S., Salter, R. and Hayford, P. The validation and refinement of measures of literal comprehension in reading for use in policy research and class room management. Albany: State Education Department, Bureau of School and Cultural Research, 1977. ERIC document ED 133 363. See Resources in Education, 1977, 12.

Peirce, C. S. Collected papers of Charles Sanders Peirce, vol. 2: The elements of logic. Ed. C. Hartshorne and P. Weiss. Cambridge, MA: Harvard University Press, 1932.

Perl, S. The composing processes of unskilled college writers. Research in the Teaching of English, 1979, *13*, 317–336.

Phillips, S. Literacy as a mode of communication on the Warm Spring Indian Reservation. In E. H. Lenneberg and E. Lenneberg (Eds.), Foundations of language development: A multidisciplinary approach. Vol. 2. New York: Academic Press, 1975.

Popper, K. The logic of scientific discovery. New York: Basic Books, 1959.

————. Objective knowledge: An evolutionary approach. London: Oxford at the Clarendon Press, 1972.

Prague School. Manifesto presented to the First Congress of Slavic Philologists in Prague, 1929. In M. K. Johnson (Ed.), Recycling the Prague linguistics circle. Ann Arbor, MI: Karoma, 1978.

Putnam, H. Mind, Language, and Reality. Cambridge, UK: Cambridge University Press, 1975.

Read, C. Children's categorization of speech sounds in English. Urbana, IL: National Council of Teachers of English, 1971.

————. Lessons to be learned from the preschool orthographers. In E. H. Lenneberg and E. Lenneberg (Eds.), Foundations in language development (vol. 2). New York: Academic Press, 1975.

————. Review of Bissex's GNYS AT WRK: A Child Learns to Write and Read. The Harvard Educational Review, 1980, 52(1), 909–93.

Reder, L. Elaborations: When do they help and when do they hurt? Text, 1982, 2(1/3), 211–224.

Redish, J. Readability. Washington, DC: American Institutes for Research, 1979.

Reicher, G. M. Perceptual recognition as a function of meaningfulness of stimulus materials. Journal of Verbal Learning and Verbal Behavior, 1969, 8, 225–280.

Richards, M. P. M. The integration of a child into a social world. New York: Cambridge University Press, 1974.

Rodgers, P. A discourse-centered rhetoric of the paragraph. College Composition and Communication, 1966, 17, 2–11.

Rommetveit, R. On message structure: A framework for the study of language and communication. London: Wiley, 1974.

————. Words, context, and verbal message transmission. In R. Rommetveit and R. M. Blakar (Eds.), Studies of language, thought and verbal communication. London: Academic Press, 1979.

————. In search of a truly interdisciplinary semantics. A sermon on hopes of salvation from hereditary sins. Journal of Semantics, 1983, 2(1), 1–28.

————, Berkly, M., and Brøgger, J. Generation of words from stereoscopically presented non-word strings of letters. Scandanavian Journal of Psychology, 1968, 9, 150–156.

Rommetveit, R. and Kleiven, J. Word generation: A replication. Scandinavian Journal of Psychology, 1968, 9, 277–281.

Rose, M. Writer's block: The cognitive dimension. Studies in Writing and Rhetoric, No. 2. Carbondale: Southern Illinois University Press, 1984.

Rosenberg, S. (Ed.). Sentence production: Developments in research and theory. Hillsdale, NJ: Lawrence Erlbaum Associates, 1977.

Sacks, H., Schgeloff, E., and Jefferson, G. A simplest systematics for the organization of turn-taking for conversation. Language, 1974, 50, 696–735.

Saussure, F. de. [Course in general linguistics]. Edited by C. Bally and A. Sechelaye in collaboration with A. Riedlinger. Trans. by W. Baskin. New York: The Philosophical Library, 1959.

Scaife, M. and Bruner, J. S. The capacity for joint visual attention in the infant. Nature, 1975, 25, 265–266.

Scardamalia, M. and Bereiter, C. Written composition. In M. Wittrock (Ed.), Handbook of research on teaching (3rd ed.). New York: Macmillan, in press.

Schaffer, H. R. The child's entry into a social world. London: Academic Press, 1984.

Schgeloff, E., Jefferson, G., and Sacks, H. The preference for self-correction in the organization of repair in conversation. Language, 1977, 53, 361–382.

Schutz, A. Collected papers, vol. 1: The problem of social reality. the Hague: Martinus Nijhoff, 1967.

Scinto, L. The development of text production. In R. Freedle and J. Fine (Eds.), Developmental issues in discourse. Norwood, NJ: ABLEX Publishing Corporation, 1982.

————— . Written language and psychological development. New York: Academic Press, 1985.

Scribner, S. and Cole, M. The psychology of literacy. Cambridge, MA: Harvard University Press, 1981.

Shaughnessy, M. Errors and expectations: A guide for the teacher of basic writing. New York: Oxford University Press, 1977.

Shotter, J. Men, the man-makers: George Kelly and the psychology of personal constructs. In D. Bannister (Ed.), Perspective in personal construct theory. New York: Academic Press, 1971.

Silverstein, M. Language structure and linguistic ideology. In P. Clyne, W. Hanks, and C. Hofbauer (Eds.), The elements: A parasession on linguistic units and levels. Chicago: Chicago Linguistic Society, 1979.

————— . Language and the culture of genre: At the intersection of structure, usage, and ideology. In E. Mertz and R. J. Parmentier (Eds.), Semiotic mediation: Sociocultural and psychological perspectives. Orlando: Academic Press, 1985, p. 219–259.

Smith, B. H. On the margins of discourse: The relation of literature to language. Chicago: University of Chicago Press, 1978.

Smith, F. Understanding reading. New York: Holt, Rinehart & Winston, 1971.

————— . Writing and the writer. New York: Holt, Rinehart & Winston, 1978.

————— and Miller, G. A. The genesis of language. Cambridge, MA: The MIT Press, 1966.

Smith, N. V. (Ed.). Mutual knowledge. London: Academic Press, 1982.

Snow, C. Literacy and language: Relationships during the preschool years. Harvard Educational Review, 1983, 53(2), 165–189.

Sommers, N. I. Revision strategies of student writers and experienced adult writers. College Composition and Communication, 1980, 31, 378–388.

Sperber, D. and Wilson, D. Mutual knowledge and relevance in theories of comprehension. In N. V. Smith (Ed.), Mutual knowledge. London: Academic Press, 1982.

Spilich, G., Vesonder, G., Chiesi, H., and Voss, J. Text processing of domain-related information for individuals with high and low domain knowledge. Journal of Verbal Learning and Verbal Behavior, 1979, 18, 275–290.

Stallard, C. K. An analysis of the writing behavior of good student writers. Research in the Teaching of English, 1974, 18, 206–218.

Stalnaker, R. C. Pragmatic presuppositions, In D. Davidson and G. Harman (Eds.), Semantics of natural language. Dordrecht, Holland: Reidel, 1972.

Steinmann, M. Superordinate genre conventions. Poetics, 1981, 10, 243–261.

Stern, D. N. Mother and infant at play: The dyadic interaction involving facial, vocal and gaze behaviors. In M. Lewis and L. A. Rosenblum, The effect of the infant on its caregiver. New York: Wiley, 1974.

————— . The first relationship: Infant and mother. London: Open University, 1977.

Sternberg, R. F. Sketch of a componential subtheory of human intelligence. Behavioral and Brain Sciences, 1980, 3, 573–614.

Stubbs, M. Language and literacy: The sociolinguistics of reading and writing. London: Routledge & Kegan Paul, 1980.

——— . Written language and society: Some particular cases and general observations. In M. Nystrand (Ed.), What writers know: The language process, and structure of written discourse. New York: Academic Press, 1982.

——— . Discourse analysis: The sociolinguistic analysis of natural language. Chicago: University of Chicago Press, 1983.

——— . A matter of prolonged fieldwork: Notes towards a modal grammar of English. Paper presented at the annual meeting, American Association of Applied Linguistics, Baltimore, December 27–30, 1984.

Swaney, J. H., Janik, C. J., Bond, S. J., and Hayes, J. R. Editing for comprehension: Improving the process through reading protocols (Tech. Report No. 14). Pittsburgh: Carnegie-Mellon University, 1981.

Szasz, T. The myth of mental illness. The American Psychologist, 1960, *15*, 113–118.

Tannen, D. Oral and literate strategies in spoken and written narratives. Language, 1982, *58*(1), 1–21.

Taylor, W. Cloze procedure: A new tool for measuring readability. Journalism Quarterly, 1953, *30*, 414–438.

Tierney, R. Writer-reader transactions: A synthesis and suggested directions. Language Arts, 1983, *30*, 627–642.

Tierney R. and LaZansky, J. The rights and responsibilities of readers and writers: A contractual agreement (Education Report No. 15). Urbana: University of Illinois, Center for the Study of Reading, 1980.

Tierney, R., Leys, M., and Rogers, T. Comprehension, composition, and collaboration: Analysis of communicative influences in two classrooms. Paper presented at the Conference on Contexts of Literacy, Snowbird, UT, 1984.

Trávníček, F. On the so-called functional sentence perspective. Slovo a Slovesnost, 1962, *22*, 163–171 [cited in Firbas, 1964].

Trevarthen, C. and Hubley, P. Secondary intersubjectivity: confidence, confiding, and acts of meaning in the first year. In A. J. Lock (Ed.), Action, gesture and symbol: The emergence of language. London: Academic Press, 1978.

Tulving, E, and Gold, C. Stimulus information as determinants of tachistoscopic recognition of words. Journal of Experimental Psychology, 1963, *66*, 319–327.

Turner, A. and Greene, E. Construction and use of a propositional text base. JSAS Catalogue of selected documents in psychology, MS 1713, 1978.

Ure, Jean N. Lexical density and register differentiation. In G.E. Perren and J. L. M. Trim (Eds.), Applications of linguistics: Selected papers of the second world congress of applied linguistics, Cambridge, 1969. Cambridge: Cambridge University Press, 1971, 443–452.

Vachek, J. Written language: General problems and problems of English. The Hague: Mouton, 1973.

van Dijk, T. and Kintsch, W. Strategies of discourse comprehension. New York: Academic Press, 1983.

Voss, J. F., Vesonder, G. T., and Spilich, G. J. Text generation and recall by high-knowledge and low-knowledge individuals. Journal of Verbal Learning and Verbal Behavior, 1980, *19*, 651–667.

Vygotsky, L. [Thought and language]. Cambridge, MA: MIT Press, 1962.

——— . Mind in society. Cambridge, MA: Harvard University Press, 1978.

Walia, J. Unpublished doctoral preliminary examination. University of Wisconsin-Madison, 1983.

Wall, C. Predication: A study of its development. The Hague: Mouton, 1974.

——— . Linguistic interaction of children with different alters. Unpublished paper, University of California at Davis [cited in Bruner, 1975].

Wardhaugh, R. Reading: A linguistic perspective. New York: Harcourt Brace Jovanovich, 1969.

Watson, R. P. M. and Olson, D. R. From meaning to definition: A literate bias on the structure of word meaning. In R. Horowitz and J. Samuels (Eds.), Comprehending oral and written language. Orlando: Academic Press, in press.

Wayne, R. The effects of peer grading/editing on the grammar-usage and theme composition ability of college freshmen. Unpublished Ph.D. dissertation: University of Oklahoma, 1973.

Weinrich, U. On the semantic structure of language. In J. Greenberg (Ed.), Universals of language. Cambridge, MA: The MIT Press, 1963.

Wells, G. Language, literacy and education. In G. Wells, Learning through interaction: The study of language development. Cambridge: Cambridge University Press, 1981.

————. Learning through interaction: The study of language development. Cambridge: Cambridge University Press, 1981.

Wertsch, J. Adult-child interaction and the roots of metacognition. The Quarterly Newsletter of the Institute for Comparative Human Development, 1978, 12(1), 15–18.

———— and Hickmann, M. A microgenetic analysis of problem-solving in social interaction. In M. Hickmann (Ed.), Social and functional approaches to language and thought. Orlando: Academic Press, in press.

Wilkinson, L. C. (Ed.). Communicating in the classroom. New York: Academic Press, 1982.

Witte, S. P. Topical structure and invention: An exploratory study. College Composition and Communication, 1983, 34(3), 313–341.

Wittgenstein, L. Philosophical Investigations. Ed. G. E. Anscombe. Oxford: Blackwell, 1968.

Wittrock, M. C., Marks, C., and Doctrow, M. Reading as a generative process. Journal of Educational Psychology, 1975, 67, 484–489.

Yussen, S. R. and Berman, L. Memory predictions for recall and recognition in first-, third-, and fifth-grade children. Developmental Psychology, 1981, 117(2), 224–229.

Zoellner, R. Talk-write: A behavioral pedagogy for composition. College English, 1969, 30, 267–320.

Index